CW01263510

Palgrave Studies in British Musical Theatre

Series Editors
Millie Taylor
Department of Performing Arts
University of Winchester
Winchester, UK

Dominic Symonds
Lincoln School of Performing Arts
University of Lincoln
Lincoln, UK

Britain's contribution to musical theatre in the late twentieth century is known and celebrated across the world. In historiographies of musical theatre, this assertion of British success concludes the twentieth century narrative that is otherwise reported as an American story. Yet the use of song and music in UK theatre is much more widespread than is often acknowledged. This series teases out the nuances and the richness of British musical theatre in three broad areas: British identity; Aesthetics and dramaturgies; Practices and politics.

More information about this series at
http://www.palgrave.com/gp/series/15105

Millie Taylor

Theatre Music and Sound at the RSC

Macbeth to Matilda

palgrave
macmillan

Millie Taylor
Department of Performing Arts
University of Winchester
Winchester, UK

Palgrave Studies in British Musical Theatre
ISBN 978-3-319-95221-5   ISBN 978-3-319-95222-2   (eBook)
https://doi.org/10.1007/978-3-319-95222-2

Library of Congress Control Number: 2018951789

© The Editor(s) (if applicable) and The Author(s) 2018
This work is subject to copyright. All rights are solely and exclusively licensed by the Publisher, whether the whole or part of the material is concerned, specifically the rights of translation, reprinting, reuse of illustrations, recitation, broadcasting, reproduction on microfilms or in any other physical way, and transmission or information storage and retrieval, electronic adaptation, computer software, or by similar or dissimilar methodology now known or hereafter developed.
The use of general descriptive names, registered names, trademarks, service marks, etc. in this publication does not imply, even in the absence of a specific statement, that such names are exempt from the relevant protective laws and regulations and therefore free for general use.
The publisher, the authors and the editors are safe to assume that the advice and information in this book are believed to be true and accurate at the date of publication. Neither the publisher nor the authors or the editors give a warranty, express or implied, with respect to the material contained herein or for any errors or omissions that may have been made. The publisher remains neutral with regard to jurisdictional claims in published maps and institutional affiliations.

Cover illustration: Macbeth, 2011: Photo by Ellie Kurttz © RSC

This Palgrave Macmillan imprint is published by the registered company Springer Nature Switzerland AG
The registered company address is: Gewerbestrasse 11, 6330 Cham, Switzerland

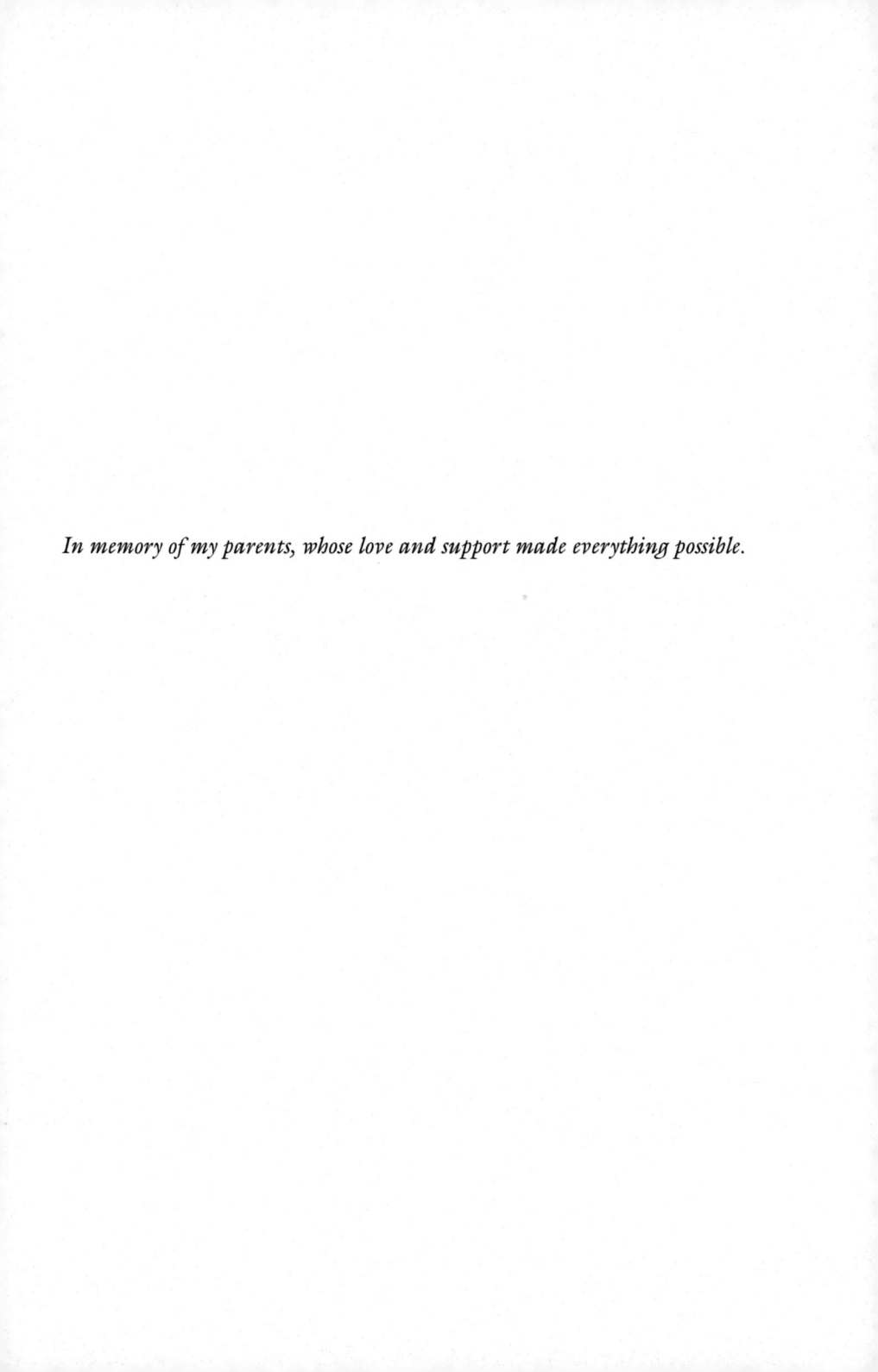

In memory of my parents, whose love and support made everything possible.

FOREWORD

The Royal Shakespeare Company (RSC), founded by Peter Hall in 1960, is one of Britain's most revered institutions, celebrating one of its most beloved writers. With a home in the picturesque Midlands market town of Stratford-upon-Avon where Shakespeare lived, it boasts quite legitimately of being one of the world's foremost theatre companies.

Stratford itself, despite its bustling traffic and its proximity to major motorways, still holds on to its chocolate box image as a quaint historic centre: characteristic half-timbered buildings and thatched cottages line the streets; a pretty canal basin dominates the Eastern edge of the town; and the imposing Royal Shakespeare Theatre presides over the waterfront, serving as a focal point for the millions of visitors who flock to Stratford every year.

It's unlikely that many of these visitors seek out Shakespeare's birthplace with music in mind—his plays are known far more for their use of language, and his legacy is as a master of the spoken word. Yet as Millie Taylor argues persuasively in this book, Shakespeare's theatre is steeped in music, creating resonant atmospheres in which to set the plays; colourful characters whose charm is often expressed in song; and, later in his career, plays whose forms adopt musical structures and present musical idioms as languages in themselves—communicative strategies through which the world of Shakespeare's imagination comes to life.

Throughout these pages, Taylor explores that world in its musical voicings, considering explicit gestures towards music that can be found in the texts of the plays; interviewing musicians, composers and musical directors who have contributed to the way the plays sound in performance; and—perhaps most significantly—arguing that the RSC over the years has nurtured a profound understanding of how Shakespeare's legacy can be articulated musically as much as through the spoken word.

In its almost 60 years, the Stratford company has created an exciting laboratory for the interpretation of that legacy. It has benefitted from significant public subsidy, as Taylor notes; from the luxury of robust resources; and from the opportunity to recruit and employ a dedicated company who over numerous successive projects have been able to explore the various languages of Shakespeare's theatre. In her strands of analysis, we learn how musical practices have been passed down as new musical directors have inherited from the past; we see how different interpretations of a single play in multiple iterations present a picture of working practices, technologies and contexts as they develop; and we gain from Taylor's close engagement with both the composers and their scores an intimate knowledge of how Shakespeare's musical imagination has been brought to life.

Readers of this book may be surprised to discover it within this book series, Palgrave Studies in British Musical Theatre, since Shakespeare's canon is typically viewed as the antithesis of musical theatre: where Shakespearean theatre is highly valued as a cultural form, musical theatre is often seen as a populist and commercial mode of entertainment; where Shakespearean texts are esteemed by principled lovers of the arts, musicals are often seen as fodder for the masses; and where Shakespeare's plays are celebrated as works of literature, musicals are often derided as trite bits of floss. Yet Taylor's resounding success in this book is to evidence the continuum that the RSC has fostered between the musicodramatic world that colours Shakespeare's plays and the same sort of landscape that creates the rich textures found in the delights of a musical. It therefore comes as no surprise to be reminded that the RSC has in fact been a driving force behind a number of the most important contributions to the musical stage in recent years. In Taylor's final chapters, she turns to the development of these works—not only the obvious examples of *Les Misérables* (1985) and *Matilda* (2010), but also productions that are not really viewed as musicals but which nevertheless construct in their formats pieces of theatre that are in everything but name, musical theatre works—*The Life and Adventures of Nicholas Nickleby* (1980) and *The Lion, the Witch and the Wardrobe* (1998). In each of these cases, she considers how their adaptation from literary texts in many ways resembles the sort of adaptations that the RSC has perennially explored in its interpretation of the Shakespeare classics.

In this sense, we can view the RSC not just as an organisation with a "straight theatre" and a "musical theatre" wing, but instead as a company with a coherent mission to further the creative possibilities of the stage using all of the tools at its disposal. And by extension, we can read into this analysis a synecdoche for British theatre more widely. For as Taylor notes throughout her book, the landscape of British theatre as a whole has embraced music in its texture throughout its history, whether that be in the traditional forms of pantomime, the innovative developments of regional, community and children's theatre, or in other institutional establishments such as the National Theatre which itself has created some of the most striking musicals of recent years (*Jerry Springer: The Opera*; *London Road*). Indeed, if British musical theatre is to be recognised as a creative idiom in its own right, it is perhaps this continuum of practices, eloquently demonstrated by the work of the RSC, that most articulately frames a national style. Thus British musical theatre creates a dialogue with the Broadway idiom, with which it interweaves but never quite attempts to clone; and with its distinct voice it generates works that are quintessentially British: from *Cavalcade* to *Cats*, from *Salad Days* to *Billy Elliot*, from *The Rocky Horror Show* to *Return to the Forbidden Planet*, and as explored in the odyssey of this book, from *Macbeth* to *Matilda*.

2018   Dominic Symonds

Acknowledgements

It's very hard to know where to start with acknowledgements on this project—there are so many people who have given their time, their knowledge and their expertise in the development of this book.

Right at the start of this project Jane Woolfenden organised a lunch at which I was able to talk to Guy Woolfenden and Michael Tubbs. This was fundamental to the development of my thinking, but was also indicative of the supportive and collaborative way in which so many people contributed to the project. At a much later stage after the chapters were largely drafted Jane Woolfenden added further stories, clarifications and corrections. The other person who contributed to the project throughout the process was Roger Howells who I saw on a number of occasions at the Birthplace Trust Archive and who not only gave interviews but sent me materials from his own records. These early supportive encounters encouraged me to develop this text in a form that is inclusive of the voices of many others.

The next group of people I spoke to were the musicians, whose work generally goes unnoticed in theatre contexts; I am grateful to James Jones, Ian Reynolds, Richard Sandland and Andy Stone-Fewings. Alongside this group I will include Stephen Brown of the Midland Branch of the Musicians' Union who filled in and clarified some of the issues the musicians had raised, and Valerie Wells who searched for and sent materials from the Musicians' Union archive at Stirling University. Several music directors, music advisors or heads of music gave of their time and memories, not least of which were Guy Woolfenden and Michael Tubbs, but this group also includes Richard Brown and Bruce O'Neil. The composer

I spent most time with was Ilona Sekacz who invited me to spend a day with her, who responded to my questions and offered memories, music clips and examples of scores. Gary Yershon also gave a detailed and deeply thoughtful interview, while Adrian Lee and Dixie Peaslee (on behalf of her husband Richard Peaslee) sent information by email.

On the development of the sound department and sound design there was Roger Howells starting the conversation followed by David Collison, Leo Leibowicz, John Leonard and Jeremy Dunn. Alongside the discussion of the development of sound, mention must be made of the pioneering work of Delia Derbyshire whose archive is being explored and analysed by David G. Butler of Manchester University. He helped me to source the documents relating to her interaction with the RSC at the John Rylands Library.

The various archivists at the Victoria and Albert Museum (V&A), Stirling University Library, John Rylands Library and the Shakespeare Birthplace Trust have all offered supportive advice as well as documents, videos and other materials. The staff of the Shakespeare Birthplace Trust archive, where the RSC's collections are housed, has been the most fundamental to this project. I enjoyed my many visits to Stratford-on-Avon, where the team was wonderful, going backwards and forwards to find obscure materials for me, showing me how to search for images, and even letting me sit in the vaults looking through programmes to discover the names and numbers of musicians at different stages of the RSC's history. My thanks to all of the team.

Julia Nottingham who licences images at the Shakespeare Birthplace Trust and Michelle Morton in a similar position at the RSC have helped me to make choices, put up with me changing my mind and worked through the mess of permissions, licences and paperwork to make sure I have been able to include appropriate photographs, scores and documents from their archives in this book. I can't thank them enough for their patience and attention to detail. And of course, my thanks also go to all the photographers and composers, as well as the performers in the photographs for granting permission to include their work. At the head of all this sits an organisation, the RSC, whose staff have been unfailingly helpful in the development of this book, demonstrating interest and offering support at every stage. Without that much of this would have been impossible.

There is one other group of people to thank, and they are the academics and editors who have offered help and feedback on various drafts, papers and chapters as the book has progressed. These include the peer reviewers at proposal and draft stage and the editors and copy editors at Palgrave. The Music Theatre working group of the International Federation of Theatre Researchers in Warwick and Stockholm, and the members of the Song, Stage and Screen conference in Toronto, especially David Savran and Adrian Curtin, all offered helpful suggestions relating to different parts of the book. Most importantly, my co-editor of this book series, Dominic Symonds, has read and re-read the chapters of this book, always offering sage and constructive advice without which it would have been much less coherent. Although the errors and omissions in this book are mine, without these people it would have been a less coherent and developed work.

Finally, to Martin for cooking, coffee and conversation as I worked out what I was trying to say, thank you.

Contents

Prologue	1
Musical Collaborations at the RSC	11
Collaborative Composition at the RSC	51
Electronics, Sound and Fury at the RSC	93
Theatre Music at the RSC	133
From *Macbeth* to *Matilda* at the RSC	175
Epilogue	217
Bibliography	227
Index	235

List of Figures

Musical Collaborations at the RSC

Fig. 1   *Henry V*, 1966. First Trumpet Book. (Music by Guy Woolfenden. By permission of the RSC)   31

Fig. 2   Sites of the backstage band boxes 1969–2007. (Drawing by Roger Howells. By permission of the RSC)   41

Fig. 3   Players in the band box, 1981. (Joe Cocks Studio Collection. ©Shakespeare Birthplace Trust)   42

Collaborative Composition at the RSC

Fig. 1   *King Lear*, 1982. (Music by Ilona Sekacz. By permission of the RSC)   56

Fig. 2   *Macbeth*, 1967. Cue list for sound and music. (Music by Guy Woolfenden. By permission of the RSC)   74

Fig. 3   *Macbeth*, 1999. Annotated script Act 1, Sc. i. (Music by Adrian Lee. By permission of the RSC)   83

Fig. 4   *Macbeth*, 2011. Onstage cellists. (Photo by Ellie Kurtz. ©RSC)   86

Electronics, Sound and Fury at the RSC

Fig. 1   Michael White and the Revox in PS Wing of RST, 1959. (Courtesy of the RSC)   99

Fig. 2   Trevor Pearce in the sound box, 1981. (Joe Cocks Studio Collection. ©Shakespeare Birthplace Trust)   103

Fig. 3   *The Winter's Tale* and *The Lion, The Witch and The Wardrobe*, 1998. Keyboard settings. (Music by Ilona Sekacz. By permission of the RSC)   107

xviii LIST OF FIGURES

Fig. 4   Setting up the sound desk upstairs in The Swan's top gallery, 1990. (Malcolm Davies Collection. ©Shakespeare Birthplace Trust)   114
Fig. 5   Henry V, 1966. (Sound plot by Guy Woolfenden. By permission of the RSC)   121

Theatre Music at the RSC

Fig. 1   *Taming of the Shrew*, 2012. Katherina Rages. (Photo by Sheila Burnett. ©RSC)   160
Fig. 2   *Taming of the Shrew* (1996), The Band in Formation. (Photo by Reg Wilson. ©RSC)   162
Fig. 3   *A Midsummer Night's Dream* (1972) Touring version showing the onstage band. (Photo by Reg Wilson. ©RSC)   167
Fig. 4   *A Midsummer Night's Dream* (1970). (Score by Richard Peaslee. By permission of the RSC)   169

From *Macbeth* to *Matilda* at the RSC

Fig. 1   *Twelfth Night*, 1969. Actor musicians performing on stage. (Joe Cocks Studio Collection. ©Shakespeare Birthplace Trust)   191
Fig. 2   *Merry Wives: The Musical*, 2006. (Photo by Stewart Hemley. ©RSC)   199
Fig. 3   *Matilda the Musical*, 2010. Workshop with band. (Photo by Manuel Harlan. ©RSC)   210

Epilogue

Fig. 1   *The Tempest*, 2017. Ariel and his avatar. (Photo by Topher McGrillis. ©RSC)   219

Prologue

As a student at the end of the 1970s I regularly went to see performances at the RSC's Stratford base—performances I barely recall at all—but much as I enjoyed the experience of the productions, the most important thing for me was that musicians were playing onstage. Live music was being performed not just for songs and dances but throughout the plays. I remember seeing the live band located at circle level at either side of the proscenium arch, making the players appear closer to the stage picture and more clearly visible than when hidden below the stage as they were in other theatres—and I was inspired by watching them work. Though this memory of their location may be overlaid with many other subsequent memories of nights at that theatre I know that the musicians certainly would not have been in a pit, though they might have been hidden elsewhere. The point is that it seemed to me then and subsequently that they were both an audible and a visible part of the theatre experience, and they were playing live every night.

The experience of live music struck me forcibly not just because of my own burgeoning interest in musical theatre and theatre music as a potential career, but because the RSC was unusual. For most theatre performances at this time music was the accompaniment to songs and dances, and live music certainly did not occur in plays whose literary quality was partially evidenced by the lack of such entertainments as music, song or dance. Some years later when writing a PhD dissertation I would still argue that in plays 'incidental' music provided an accompaniment to song and dance; signalled and covered entrances, exits and scene changes; and cued applause with suitably atmospheric and contextual music that would frame the dramatic scene, though in the awareness that music was able to work with or in juxtaposition to the action. But this was later after a number of years as a Musical Director (MD) in musicals, pantomimes and plays that had included deputising (depping) on keyboards at the National Theatre (NT) but never, sadly, at the RSC. Back in the late 1970s as a student I began to experience new types of experimental performance for the first time, seeing works that incorporated sound in new ways—though in my mind at this time there was still a clear distinction between music and sound, as I was only just being exposed to Russolo and Cage and the twentieth century's democratisation of sound. Where the RSC made a fundamental impression on me was in its difference from either of the models of theatre I knew—the popular musical theatre and the experimental music theatre performances. The music I was hearing at the RSC was like both of these and neither. Music, or a combination of music and 'sound', was used to accompany song and dance as well as being used in all the ways I imagined of 'incidental music' and more; it was more pervasive than I had been aware of before, and unlike the idea of filmic 'incidental music', it was live.

The consequences of music's liveness and how that has been maintained and adapted in various productions is one aspect of the story this book will tell. This is the part of the story that focuses on the development of what I'm calling 'theatre music'. David Roesner explores this term, choosing to refer to theatre music as the combination of music and sound for a theatre production that incorporates live, recorded and digitally created sounds (Roesner 2016, 202–3)—combinations that in the UK have in the past been termed 'incidental music' (if written by a composer and played on instruments whether live or recorded) or 'sound design' (if created through recorded or digitally manipulated sounds). Often the separation of these roles and the sounds they create, whether for the creators and certainly for audiences, has not been clearly defined in the UK, and is certainly far from clear in many productions at the RSC, though there are people credited in the programme for each aspect. At the time the RSC was inaugurated in 1961 the sound department as such did not even exist, but since that time the artistry of the creators, their job titles and what the technology makes possible have all continued to evolve, and part of this story is the story of that evolution told from the perspective of theatre music. Overall, however, Roesner is right to question the term incidental music (though his reasons for doing so relate to his interest in studying postdramatic theatre). Can music or sound of any sort ever really be considered 'incidental' to the dramatic action?

In the Shakespeare canon, as recorded in the various Quartos and Folios, there are songs and/or dances and military signalling in many of the plays; even the tragedies offer such instructions. Out of the 37 plays 32 contain interesting references to music and musical matters in the text itself, including instructions to play, sing or dance, and there are over 300 musical stage directions in 36 of the plays (Naylor 1965, 3). Musical occasions include pageants, wedding processions, banquets, masques and occasionally dreams or just the accompaniment of speech (Naylor 1965, 162). Although most contemporary productions contain more or less music than that suggested by the various editions of the texts, Naylor's extraordinary cataloguing of the occasions of music does give a sense of the importance not just of music but of a sound world within this canon of plays. In most productions there are frequent interjections of sound cues that are also atmospheric and contextual, some of which could be created either by a musical instrument or a sound tape, and then there is the voice that moves between speech and song, acoustic or digitally enhanced. Surely then, the work of the sound department and vocal practices all require consideration in a study of the musical and sound worlds of the theatre, none of which is really 'incidental' to the action. All in all the sound of the theatre is hard to contain or to isolate, and it is even more difficult to understand what its effects and affects might be on audiences.

At the time I began attending RSC productions the music was often composed using the melodic and harmonic structures of tonality and the orchestral sounds of the wind band employed at the theatre, but the sound world was already moving beyond these limits. Although I was not then aware of it, this sound world combined tonal music with fast developing electronic and digitally created sounds to produce new possibilities for live theatre performance. This theatre music was produced as a result of the collaboration of composers and musicians with the emerging practitioners of sound design, a field that has developed gradually over the last 40 or more years.[1] So now, after another long gap since the PhD dissertation in

---

[1] Adrian Curtin, writing in 2016, talks of the growing importance of sound design over the last 30 years. Although the job title may have emerged in the 1960s the practice really became significant from the late 1970s onwards.

which I first began loosely to grope around this topic, I've again returned to question the ways in which music and sound work together with the visual elements of theatre to create a total experience of theatre. There are several questions that this book asks: what are the practical working processes within which live and recorded, onstage and offstage music performance have been produced since the inception of the RSC in 1961? What are the consequences of developments and alterations in these processes for creative teams, performers and audiences? How has the development of sound design and the collaboration of sound and music changed the way music and sound signify in performance? Have the functions of theatre music and sound altered as a consequence? Can the vocal sound of performers be excluded from a discussion of sound and music, and if not, where are the limits of the sound world?

That question raises a corollary already intimated above, which is that sound and music are perceived in a theatrical context that is visual, and attempting to separate the visual from the aural is not only impossible but also unhelpful in a contemporary context that values the theatricality of performance. Interestingly, Roesner explores the tension between a naturalistic theatre in which music and sound are designed to support the dramatic action and remain 'unheard'[2] and a modern turn in postdramatic theatre that foregrounds what he calls the 'retheatricalisation' of theatre through the interaction with another art form: music (Roesner 2014, 5). In his discussion of 'musicality' he addresses some of the ways in which a postdramatic theatre has moved from a model in which specialists are responsible for their own areas, such that 'actors only know how to act, musicians how to play their instruments, designers how to model and build a set, create costumes or devise the lighting' and so on. In this model the director accumulates all the integrative power and retains the interpretative sovereignty (Roesner 2014, 9). Instead there has emerged a series of practices in which art forms interact, such that the structures of music might, for example, influence the dramaturgy of a devised work. While I'm not proposing to introduce Roesner's approach to musicality into this study, especially since he references a very different body of theatrical practices, the notion provides a stepping stone to consider the interdisciplinary interactions of the aural and the visual. In the cultural and artistic context

---

[2] This is a reference to Claudia Gorbman's book *Unheard Melodies* in which she makes the case that film scores are designed to influence and manipulate audiences without their presence actually being noticed (1987).

of the RSC a similar pattern emerges, where the practice of collaboration, the involvement of music and sound staff at an early stage of the rehearsal process, and the integration of the visual and aural elements of a performance can lead not to the subordination of separate disciplines but to the heightened theatricality of the whole as a combination of the visual and the aural.

Such combinations rely on new thinking about ways of understanding and speaking about theatrical performance that incorporate the aural and the visual into audience experience. It is the interaction between these two ways of 'attending' by audiences that George Home-Cook explores in *Theatre and Aural Attention*. One of the issues he discusses is the question of how our experience of sitting in the theatre in silence is 'shaped by designed sound, darkness, and the intersubjective act of attending' (Ibid., 10). Although the experience of audiences is not a priority in this book, the understanding and experience of performance is implied throughout when discussing the creation of meaning, atmosphere or emotional connection. None of these can be explored in isolation from the narrative context and the performance of actor/characters or the collaborations that have generated the production.

Since addressing all these interrelated questions is already a herculean enterprise given the way in which historical context and artistic aims affect each production there were two limits I placed on the enterprise from the start—time and place. The RSC is unique: most theatres, other than the RSC and the National Theatre (which was formed more recently) do not maintain a music department or employ freelance composers or musicians for plays, but rely on sound designers to provide a soundscape and appropriate effects for each production. Such soundscapes might be created from library music and effects, extant recordings or newly created samples and music. The sound designer is responsible not only for putting that score together or working with a composer, but also for overseeing the placement of microphones, the processing of speech and live music and the placement of speakers to achieve an aesthetically desirable effect on audiences—directing the audience's attention or understanding. Given the smaller level of continuity of staff, and the absence of permanent music teams at most other theatres, the development of a relationship between sound and music is inconsistent at best beyond these two national theatres. Filter Theatre is one of the recent exceptions: founded in 2003 by actors Ollie Dimsdale and Ferdy Roberts and musician Tim Phillips, music and sound play a central role in the creative process and in the performance of classic texts including Shakespeare (Roesner 2014, 240).[3] However, the RSC's longer history and its strategy of employing many freelance composers and sound designers alongside its in-house teams allows for interactions with the wider theatre, film and television world. It is likely therefore that practices at the two national theatres may overlap with, influence, or indeed follow innovations elsewhere. However, this study does not attempt to trace those wider influences, rather, its strength is that it focuses on one important institution in order to analyse a coherent but developing practice over a significant period of time in detail.

The choice of the RSC over the National Theatre as the subject of this book was based on something more than my own early interest in the company's work. That the RSC is based in the Midlands, well away from the commercial heartland of music and theatre in the UK, was a deciding factor, since staff teams tended to relocate to the Midlands and stay at the company for longer periods of time than the freelancers in London. This meant that there were likely to be consistent practices that could be identified as such. These practices include the fact that the RSC has, since its inception in 1961, retained a live band, employed a composer to create a new score for each new production, focused on a fairly discrete body of texts, and even more importantly for a researcher, archived the scores with the production materials at The Shakespeare Birthplace Trust. The National Theatre has a similar archive, but its inauguration is more recent and the breadth of the company's programming makes some aspects of comparison almost unimaginably complicated. The programme of the RSC with its regular re-envisioning and re-sounding of a discrete group of plays allows the variability of the aural world to be compared across productions of the same play. Detailed analysis will explore how sound and vision interact in new readings of the same text, and how the functions and aesthetics of the aural affect emotion, atmosphere and audience response across different productions. Then as the same company branches out into new fields (Christmas shows and musical theatre) it is possible to analyse the influence of the core practices beyond the core activity.

By contrast Shakespeare's Globe Theatre, which has an even more limited range of programming than the RSC, has, since its 'Prologue Season' in 1996, also employed a permanent music director, Claire Van Kampen, and it focuses predominantly on the works of Shakespeare and his contemporaries. Productions of Shakespeare's plays performed there from 1997

[3] For more on the work of Filter Theatre see Roesner (2014) and Curtin (2016).

began from research that identified 'the practice of Renaissance music, and, work[ed] with early music practitioners, to marry modern reconstructions of Elizabethan and Jacobean music to Shakespeare's texts for performance in the Globe using only reconstructed period instruments without amplification or electronic aids' (Van Kampen 2008, 80). That remit has expanded in recent years to explore how modern musical sources and conventions might be combined with Renaissance ideas, especially in incorporating known songs and music into scores to create intertextual reference. Because of the particular focus of this book on the development of music theatre and sound design in theatre, and because of the reconstructive efforts at Shakespeare's Globe that promote a greater sense of historical accuracy, I have chosen not to include it in the discussions below. It is particularly interesting to note, however, that in contrast to the RSC's strategy of embracing electro-acoustic music and popular forms Shakespeare's Globe was initially moving in the opposite direction, expanding on the understanding of how 'authentic' music might have sounded and operated in relation to the same group of plays (Ibid.)[4] before moving on to try to recreate the experience of the early modern theatre rather than simply its sound.

As David Lindley notes, music at the RSC has, in the last 50 years or so, made a significant contribution to a specific directorial perspective and supplies a consistent 'soundscape', assisting in historical relocation of Shakespeare's plays as well as reinforcing emotion and feeling (Lindley 2006, 111). During this period (since 1961) the music for each production has generally been entrusted to a single composer working with the director and is different from the seventeenth and eighteenth century practice when scores were often 'assembled from a variety of pre-existing music, only sometimes with new additions' (111). Whether or not the score is created in a similar fashion to that in the early modern period, the way sounds communicated to the early modern ears would have been entirely different as Bruce R. Smith notes in his account of *The Acoustic World of Early Modern England* (1999). As such, all that I can attempt here is to document the changes in the contemporary period without fully accounting for any parallels with early modern practice.

---

[4] As Van Kampen remarks this work was pioneered in England in the 1960s by the Early Music Movement and the pioneering work of David Munrow, who was a contracted player at the RSC in the 1960s.

Crucially, though, the decision to retain a permanent music department at the RSC since the 1960s that could instigate collaborations between music, sound, direction and design, even when the financial stability of the company was in doubt, points to a commitment to music and sound for more than reasons of historical authenticity. There was clearly a commitment to a total theatre experience well before the term became fashionable. Although this total theatre experience might have had much in common with the early modern period when The King's Men performed together over a significant period developing a company ethos and collaborative practices, it is the collaboration in the contemporary period and what that facilitates that is of interest. Being in the Midlands somewhat isolated from the commercial London 'scene' might have brought about some unexpected and productive interactions and an ethos particular to the company. It is worth considering how changing communications infrastructure (road transport as well as computer technology) might have affected working practices especially since the turn of the twenty-first century.

The discussions in this book arise from a combination of archival research, new and unpublished interviews, performance and musicological analysis, reviews and other post-performance materials in a mixed method approach that is often ephemeral and anecdotal, making use of the full complexity of the cultural archive surrounding performances. This method allows consideration of the stories of the participants and the practices they undertook always in the awareness that memories are fallible and each perspective has an unknowable context. Alongside this important body of knowledge I made choices about which scripts, scores and performances to analyse from my own subjective position. This combination of historiography and analysis is necessarily partial, not least because of the choices I made about which leads to follow, which shows to analyse, which composers to interview. What it produces, though, is a series of stories about the development of practices in music and sound design that provide a provocation to further research into a field that is ripe for investigation.

This book's strength, therefore, is its focus on a uniquely important British company revered for its literary tradition but which demonstrates a consistent commitment to innovation in music/sound for theatre. It explores the contexts, the material conditions, the nature, quality and character of music/sound produced for theatre productions at the RSC from 1961 up to the contemporary period. Because of the opportunity provided by a continuity of practice in the music department under long serving music advisers and music directors, this book is also able to question the extent to which theatre music responds to changing social, cultural and material circumstances, and how the aural interacts with the visual in a discrete group of theatre performances. New and exciting discoveries begin to emerge about the work of the RSC; how the practices and aesthetics of that company changed over several decades, and how the arts of theatre music and sound design have been transformed. It demonstrates how the meanings of contemporary productions of Shakespeare's plays are shaped by sound/music, and how similar practices might be used in the development of musical theatre. Throughout all the analysis of theatre music and sound, one issue that is abundantly clear is that it is impossible to separate sound from vision, any more than music from sound, demonstrating the importance of interdisciplinarity in the analysis of theatre production and the reception of performance.

The book's structure moves broadly from the practical via the analytical to the theoretical, though none of these is really discrete. "Musical Collaborations at the RSC" explores the working practices of composers, MDs and musicians and the negotiations of time, space and collaboration that frame the practicalities of working in theatre from the 1960s to the present. "Collaborative Composition at the RSC" continues to use a historical perspective in order to analyse a sequence of productions of *Macbeth* in chronological order. This very limited historical overview raises some issues about the interactions of music and sound, and their effects on dramaturgy as well as how electronic and digital instruments and timbres affected composition. Considering the importance of electronic and digital production is the focus of "Electronics, Sound and Fury at the RSC", which documents the development of sound design and the consequences of the introduction of different technologies at the RSC. It explores the perceptions of sound design in relation to collaboration and job title as well as the audience experience of performance. "Theatre Music at the RSC" builds on the arguments in both the previous chapters in considering the work of theatre music (as a composite whole created by composer and sound designer) in relation to specific productions, documenting some of the ways the sound world interacts with narrative and visual performance, not just by signifying meaning, location and atmosphere, but in contributing to dramaturgy and the awareness of theatricality. Since the RSC has had some notable successes in musical theatre, and since many of the Shakespeare plays contain song and dance,

"From *Macbeth* to *Matilda* at the RSC" explores the place of voice in the sound world of the theatre, especially in song, a discussion that expands to consider the question of musicality in plays with songs and the continuity of practice in the RSC's musicals.

As the work of the RSC continues, with new productions like Gregory Doran's version of *The Tempest* (2017), with its computer generated avatar and enhanced sound, it is increasingly clear that it will be impossible to document all the innovations of the company even over a specific period. It is also impossible to spend the time inside every rehearsal and production meeting in order to conduct an ethnographic study of all that goes into even one production. What this book does, though, is to identify significant trends that reveal a developing aesthetics of theatre music at the RSC that may be paralleled more widely in British theatre and media.

Musical Collaborations at the RSC

> *Mark how one string, sweet husband to another,*
> *Strikes each in each by mutual ordering;*
> *Resembling sire and child and happy mother,*
> *Who, all in one, one pleasing note do sing:*
> *Whose speechless song, being many, seeming one,*
> *Sings this to thee: "Thou single wilt prove none".* Sonnet 8.

I began with this quotation as an example of collaboration; of strings in the production of music, of members of a family in the production of a pleasing unison, and of a moral epithet from Shakespeare's 8th sonnet. This quotation therefore introduces both the theme of collaboration and the subject of music at the Royal Shakespeare Company (RSC).

Most music requires collaboration or at least interpretation. At the very least, and excepting singer/songwriters, a musician or group of musicians is likely to play the music of a composer. Though sometimes the composer is not present the written score provides the point of contact, though this could be mediated through a conductor or music director as is the case at the RSC. There is also a very particular non-verbal understanding between musicians who develop a close relationship as they play and share the experience of performing together. Aside from these features of all music performances, music in theatre always requires a much greater number of collaborative partners. The director and composer might agree on a musical vision for the piece, the music director may or may not be involved at that stage. Many of Shakespeare's plays contain dances or songs that will not only be composed to fit the production, but must be taught to performers by a music director and choreographer, who liaise with director and composer over dance arrangements. The music itself will be played by musicians, part-time or full-time, on contract or freelance, onstage or elsewhere in the theatre building, live or recorded. It will mostly be conducted by a music director (who is alerted by stage management cues) so that it occurs at exactly the right moment in the performance in association with the actors and sound department. In fact music needs to be completely integrated into the creative process so that it works most effectively in performance.

Later chapters will focus on the musical dramaturgy and the issue of the contexts and aesthetics of the music itself, but for the moment this chapter will concentrate only on the production of music; who is involved in that process, and what are the structures within which they work. Understanding the material circumstances for the production of music creates the environment within which to understand the creativity of the music department. In *Group Creativity: Music, Theater, Collaboration* R. Keith Sawyer describes the concept of group flow as 'a collective state that occurs when a group is performing at the peak of its abilities' (Sawyer 2003, e-book). He suggests that group flow is more likely to occur when there is an extrinsic collective goal that the group must attain (such as a performance scheduled to open on an advertised date) and a number of structures shared by the performers (such as the working practices, time pressures and the quality imperatives of the company). Creativity theory also reminds us that the contribution of different members of the team must be complementary; there is a clear division of roles that results in a fluid process towards the shared goal of a unified performance. Clearly that applies to the members of a band in the performance of music, but it also applies to the collaboration of musicians with composers, directors and actors. Finally, Sawyer also notes that 'creativity is fundamentally social and collaborative, that it involves preparation, training, and hard work, and that the process is more important than the product or the personality' (Ibid., 259/356). The research enquiry that underpins this chapter explores the social and collaborative processes in the production of music at the RSC since its inception in 1961. The facets of this enquiry include questions around the nature of music management, the employment practices around composers and musicians, the economics of music production and the working practices for musicians in performance. The findings reveal that the slow pace of evolution during which individuals worked together for several years, and in some cases decades (despite the fact that some collaborators were on freelance contracts) had a positive impact on the creativity and the nature of the ensemble produced among its members.

Music Management: A Timeline

In 1948, when Stratford's Shakespeare Memorial Theatre played host to the annual Shakespeare Festival, the Music Advisor was Leslie Bridgewater who continued in this role until 1958 by which time he had written scores for 16 Stratford productions. During these years a number of highly respected composers were employed to write scores for specific productions including Roberto Gerhard, John Wooldridge, Antony Hopkins, Julian Slade, John Gardner, Christopher Whelan, Alexander Gibson, and in 1959, Humphrey Searle and Lennox Berkeley. Raymond Leppard (who in 1956 was only 28) first appeared at Stratford as a composer for the then 25-year-old Peter Hall's production of *Love's Labour's Lost* in 1956. *Cymbeline* followed in 1957 and *Twelfth Night* in 1958 as the two, who had met while studying at Cambridge University, developed an ongoing collaboration. When Peter Hall became Artistic Director of the theatre and company in 1959/60 Raymond Leppard took over from Leslie Bridgewater as the Music Advisor to the Shakespeare Memorial Theatre and Brian Priestman was appointed as Music Director. It appears that until this time the music advisor role related to composition of scores and the employment of freelance composers as well as having oversight of productions, while the music director was responsible for conducting or playing for productions and managing musicians. At no stage are these roles clearly separated or defined, however, it is especially so after this point, since music advisors have also been composers, players and conductors. In fact as time went on and the number of productions increased, composers were sometimes drawn from the pool of players and music directors as well as from outside the company, while the conductor was very soon replaced by a keyboard-playing music director.[1]

However, a pattern was emerging that new appointments of artistic directors arose from within the bank of directors already working with or

---

[1] There are occasional exceptions to this practice, when a percussionist, accordionist, or other instrumentalist has led the band, but they are relatively uncommon.

for the company. They were likely to have brought in composers with whom they had worked previously, as did freelance directors. This meant that there were comfortable working relationships within the creative team between director and composer, while at the same time new ideas were being introduced into the company by the freelance staff. This type of process can be seen in musical styles and genres as they evolve, in the introduction of electronic synthesisers and samplers and in the development of the sound department, but what is interesting in this institution is the extent to which a gradual process of renewal and evolution is also apparent in the working practices of musicians, the instrumentation of the house band, and even, as argued here, in the recruitment practices for directors, music directors and musicians from within freelance staff who are already known to the company.

Music directors were sometimes drawn from players employed in the band, a few of whom also composed scores for the company opening up the potential for progression for players. In many ways the pool of players and the instrumentation within that group provided one aspect of continuity, as did the practice of repeatedly employing the same freelance composers and players known to the company. At the same time since composers and musicians were actually on annual or freelance contracts there was also the potential for innovation, for varying the instrumentation, musical genres and timbres. Overall, the regular use of many of the same personnel maintained the sense of continuity, even while transformation and variety was encouraged by the nature of freelance employment.

The most important figure in the evolution of music over the period 1961–1998 at the RSC was Guy Woolfenden who remained in a leading role as composer and later Head of Music for 37 years: there would not be another Head of Music until 1999.[2] In 1961 Woolfenden had been booked as Deputy Music Director for the company and became Music Director when Brian Priestman left in 1963. Raymond Leppard was booked to compose the music for *The Wars of the Roses* (*Henry VI*, *Edward IV* and *Richard III*) to be directed by Peter Hall, but the show was postponed by six weeks when Peter Hall was ill. The result was that the rehearsal period coincided with that of *The Beggars Opera* that Leppard

---

[2] After reading music at Cambridge and studying conducting and horn at the Guildhall School of Music and Drama, Woolfenden joined the RSC in 1961. By the time he retired in 1998 he had composed more than 150 scores for the company, leading the development of music and sound for that entire period.

was also working on at the Aldwych in London—so Woolfenden was suddenly asked to write the score when all he had done at the RSC so far was to write five jazz cues, a little incidental music for *Julius Caesar* and a song in *Measure for Measure* (Woolfenden et al. 2013).[3] Jane Woolfenden records that Peter Hall came to their flat late one night to ask Guy to write the music. Woolfenden refused as the time was now so short, and when asked which composer could was told that 'no-one would think of trying to write the music for three plays which were due to open in less than six weeks'. Hall apparently replied that that was the reason he was in their flat asking and 'he knew that Guy would do it wonderfully!' (Woolfenden 2018).

Woolfenden was made Music Director of the Royal Shakespeare Theatre Wind Band the following year, and in 1968 became an Associate Artist of the RSC. In 1967 he was joined by Michael Tubbs who became Deputy Music Director in 1969.[4] Tubbs was also very long serving and retired in 2006. Within this continuity other roles were developed and other long-serving players and music directors appeared, but Woolfenden and Tubbs must be considered a hugely influential collaborative partnership.

As noted above, artistic directors of the company were generally appointed from among the associate or freelance directors who had worked with the company and were fairly long-serving, again providing a high level of continuity. In 1958 Peter Hall had become Artistic Director of the Shakespeare Memorial Theatre which in 1961 changed its name to the Royal Shakespeare Theatre (RST), home of the RSC (Beauman 1982, 239). The theatre had been incorporated by Royal Charter in 1925 'so it virtually belongs to the nation' (Quayle 1952), and Peter Hall's first years at the company involved not only choosing plays, directors, casts and other artists for his first season, but also following through with plans for altering the Stratford stage which included removing the pit, an important decision that affected the way music developed subsequently. Simultaneously he needed to elicit a subsidy from the Arts Council[5] and

---

[3] Interviews will be referenced throughout with the subject's name and the year of interview. The date and type of communication is listed in the bibliography.

[4] Michael Tubbs read music at Cambridge and studied conducting and oboe at the Guildhall School of Music and Drama before joining the RSC. At the RSC he was a music director and composer, a job that he extended to include creating musical instruments, sound effects, coaching actors in singing roles and liaising with composers (Tubbs 2013).

[5] For more on the convoluted battle with the Arts Council in light of the development of the National Theatre see Chambers (2004), 23–30, 81–5.

find a London theatre for his expanded vision of the company which he achieved in 1960. In addition, since the company was subject to Royal Charter, Hall also needed to enter discussions with Buckingham Palace to agree to the change of name for the theatre and company (Chambers 2004, 11). He was successful and continued with the company until 1968 when Trevor Nunn took over, a role he enjoyed until 1978. Since the company had by then expanded enormously he invited Terry Hands, who had been with the company since 1966 running TheatreGoRound (TGR), to join him as Co-Artistic Director until 1986. Together they faced the difficulty of managing a growing deficit as well as running the company. Terry Hands then remained until 1990 before Adrian Noble took charge for just over another decade until 2002. Michael Boyd served from 2003 to 2012 and was followed by Gregory Doran who remains Artistic Director in 2018.

By 1982 when Heads of Department are first listed in the theatre programmes, Woolfenden was named as Head of Music with Nigel Hess as the Company Music Director, Michael Tubbs as Music Director for Stratford and Richard Brown as London Music Director. What had started as a seasonal festival in 1879 was by the start of 1960 the operation of seven productions a year in two venues (Stratford and the Aldwych in London). A series of national and international tours followed as well as the opening of The Other Place (TOP)—a studio theatre in Stratford-upon-Avon, and the opening of the Swan Theatre in 1986. In the early 1980s the company was leasing the Aldwych and putting shows into other London theatres (the Warehouse, Wyndham's Theatre and the Piccadilly Theatre in 1980) as well as touring to New York, Europe and nationally. The London schedule was streamlined by the opening of the Barbican in 1982 which had its own studio theatre, The Pit, but by this time the RSC operation was enormous. In 1984, for example, there were five productions at the RST, seven at TOP, eight at the Barbican, eight at The Pit, as well as two productions doing a small-scale tour, and two productions on tour to the US. Of course, these were not all new productions; productions were retained for two or three years in different venues or on tour, but still the organisational administration for the employment of directors, actors, stage staff, designers, technicians, composers and musicians was vast. The need for music directors at each venue to co-ordinate musicians in so many performances and productions, while oversight of music across the whole company was maintained by the Head of Department, can thus be explained.

And the pattern of internal promotion and evolution continued as, aside from Guy Woolfenden who remained as Head of Music, writing scores until 1998, other composers who moved into leading roles in the music department were Nigel Hess who was Royal Shakespeare Theatre Company Music Director and a staff composer for a time from 1982; Richard Brown who was Director of Music in London from 1982 to 2002; and Stephen Warbeck who was briefly Head of Department in 1999. On the playing side John Woolf joined the band as an oboist in 1974, and by 1982 was mostly working as a production Music Director; in 1990 Michael Tubbs became Director of Music with John Woolf as Music Director. Tubbs seems to have managed what had by now become the very complicated logistics of making sure contract and freelance musicians were paid correctly in line with the Musician's Union (MU) contract as well as acting as Music Director on many shows. Woolf composed and was MD on many productions, while Woolfenden had oversight of composers and music in all the various venues and on tour.

Guy Woolfenden retired in 1998 having written around 150 scores for the RSC and was awarded an OBE[6] in HM Queen Elizabeth II 2007 New Year's Honours list for services to music. When a comparison is made with the previous music advisor, Leslie Bridgewater's 16 scores, the scale of Woolfenden's achievement and his influence on theatre composition can be understood. But to return to the timeline, at that point Stephen Warbeck was recruited as Head of Music and Associate Artist. Richard Brown was still in post in London as Director of Music with Tony Stenson as Music Director, while at Stratford, Michael Tubbs and John Woolf remained in their posts.

In 2001 for the first time a Music Manager, Kate Andrew, was appointed in Stratford to oversee the complicated logistics of players, hours and contracts and to streamline the employment of musicians, though she had effectively been doing this job for several years already as Music Officer. This occurred shortly before the RSC pulled out of the Barbican in 2002. In 2006 Michael Tubbs retired and in 2008 another former player, Richard Sandland, became Music Coordinator and then Music Operations Manager. In 2014 John Woolf stepped down from management (he had followed Warbeck as Head of Music) though he remains a regular music director and composer with the company. Meanwhile Bruce O'Neil, now Head of Music, first worked for the RSC as a freelance music director in

---

[6] OBE—Officer of the Most Excellent Order of the British Empire.

2002 for *Antony and Cleopatra* (Attenborough)[7] and *Much Ado About Nothing* (Doran 2002). He continued to be employed as a freelance music director until 2006 when the RSC did a festival of the complete works before the building was closed for redevelopment. He was offered a year-long contract that included *Merry Wives The Musical* (Doran 2006). After that year he was asked to stay as a full-time music director, during which time he worked on *Matilda the Musical*. In 2013 when Gregory Doran was appointed Artistic Director, O'Neil became Head of Music.

In the course of 55 years the music department's work had grown exponentially, and for most of that time it had been led by Guy Woolfenden who provided a sense of continuity while expanding the department enormously, introducing innovation and supporting a gradual evolution of practice. The process of evolution continues, however, and many of the newer players, music directors and composers are no longer aware of that remarkable legacy, even as they continue to operate within the framework Woolfenden established.

Freelance and Staff Composers

The process of evolution was initiated to some extent by the choice of composers who might be suggested by directors coming into the company. Most composers were freelancers, though some were used a great deal (apart from Nigel Hess who was on the staff for a time). Composers would be chosen because of the musical styles in which they worked and the ways in which that style might expand the director's vision for a particular production. Since many freelance composers worked across companies and media, often working in theatre, film and television, and might have a particular interest in, for example, the electronic generation of sound, authentic instrumentation or world music practices, the sound world of the company was continually changing as each new composer was contracted.

Company music directors often wrote music for a range of directors, as Guy Woolfenden had done; John Woolf, Richard Brown and Michael Tubbs fall into this category. Nigel Hess, now best known as a conductor and composer for film and television, was house staff composer for the RSC before he became Company Music Director. He composed 20 scores,

---

[7] Throughout this book a production will be identified by the name of the director and date of production in brackets if not mentioned in the text.

especially for Terry Hands. Most recently he returned to the RSC after a long absence working for other companies to compose scores for *Love's Labour's Lost* and *Love's Labour's Won* in 2014 for director Christopher Luscombe, a process which will be documented in the next Chapter.[8] As noted above, many directors have composers with whom they work well, and so when a director is employed they may ask for a particular composer to compose the score. Gregory Doran, for example, works often with Paul Englishby, while Adrian Noble is notable for the number of different composers he worked with. Peter Hall worked frequently with Raymond Leppard and later with Guy Woolfenden, as of course did many of the directors. Derek Oldfield wrote two scores for John Barton for *All's Well That Ends Well* (1967) and *Julius Caesar* (1968), while James Walker composed many scores for Barton including *Richard II* (1974), *King John* (1974), *Much Ado About Nothing* (1976), *Love's Labour's Lost* (1978) and *The Merchant of Venice* (1981). Carl Davis, a very experienced composer for film and television, wrote the score for Richard Eyre's production of *Much Ado About Nothing* (1971), and there were a number of other composers whose work spanned theatre, film and television who were brought in for individual productions by directors. New ideas and trends were thus introduced in composition as well as direction, and this increased the diversity of music within the theatre.

The other group are the composers who arrive, perhaps with a director or because notice has been taken of their work elsewhere, and who return frequently building a considerable reputation for their work with the company. Stephen Oliver arrived with Keith Hack for productions of *Measure for Measure* in the RST and *The Tempest* at TOP in 1974. He returned in 1977 (*As You Like It* [Nunn], *Tis Pity She's A Whore* [Daniels], and *The Lorenzaccio Story* [Daniels]), 1979 (*Much Ado* [Davies], *Othello* [Eyre], *Pericles* [Daniels] and *The Caucasian Chalk Circle* [Caird]), 1980 (*Romeo and Juliet* [Daniels] and *Nicholas Nickleby* [Nunn/Caird]), 1981 (*A Midsummer Night's Dream* [Daniels] and *The Winter's Tale* [Eyre]), 1982 (*Peer Gynt* [Daniels], *Peter Pan* [Caird/Nunn], and *The Tempest* [Daniels]), 1986 (*Richard II* [Barry Kyle]), and 1987 (*The Taming of the Shrew* [Jonathan Miller]). Oliver was best known for his operatic music but he was also a prolific theatre composer especially in collaboration with Ron Daniels, as well as a composer for the concert hall and television until his sadly early death in 1992.

[8] He has also composed several scores for Shakespeare plays at The Globe in London.

David Thacker (Director) worked with Mark Vibrans (*Pericles*, 1989, *Julius Caesar*, 1993) and Gary Yershon (*As You Like It*, 1992, and *Merchant of Venice*, 1993), while Dominic Muldownney, Director of Music at the Royal National Theatre, also composed many RSC scores, often when his wife, Di Trevis, was directing. George Fenton began writing for the theatre in 1974. He had begun his career as an actor and because of his interest in working as a recording artist with various rock and folk bands, he was often asked to play instruments or help with music in the theatre, so he decided on a career switch to theatre composition, and given his understanding of theatre and performance this proved extremely successful. Richard Brown remarked on the ingenuity of Fenton's orchestration and the innovative timbres and textures he was able to imagine, speculating that this might have resulted from his less classical music education (Brown R. 2014). Fenton first worked at the RSC in 1974 on *Twelfth Night* directed by Peter Gill with whom he collaborated on several other occasions elsewhere.[9] He later worked at the RSC with Howard Davies in 1981, 1982 and 1985, Adrian Noble in 1982 and Michael Attenborough in 1999, as well as becoming a prolific composer for television and film.

Gary Yershon is another composer who sidestepped from working as an actor into a very successful career as a composer for theatre, film and television (Yershon 2016). Most notable among his works outside the theatre are several films for director Mike Leigh. He arrived at the RSC with Phyllida Lloyd, with whom he had worked at Manchester Royal Exchange, for a show called *Virtuoso* for which he used a saxophone quartet. He wrote 20 shows for the RSC including a number of modern shows as well as Shakespeare productions, the latter of which included two versions of *As You Like It* (Thacker 1992 and Cooke 2005) and two of *The Winter's Tale* (Boyd 2002 and Cooke 2007). Directors he worked with other than Phyllida Lloyd include David Thacker (as mentioned above), as well as several shows with Lindsay Posner, Dominic Cooke and Matthew Warchus. In the course of our interview he remarked on the expertise and professionalism of the RSC's in-house music directors and sound engineers in supporting composers and having 'great taste and judgement' when dealing with the spaces in which they're working, while demonstrating his

---

[9] His first television score was also for a production directed by Peter Gill, *Hitting Town* (1976) by Stephen Poliakoff.

own deeply philosophical approach to thinking about the interactions of music and action (Yershon 2016).

Ilona Sekacz is a rare female composer at the RSC who also writes for television and film (Sekacz 2016). She is one of the most prolific composers for the RSC, for whom she has worked repeatedly since 1982, and her scores are praised by the musicians for their flexibility when working on the live performance of plays (Reynolds 2016b). Her first production was *King Lear* directed by Adrian Noble with Antony Sher as the Fool in 1982, and her most recent production sees her revisit that play with Gregory Doran directing, and this time Sher is playing Lear (2016). She worked predominantly for John Caird and Adrian Noble, and was one of the instigators of the use of synthesisers and samplers in the 1980s. In interview her understanding of the creation of musical dramaturgies proved fascinating.

Other important composers introduced to the RSC by Woolfenden include Edward Gregson and Howard Blake. Latterly a host of new composers has been employed including Paddy Cunneen, Michael Bruce, Jason Carr, Adrian Lee, Shaun Davey, Corin Buckridge, Craig Armstrong, Dave Price, Stephen Warbeck and Adam Cork. As an example of this younger group, Adrian Lee first worked at the RSC on *The Comedy of Errors* (1996) after already spending around 15 years developing a viable way of devising theatre music scores. His devising process will be detailed in "Electronics, Sound and Fury at the RSC" below, but his score for *The Island Princess* (2002) is notable for including an onstage percussion orchestra of Central Javanese Gamelan instruments played by the entire acting company.

Occasionally in recent years a composer from another field has been brought in for one production as Laura Marling was for *As You Like It* (Aberg) in 2013, John Boden of Bellowhead for *The Winter's Tale* (Bailey) in 2013, Dave Maclean for *White Devil* (Aberg) in 2014, and most recently Perfume Genius for *Salomé* (Horsley 2017). In these cases the director is 'interested in doing something quite interesting and different with the music' (O'Neil 2016) and asks for a particular composer to add a very specific sound world to the production. In addition several of the musicians and music directors have written scores for the company, including John Woolf and James Jones. Jones composed scores that were partly devised in rehearsal with the actors and then scored to include a larger number of players and for which he led the production as a rare percussion/MD. These productions include Michael Boyd's *Henry IV* parts 1–2 (2000) and *Richard III* (2001) (Jones 2016a). It is this type of collaboration drawing on many years of experience with the company that is one of the features of theatre music composition and its evolution at the RSC.

Although these are by no means all the composers who have worked for the RSC this list exemplifies something of the diversity and continuity of practice at the company. Many composers work across media, and as such there is a continuity of signifying practice to communicate with a mainstream audience, while each has his or her own style and influences. Although many composers alter their style and musical genres for each production, some have a distinct musical language that is always apparent; this is particularly true of Guy Woolfenden whose work has a distinctive sense of English identity, and Shaun Davey whose work always carries inflections of an Irish folk heritage (Jones 2016a). Alongside these freelance composers are a vast number of scores by the house composers and music directors so that a gradual evolution of practice was stimulated.

The Band

Music at the RSC in Stratford and later in London and on tour was played by a group of musicians employed on a number of different contracts and using different working patterns, in many different instrumental configurations during the 55 years of this study. In a comparison with the early modern period there is a somewhat similar situation of uncertainty and variety: the practice at the indoor hall theatres and the outdoor amphitheatres differed fundamentally and its exact nature is uncertain. Before 1608, in the plays written for the outdoor theatres, although the location and details of much of the music is uncertain, it is surmised that there was rather more played than is noted in the stage directions (Lindley 2006, 94). The instruments would certainly have included brass instruments and drums for military signals as well as fiddles for dancing, pipes and tabors for dancing and clowning, plucked strings, such as the lute and later viols, or recorders to accompany singing. Despite the amount of music, though, and since the adult companies were performing different plays every afternoon with no requirement for pre-show or act music, it is thought unlikely that the adult companies would have had a permanent band (Ibid., 100). Rather, many actors would have had some musical expertise and apprentices would also have been taught a variety of instruments so that the actors with smaller parts might accompany scenes, or actors accompany their own singing. In the later period, Lindley concludes that it is perfectly possible that a theatrical company might hire musicians for particular performances. Especially for touring, hiring musicians at each venue or for specific performances would keep the touring company size and costs to the minimum (Ibid., 102).

However, professional musicians might have been employed throughout and it is likely that musicians were employed in the later period. The town 'Waits' was a group of professional musicians who numbered about 11 men and 20 apprentices by 1620. They played shawms, sackbuts, viols, recorders and cornetts 'together with other unspecified instruments', and the group later also included singers (Ibid., 55). They played at ceremonial and civic events and festivals as well as giving regular public performances on Sundays for a guaranteed annual salary and livery, and 'their privileged position and musical expertise meant that they were best placed to be recruited [...] by the theatres' for which they would be paid additionally (Ibid., 55). The Waits were the players at some wedding ceremonies, and they were regarded as excellent musicians, foremost of which were the London Waits (Ibid., 56). In the end, though, Lindley can only point to the available information about payments to musicians before reiterating that we simply don't know who was playing the music in the theatres during the original productions of Shakespeare's plays, though it is thought that the quality and professionalism of musicians increased in the indoor theatres, that distinctions must be made between those plays written before and after 1608, and that the written texts represent later rather than earlier practice.

There is a lot more information available about the modern period, but it is also somewhat convoluted. Just before the start of the period of this study in Stratford there was a contracted orchestra who played pre-show music and concerts as well as recording specially composed music for performances at the Memorial Theatre. Their names are not listed in the Souvenir Programmes until 1957 when the orchestra consisted of 13 players plus the director. That music director was Harold Ingram and the orchestra consisted of a Leader (violin), viola, cello, bass, flute, oboe, clarinet, horn, two trumpets, trombone, percussion and a player doubling harp and piano. Peter Hall's arrival as Artistic Director in Stratford was quickly followed by a change in the institutional structure with the addition of a London theatre and an increase from five annual productions in Stratford to six in Stratford plus a further eight or nine at the Aldwych. The company of around 60 actors was increased to over 100 (Beauman

1982, 242). All this created a strain onstage staff and the managerial team as well as on the financial resources, and sat alongside changes to the musical line-up.

In 1959 the Shakespeare Memorial Theatre Orchestra was renamed the Shakespeare Memorial Theatre Wind Band, and for the 1960 season the line-up was changed removing the string section. This group now consisted of a leader, five woodwind players (1 oboe, 2 flutes, 2 bassoons), a percussionist, five brass (2 horns, 2 trumpets, trombone), double bass and a single player who is credited in the programme as playing harp, harpsichord, piano and lute. There was almost a clean sweep of new players in an ensemble that continued to play before the show and between the acts, and who recorded incidental music that was played on discs and later tape during the show. Peter Hall told Woolfenden that the band composition would change for the 1963 season and from then on a group of about ten regular players is listed in programmes of the period drawn from a larger pool that included Gordon Bennett, Martin Best, Richard Callinan, Gilbert Cobbett, Richard Lee, Geoffrey Mason, David Munrow, Derek Oldfield, Robert Pritchard, Gareth Richards, William Salaman, James Walker, Edward Watson and Robin Weatherall (Woolfenden 2018). There were some changes of personnel each year, which supports the idea of insecurity of contract or seasonal employment but, for example, Peter Morris and David Statham on horns with Gareth Richards on trombone can be traced playing together from 1969. Richards left in 1990 when Kevin Pitt took over on trombone, but the other two brass players appear in programmes until 2001, when Morris' name disappears as part of the 2001 redundancies. Although the contracts were seasonal and caused some insecurity to the players themselves (Reynolds 2016a) the practice was that these players were in permanent employment for many years, a practice that was extremely unusual in the sector and may have been accounted for by the requirement of living in the area. However, it was not only the employment contract that changed but the working practice.

Fairly early in the 1960s, under Peter Hall's artistic directorship, there was a transition so that first onstage music was played live, and shortly afterwards offstage music was also performed live—music during the performance had been recorded until this point. This gave composers the freedom to continue developing the music up until, and even after, the opening night, so that it evolved with the production, allowing for extensions or reductions in the length of scene changes, alterations of pace, or other cuts and adaptations through the technical and dress rehearsals, previews, and even during the run of the show. Woolfenden remarked, 'songs are introduced earlier because they have to be learnt, but it's dangerous to provide the score too early as it is likely to change' and having a group of regular musicians under contract with whom he was well acquainted meant that he was able to make changes without difficulty drawing on known strengths and developing the sense of a creative collaboration (Woolfenden et al. 2013). In fact Woolfenden and Tubbs both recalled scoring and rescoring cues overnight immediately before the opening of many productions and relying on players they knew well to be able to adapt appropriately. Jones and Ian Reynolds both comment on the importance of keeping the incidental music and scene change music fluid so that it could be adapted during technical rehearsals, and noted the skill of the regular players in contributing to this flexibility both in rehearsals and in performances (Reynolds 2016b; Jones 2016a).

But to return to the composition of the band, according to Woolfenden and Tubbs, trumpets seemed to 'go out of fashion' with composers for a while in the late 70s and early 80s, though they were always needed for the history plays. Stephen Oliver is identified as one of a group of young composers who wanted to work with different combinations of instruments. A cellist re-appeared in 1974 and other stringed instruments followed, some of which were occasionally played by the core group as extra instruments. For example, when George Fenton wrote a score for *Twelfth Night* in 1974 for guitar, violin and harp, Fenton played guitar, while violin and flute were played by Ian Reynolds (a flautist), Michael Tubbs (an oboe and keyboard player) played Celtic harp, and one of the actors joined in on mandolin. This type of improvisation meant that there was flexibility for composers, and since more shows were being performed and more freelancers being brought in the instrumentation could be expanded, but at a cost. Freelance musicians were being brought in to play because of the demands of composers, but sometimes the core group was not fully employed on other shows, so the question began to be raised as early as the late 1970s about how important it was to maintain the regular full-time employment of the core musicians (Woolfenden et al. 2013). This had become more pronounced with the inauguration of The Other Place (TOP) in 1973 which meant that the band was spread even more thinly among productions and more freelance players were employed. Reynolds[10] records that there was some discussion of dispensing with the musical contingent entirely or alternatively a question as to what the composition of a new 'nucleus' band should be (Reynolds 2016a). So, as Woolfenden recounts, before the 1981 season a conference was held asking all the composers what they thought the ideal musical combination for the core group should be (Woolfenden et al. 2013). At that point it was decided that violin, cello, flute, clarinet and horn would have the most flexibility, but that change appears not to have been implemented as the resident band carried on into the mid-1980s serving all three theatres, though there certainly seems to have been a much greater use of freelance string players and guitarists in the many productions. Michael Tubbs notes that there was still a little wastage (i.e. core players not being fully utilised), but the budgets for extras grew and the road transport links to Stratford improved so that a much greater range of musical sound combinations could be produced (Tubbs 2013).

Richard Brown also describes the gradual attenuation of the band in London during the 1980s and 1990s which resulted partly from the failure to replace members who left, instead using freelance players from the enormous pool of instrumentalists available in London (Brown, R. 2014). The contracts for full-time players at the Barbican were discontinued completely in the late 1990s. However discussions with the MU also affected the ability of the company to maintain a contracted band. The MU policy was to support its members and to achieve fair and equitable rates of pay for them, but the RSC could not afford to pay West End rates for transfers to London. Special rates were negotiated with the MU since the consequence for the company was that a play, which had a smaller profit margin than the commercial musicals with which they competed in the West End, could not break even. Even though both Woolfenden and Brown argued that musicians working in London should be paid the same as other players in the West End, they had to accept that it simply was not viable for the company. As a result a special agreement was negotiated with the MU for the National Theatre, the RSC and Shakespeare's Globe, and the contract band in London was dispensed with in favour of freelance players.

[10] Ian Reynolds was a band member from 1974, band steward, and MU rep from about 1990–2009. He was employed as a dep in April 1974 and took over as full-time flautist shortly afterwards. His first show was *Cymbeline* in June 1974 and he left the RSC in August 2015 after receiving a 40-year long-service award in November 2014. Emails were exchanged in December 2015 and January 2016.

Nonetheless there was a high level of continuity among players who returned repeatedly even in London, and the success of *Les Misérables* (1985) which fed funds back into the RSC coffers for many years brought an easing of the budgetary issues.

From 1977 to 1996 the seasonal pattern didn't change much; four or five productions were produced at Stratford from April to January, then these productions went to Newcastle with the band. The band returned to Stratford while the productions went on to London where a separate band was employed with the same instrumentation. The schedules in the Stratford theatres were aligned so that whatever was on in the main house would always run against the same show in The Other Place (and from 1986 the Swan Theatre), and that way both an acting company and the contracted band were deployed across two/three theatres and could always be fully utilised. Ian Reynolds notes 'I don't think I had a night off in my first twenty years' (Reynolds 2015 and 2016a). In 1997 there remained 12 contracted players (11 plus Music Director)—a group that Andy Stone-Fewings referred to as 'The Apostles' (Stone-Fewings 2015).[11]

From 1997 the pattern of performances changed under Adrian Noble's directorship to maximise the potential for touring and transfers. Separate summer and winter seasons evolved and the schedules of the Swan and main house became independent making it easier to plan tours and transfers of individual productions rather than seasons. An acting company would now only work either at the RST or at the Swan rather than across both, and that meant that musicians could only work in one house too, since if they were performing in a show in one house it could no longer be guaranteed that the dates would not clash with a different show in another house. This change to the way the company programmed its repertoire meant that a player might only be performing in one production in a season if the composers only requested that instrument in one show. This left the player underused at a cost to the company, which ultimately led to a further reduction in the number of contracted band members in 2001. In what one interviewee referred to as 'the Stratford cull', the contracted band was reduced to just six players (flute, clarinet, trumpet, horn, trombone and one percussionist).[12] In further reductions to the old house

---

[11] Andy Stone-Fewings was principal trumpet and MU steward at the RSC at the time of our conversation in 2015.

[12] The final stage of this 'cull' is mentioned in the MU minutes noted below: after protracted negotiations a new agreement was finally reached in 2003.

band, the clarinettist left in 2008 to be replaced by a guitarist in 2009, and the horn player left in 2011 to be replaced in that year with another percussionist, so by 2011 the 'house band' was flute, trumpet, trombone, guitar and two percussionists. There was a further round of redundancies in 2015 and two more jobs were removed: the flute and trombone players were both due to leave in 2015/16, but since a trombone was required for the 2016 season the band remained at five players at the time of this writing. There has been no reduction in the total number of musicians employed on freelance contracts, however, only in the form of employment, which has increased in flexibility at the expense of continuity and job security for the players.

Bruce O'Neil talked about this process in an interview in 2016, describing the change in programming that meant that musicians were no longer able to be fully utilised in the way they had been formerly. However, he reinforced the importance of maintaining live music performance, but expressed the desire of the company to 'widen the options for composers in terms of instrumentation'. He commented on the excellence of young musicians who are able to excel across a wide variety of instruments; 'a wind player, for instance, who plays flute, piccolo, clarinet, saxophone, a few whistles and recorders', while a cello player he was working with also plays 'mandolin, he plays chromatic harmonica and he plays whistles'. He concluded that if each chair gives you that sort of variety it really opens up the possibilities, and by using freelance players each composer can bring a completely different aesthetic to the production. As O'Neil explained,

> I think for composers one of their really key choices is instrumentation. Particularly with doing the Shakespeare plays and reinterpreting a relatively small number of plays those decisions that the artistic team make, the director and the composer, the sort of musical language that the composer might use is one thing. What really gives them a very specific choice, sound and timbre is the instrumentation (O'Neil 2016).

The Economics of Music Performance

In November 1962 a Minute from the meeting of the National Executive of the Musicians' Union (NEC) records that the Assistant General Secretary of the MU, the London Branch Secretary and Chairman, and the management of the RSC had gathered 'to discuss the company's proposed arrangements for employment of musicians in the future' (NEC

1962, 397).[13] The note mentions that the intention of the company is to use musicians 'as often as possible in all theatres in which it played, and that a nucleus of these should be on long-term contracts' (Ibid.). A proposal had been made for an overall contract for musicians employed by the company whether in London, Stratford or elsewhere that stipulated a minimum salary. The contract would include the freedom for the company to continue to use recorded music as part of the action, and in exchange the company would employ this number of musicians (based on the average annual full employment of musicians) on 12-month contracts even though the Stratford season then lasted for only nine months. The company also agreed to pay touring allowances and holiday and sickness benefits. This is the basis for all the subsequent contract negotiations that followed, though changes to the structure continue to be made. At the Midland District Council meeting of 14 June 1964 it was noted that 'a rate of £25 per week of eight performances had been agreed. "Onstage" appearances for certain historical plays were to be paid for at a rate of 15/- per performance.'[14] This appeared settled, but annual negotiations for pay increases doubtless continued so that in 1970 a further Minute records that a draft agreement had been received from the management of the RSC. There does not appear to be any dispute, simply the regular updating and adapting of agreements and contracts.[15]

Musicians have always expressed some dissatisfaction about salaries; an example is recorded in the 1963 Minutes of the Midland District Council of the MU, but in general the absence of Minutes relating to the RSC may indicate a good level of satisfaction overall, though equally it might simply demonstrate the difficulty of obtaining this information. However, in 2003 when difficult negotiations had been proceeding for some time the Minutes of the Midland District Council of 2nd February note that the RSC contract negotiations are 'protracted and on-going' and that a meeting with the band had been scheduled for 25 February. The main sticking points were the new RSC subsistence proposals of 2001 and the application of backdating payments in the 2003 pay offer, all combined with the fall-out from the 2001 redundancies. Three of the affected players

---

[13] Minutes of the MU National Executive Committee meetings are held in the Musicians' Union archive at Stirling University. Those that relate to the RSC were kindly forwarded by Valerie Wells.

[14] 15/- in the LSD currency translated to 75p when the country converted to decimal currency in 1971—or an additional 3% of salary.

[15] A minute of the Midland District Council dated 4 October 1970.

(percussion, trumpet and horn) were all used in the revival of *The Lion, the Witch and the Wardrobe* which ran over the Winter of 2002–03 and so the players didn't actually leave until 18 months after the redundancies were first mooted (Reynolds 2016a). By 27 April the Minute of the same Council notes that a report had been made to the Executive Council and a ballot on the settlement was held. Since there was no further comment, and in all my conversations with music staff and players no further mention of this was made, it must be assumed that an agreement had been reached.

From 1967 when Tubbs joined the company the core group of musicians was contracted for the season and was paid a retainer for the off season in accordance with the MU contract. One reason for employing a contract band in the first place may have been that there were not many freelance musicians in the area in the early days. Since players were obliged to live within 25 miles, and received no travel, touring or subsistence allowances when playing in Stratford, it made sense to encourage musicians to be based in the Midlands by the offer of semi-continuous employment. Many players were recruited from the Birmingham Conservatoire (Brown, S. 2015)[16] and as music in the Midlands developed through the appointment of Simon Rattle as conductor of the City of Birmingham Symphony Orchestra (CBSO) in 1980, freelance musicians became more available who could find enough work to be permanently based in the Midlands. Freelance musicians also became available as a result of the demise of the various BBC Midland staff orchestras in the mid-1970s. This altered the landscape and introduced more flexibility for composers and the company to increase the diversity of instrumentation. Some RSC composers also needed specialists who could play early instruments or strange combinations of instruments. For example, David Munrow played bassoon, rauschpfeife and crumhorn—instruments he employed to great theatrical effect in Woolfenden's score of *The Taming of the Shrew* (Williams 1973); trombonists might double on euphonium and tuba or learn another early music instrument, while music directors played a combination of keyboard instruments, accordion and perhaps guitars or lutes as well as their own instrument. All this made it very hard for such players to take a night off from the production to maintain their freelance careers since finding another musician to deputise (dep) for that combination and any onstage performance would be extremely difficult.

---

[16] Stephen Brown was Midlands Regional Organiser of the Musicians' Union when I spoke to him on 14 December 2015.

MUSICAL COLLABORATIONS AT THE RSC   31

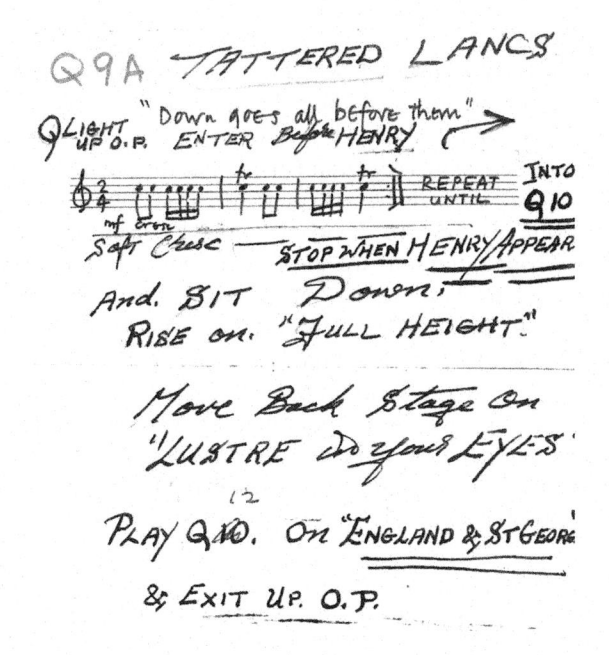

Fig. 1 *Henry V*, 1966. First Trumpet Book. (Music by Guy Woolfenden. By permission of the RSC)

From the mid-1960s, under Peter Hall's leadership, musicians began to appear onstage and in costume. Figure 1 contains an image of the music played by the First Trumpeter during the production of *Henry V* in 1966. The musicians' parts were each written into a tiny cardboard bound book that could be carried in a pocket as the players moved around the theatre and contained not only the music but instructions about where to enter, which costume to wear, and how long a gap there was before the next cue. The books could be attached to some instruments with the clips used by marching bands for playing onstage. The page for Q (Cue) 6[17] includes the fanfare to be played followed by instructions about the quick change the player must make immediately after playing. The players for this production appeared as both English and French bandsmen and so had to keep changing tunics and entering from different sides of the stage.

---

[17] Across the sector cues are routinely written into scores in musicians' shorthand using the symbol Q as in the example from the score here.

In later productions more and more music was memorised, but for marching bands it was always possible to mount music on instruments. Wearing costume, memorising music and appearing onstage, all of which were now required of the musicians, attracted extra payments as stipulated by the MU contract.[18] Such requirements reduce the possibility of employing deps since they not only have to play the music, but need to be at the correct location for entrances and exits and fit the costume. There's a circularity here—contracted staff are less likely to put in deps because they're not maintaining a freelance career outside the company and so it is much easier for them to be available to rehearse and perform onstage and in costume. Equally, the desire of directors to use musicians onstage, who were willing and able to perform onstage, might have increased the importance of maintaining a fixed group of musicians who became comfortable performing in sight of the audience. This fixed group were then more likely to be involved in an ongoing collaborative project.

As Ian Reynolds noted,

> The first advantage of a contract band … is that we were all self-sufficient. Quite often (usually at the Other Place) small groups of us would be entirely responsible for working with composer/director and running the shows ourselves. Being on-stage with an acting company, playing from memory, taking our own word cues, pacing the music etc., became second-nature to most of us old lags. Indeed, some of us rather resented the rise of the MD—I know I got a bit shirty if anyone tried to conduct me in solo cues that I would regard as my responsibility! (Reynolds 2015).

As was apparent in the band book in Fig. 1 the player had to be responsible for his track through the show without a conductor telling him where to go (and it was always a 'him' at this stage), though in practice a small band went through the show together with one designated to lead the band, setting the tempo and indicating the start and end of the cue.

So being in the Midlands was one strong reason for retaining a resident band, another was that it made it possible to achieve the goal of onstage live performance of music. The result was that there was loyalty, continuity and the ability to develop onstage performance techniques. The longer this continued the more expectations of employment grew and patterns solidified becoming ever harder to shift, but this had the advantage that an

---

[18] At some point payment for onstage duties was incorporated into the session payment so that by the 2013 agreement it is assumed to be a standard requirement of players at the theatre.

ongoing collaboration between music department, composers, directors, designers and actors developed so that composers and musicians could be involved earlier in rehearsals than was normal practice in many other theatres, allowing flow to be generated between the collaborators that resulted in a creative interaction between musicians and other members of the creative and performance ensemble.

When Trevor Nunn took over as Artistic Director in 1967 the same group of musicians was retained. It wasn't until the 1970s that new working practices began to be introduced. The records of finance meetings for 1972/73 in the Arts Council papers contain the information that retainers for the band are provided for in the budget, but that most band members' contracts have been terminated.[19] It is assumed that the termination applies to the annual end of season arrangements since there is no other mention of a substantial reduction in players at this time. The core group that Ian Reynolds joined for *Cymbeline* in 1974 still consisted of four woodwind, five brass, two percussionists, the MD (unusually) playing harp and a cellist, which suggests the same level of employment as in previous years. All the 'contracted' band members were actually on 12-month contracts and could be given five weeks' notice of termination, and the full-time contract differed only minimally from the part-time contract in this respect, but, in practice, the regular composers would write for 'the band' and as the years rolled by the players accumulated very valuable employment rights. Even though the regular members legally had 'a job' there was some anxiety at the end of each season until the line-ups for the next season were known (Reynolds 2016b).

Throughout the decade concerns about the costs of the band—whether over or underspent against the budget—are expressed in the balance sheets, but do not seem to be more concerning than the state of the overall deficit of the company and the ongoing negotiations over Arts Council grants. In the report of the accounts for 1974 at a meeting dated December 1976, for example, it is noted that a greater number of freelance players were required for *Cymbeline* at Stratford and the Aldwych 'and making allowance for *King John*'.[20] In the audited accounts for 1974/75 there is

---

[19] RST Balance Sheet as at 2 December 1972 carries this note (Arts Council of Great Britain (ACGB) 1972).

[20] Both *Cymbeline* and *Richard II* transferred to the Aldwych from Stratford, but *King John* didn't transfer. Given the pairing of productions and band members discussed above it may be that this partial transfer had some impact on the budgets and utilisation of band members, but I haven't been able to discover any more detail about the meaning of that clause.

a note that inadequate allowance was made in the estimates for holiday pay due to band members after their return from the USA, but later, that retainers for the band that had been provided for in the budget were not required and that *Macbeth* had used fewer musicians than budgeted for. In both cases savings were consequently made.[21] Likewise in 1975 the production of *Travesties* spent over budget on the band, but this was subsequently rectified by savings elsewhere; the extension of the Stratford summer season by a week led to additional costs in salaries and holiday pay that were recompensed by increased box office receipts. Far more important than the meagre under and over spending against the band budget at this time was the struggle by the company as a whole to maintain its operations with a substantially smaller grant than that received by the National Theatre, and the ongoing threat of bankruptcy that had first emerged in 1967.[22]

Since 1962/63 the RSC had been substantially underfunded, and by the end of the 1970s the disparity of funding between the RSC and National Theatre was immense, partly caused by the way the National Theatre had been created (Beauman 1982, 347). As a comparison, in 1979/80 the National Theatre held 909 performances of 16 productions for an Arts Council subsidy of 4.1 m (plus 0.5 m of GLC funding) while the RSC gave 1209 performances of 20 new productions for an Arts Council grant of just 1.9 m. The box office receipts of the RSC were 2.785 m compared to the National Theatre's 1.611 m (Ibid., 348). This was the result of Trevor Nunn's review of the RSC as a business in 1971. Although it took some years for the ship to be steadied, it had begun to turn around by 1974 and for the rest of the decade maintained its position. Things deteriorated again quite drastically after the election of a Conservative government in 1979.

By 1981 the figures reveal the gap between RSC and the National Theatre was widening again and the RSC's position deteriorated sharply. The RSC had generated income with hit shows, transfers, touring and the sale of television rights as well as introducing commercial sponsorship, but despite this commercial instinct 'unrivalled by any other subsidized British theatre' (Ibid., 348) its financial position declined. By 1979–1980 the grants of the other three major companies (the National Theatre, Covent Garden and the English National Opera) rose by 20%, whereas the RSC

---

[21] ACGB/1/3077 Minutes 1973/1974 and 1974/1975 available at the V&A archives.
[22] This is documented by Beauman (1982) and Chambers (2004).

received an increase of only 7.46% against an inflation rate of 15%. That grant was supplemented later in the year to 13.4%, but the deficit for the year was 61k, and the accumulated deficit when the company finally began operations at the Barbican was 300k (Ibid., 349). It seemed that the more successful the company was at raising funds, the less inclined were the Arts Council and government to increase funding. Here, though it is most important to note that the budgets for band salaries and expenses were largely maintained throughout the 1970s, but fell slightly from 16% to 14% against Company salaries and expenses.[23] This imbalance may be explained by an increase in company sizes but it does provide a sense of perspective on the relative costs within the company. By another measure, though, the proportion of band salaries against production costs fell from 22% to 14.8%. This suggests that productions became more expensive in comparison to company salaries; there could be many reasons for this, but it does present an interesting picture.

As Ian Reynolds noted, at one time Stratford was the heart of the organisation and a contract band could be fully utilised, but gradually, bit by bit, and especially from the late 1990s with the shift in organisational structure productions were constituted with an eye to commercial transfers/touring. This meant that the focus shifted from a full utilisation of the band members in Stratford since, according to the MU contract, a touring production must use the same number of musicians for the tour. This would increase the costs on the tour either through employing freelance players for the tour or to replace the contract band at Stratford, either of which would need additional touring allowances and subsistence. It would be financially advantageous for the RSC to take a smaller band on tour, but because of the MU contract that required the same number of players on the tour as on the original production, it meant a smaller band had to be employed for the whole production from the start, leaving some players out of the equation for the Stratford production of a potential tour (Reynolds 2015 and 2016a). As a result the presence and function of a contract band was again questioned. There was also a constant background discussion about the exact employment/tax/NI status of these annual contracts. This resulted from the fact that the RSC appeared not to be able to decide if it wanted this set-up and if so what instruments it should consist of or to what extent the players should be treated as 'staff'.

---

[23] These percentages are deduced from audited accounts held in the Arts Council papers at the V&A archive, Olympia London.

In fact Andy Stone-Fewings recalls that in the 1990s and later at least two of the company music directors were asked how important the full-time band remained (Stone-Fewings 2015). They, unsurprisingly, supported the players' continued employment.

The working agreement was very complex and fully understood by only the MU stewards and managers, so it required one of the contract band members who understood how the contract worked in relation to doubling, overtime and so on to note what everyone else on the show was doing and communicate this information to Michael Tubbs and later to the music office staff. By 2015 the office was grappling with the problem of how to manage an almost fully freelance band and ensure payment according to the agreed contract. This was especially difficult during a tech week; how were the music staff to collect information in the right format about the numbers of hours played by each player? This was made more complex by the fact that musicians work eight three-hour sessions in a week, any remaining hours are added based on a calculation referring to various different overtime rates. In the same rehearsal the actors are working to an Equity contract that calculates sessions in four hour blocks, and preparation, overtime, breaks and so on are all at different rates. Technicians are on yet another contract working in four hour sessions. So the schedule for bringing together actors, musicians and technicians generally works to a four hour session format. This makes working out the musicians' overtime incredibly complex. Given that there might be several productions being played by any number of musicians on different full, part-time and freelance contracts in each week this becomes a very difficult payroll process.

In addition, although the special RSC contract negotiated with the MU by now included onstage appearance and memorising music in the basic fee, there are additional payments for trebling (i.e. playing three instruments in a show: playing two instruments—doubling—is covered by the basic session fee). These are calculated according to a list in the contract that anticipates, for example, that a flautist will double on piccolo and alto flute, but might also be expected to be able to play any other transverse flute or fife. If they are asked to play an unrelated instrument, for example, a drum or learn a keyboard part, additional payments are made depending on the groups to which the instruments belong. Percussionists have an even more complicated categorisation of instruments into four groups—(i) indefinite pitch and reasonable 'effects', (ii) definite pitch,

(iii) timpani, (iv) drum kit.[24] Those players on a full-time contract are expected to play instruments from three of those categories, but receive an additional payment, while the calculation for part-time players in the third category is slightly different.

A system may evolve where there is no contract set up and each production has only freelance musicians employed. This would have the advantage of simplifying the contract as all musicians would be paid at the same rates, and so the payments would be simpler to calculate. However, because of the difference between the way actors and musicians earn their living it is unlikely that musicians would be so willing to give up their circle of freelance work for a one-off RSC production, so it is possible that the number of deps playing on a production might increase and the system of onstage players in costume might become impossible to sustain (Brown, S. 2015). Although the contract currently limits the number of deps and stipulates a level of loyalty to the RSC contract and production (MU 2013), once the full-time core team is removed this may create increased tensions. There is a further issue that once a musician is on a full-time contract with a nominated base at Stratford the RSC is not liable for any expenses. The pool of players in the Midlands is relatively shallow in comparison with London and, as noted above, this may have been one of the reasons for establishing a full-time group in the first place (Brown S. 2015).[25] If the RSC is required to pay travel and accommodation expenses for a large number of freelancers who are not based in the Midlands then despite any savings in the full-time budget they could end up with a smaller number of musicians costing more overall. So the benefit of greater economic and instrumental flexibility may come at the cost of some of the creativity, established working practices for onstage performance that the core group have developed, and may not, in fact reduce costs.

All that being said, Stephen Brown remarked that the RSC is not only a big employer—employing an average of almost 30 musicians a year—it is also a good employer in sticking to the contract and paying the musicians fairly. However, he explained that freelance players complain that the pay for an eight session week leaves them working for much less than they would earn as freelancers doing eight sessions

---

[24] All information is derived from the *Agreement Between The Royal Shakespeare Company and The Musicians' Union* 2013.

[25] Stated by Stephen Brown and confirmed by Reynolds 2015 and 2016 and Jones 2016.

elsewhere. At the time of writing a new contract was being negotiated that may remove all contracted players and turn entirely to freelance players (Brown S. 2015). It remains to be seen what effects this may have on music at the RSC.

Musical Spaces[26]

One of the distinctive features of the performance of music at the RSC is the presence of live musicians; their involvement in performance or their presence in a band box in the auditorium, or in a variety of locations backstage. This may not be inconsistent with the practice of the early modern theatre, since David Lindley surmises that, for the earlier part of Shakespeare's career, music was provided by the actors themselves playing in cramped offstage conditions (Lindley 2006, 103). As James Jones, a member of the RSC band from 1979 to the present, records:

> I [...] remembered an unusual place where we played. It was the gents toilet in the original "The Other Place". The old "tin shack" was very limited for space and the gents was used for some off stage cues. I think the play was *A New Way To Pay Old Debts* by Philip Massinger and we performed it in the early 1980s. The patrons, when using the facilities, would have to squeeze past a piano, drums and music stands. (Jones 2016b)[27]

The reality of contemporary theatre practice is that it is not always convenient for players to be located in view, but the placement of musicians can affect the perception of the function of music and the dramaturgy of the work as we will discover later. However, in order to play well and to adapt to the pace and immediacy of the play the musicians need to see and hear each other clearly, to see and hear the action onstage and watch for cues from the music director.[28] There is always a negotiation over space in

---

[26] Much of the information in this section is derived from a series of interviews with Roger Howells, Stage and Production Manager at the Aldwych and at Stratford from 1962–1994, that took place between August 2013 and August 2017.

[27] It was directed by Adrian Noble in 1983.

[28] The musicians have referred to occasions when they took cues, timed music and performed on stage without reference to the music director, but in general one of the musicians will be the music director for every production. Even when there is a designated music director it may be decided that an individual player is in a better position to take responsibility for certain parts of the music, especially in a difficult location, on stage, or when following the action.

a working theatre, with so many departments fighting over the premium locations close to the stage, and so musicians can work in some very strange locations. Although this sometimes creates momentary difficulties it contributes to the sense of shared experience among the band, and to the spirit of collegiality, though not many productions place musicians in the lavatories!

In the early modern period it is thought likely that a group of instrumentalists played from 'within', that is from 'behind the *frons scenae* at stage level', whereas in later plays performed at the indoor theatres first, the musicians are referred to as being 'above' (Hosley 1960). This suggests that the musicians used a central space in the gallery over the stage, a practice that was then imported into the open-air theatres sometime after 1608. As Lindley notes, it is only after this date that there was likely to have been a fixed band of musicians requiring a permanent location using a curtained music room over the stage at the Globe (Lindley 2006, 93).

> [T]he new music consort brought the largest single alteration to the King's Men's practices when they took over the Blackfriars playhouse. The housekeepers immediately altered the Globe's stage-balcony to make a curtained music-room over its stage so the musicians could play there as well as at the Blackfriars ... In the next few years, stage-music and song was what differentiated the King's Men at the Globe from the other amphitheatre companies. (Hosley 1960 quoted in Lindley 2006, 93)

Before that it is possible that music was performed at least partly by actors in whatever locations were most convenient.

In modern times theatre pits were more common and a photograph in an edition of *The Architect* Journal in 1932 shows that the old Festival theatre had an orchestra pit that was partly uncovered for the winter season of touring shows. Most of the pit was covered by an apron to make a thrust stage with the space below used for traps and the steps down into the pit used as an acting area. In 1948, for example, Robert Helpman, who was playing Shylock in *The Merchant of Venice*, disappeared forward down the steps into the void when banished from the court. That space under the stage remained even when Peter Hall covered the underused pit in the 1960s, as the empty understage cavern was instead the perfect location for exits and entrances to and from below; using lifts and traps for special effects.

One reason for the gradual development of the sound department (apart from the provision of sound effects) was that alongside the introduction of live musicians performing onstage in the early 1960s, some cues were performed in the wings with or without microphones for amplification.[29] For the 1965 productions of *The Jew of Malta* and *The Merchant of Venice* the band was seated behind the back cloth. The instruments needed to be miked and the sound mixed through amplifiers and speakers out to the auditorium. Consequently it was at about this time that an Assistant Stage Manager (ASM) might choose to specialise in sound, a path taken by Julian Beech who became head of the sound department at the RSC.[30] In the meantime the musicians had become used to walking onstage for fanfares and drumming, but in *Love's Labour's Lost* (1965) they were required to be onstage as part of the action with the drummer using a 'hobby-horse' to carry his drums. Roger Howells suggests that some musicians were not used to this extension of their role and seemed rather uncomfortable, though it is a skill that the regular RSC musicians very quickly developed (2013–17) (Fig. 2).

By 1968 and Trevor Nunn's production of *The Winter's Tale* the band was often sited behind the backcloth which was convenient for their occasional appearances onstage, but this was a 'hippy' production, and Guy Woolfenden's rock-inspired score needed to be played loud. In fact David Addenbrooke describes how, in this production Autolycus bounded on to the stage to 'beat music' with strobe lighting and the company was transformed into the men of *Hair* (Addenbrooke 1974).[31] This production revealed the problems of sound amplification required by high volume popular music in competition with the acoustic voices of actors, and for the whole season the band was enclosed in a specially arranged area behind drapes to muffle their acoustic sound which was mixed through speakers in the auditorium. As a result of this, the following season (1970) a space upstage in the Opposite Prompt (OP) or Stage Right (SR) wing was set aside—as seen in the diagram—and a band box was built with a short wooden staircase leading to a platform for the timpani above.

---

[29] This will be discussed further in relation to *Macbeth* (1962) in "Collaborative Composition at the RSC" and the development of sound as a separate department will be continued in "Electronics, Sound and Fury at the RSC".

[30] He later worked in commercial musical theatre in London and on Broadway, becoming a company director of Autograph Sound from 1981–1998.

[31] *Hair* had recently arrived in the West End (1968) from New York and taken the town by storm.

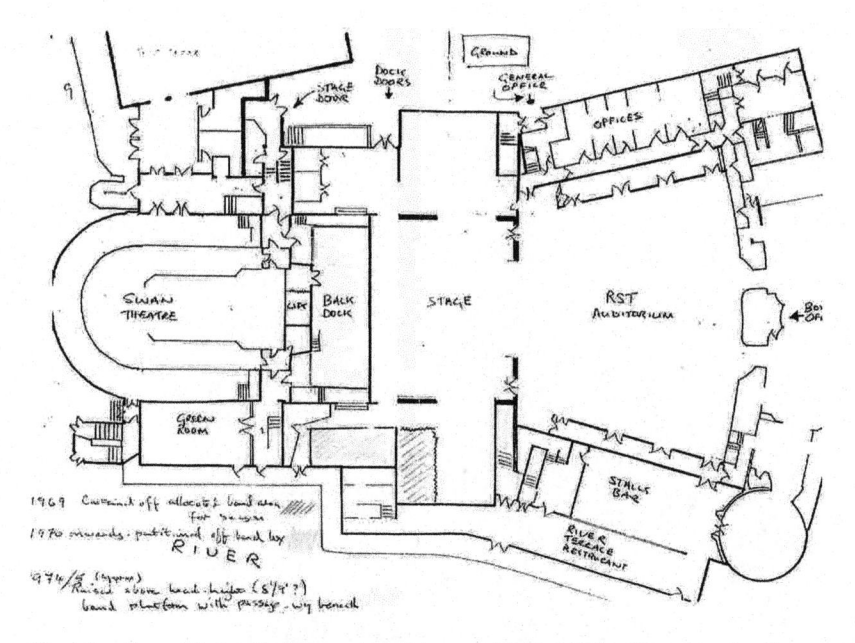

Fig. 2 Sites of the backstage band boxes 1969–2007. (Drawing by Roger Howells. By permission of the RSC)

There was an opening high up on the inside wall which gave some connection with the stage, but closed circuit television (CCTV) (seen on the shelf at the back) and cue lights were also in use. Figure 3 is a photograph of the band playing in the early band box in 1981 demonstrating the relatively small space and the separation from involvement in the stage action, which the players would only have seen on the television at the back of the picture for cueing. The presence of newspapers and playing cards demonstrates the ways in which players kept themselves occupied during the long gaps between some cues. Interesting too, and amusing to current Head of Sound Jeremy Dunn when he saw this picture, was the rank of egg boxes stapled to the wall as a rudimentary and ironic nod to any attempt at sound-proofing or deadening the volume within the box.

This semi-permanent structure allowed for amplification to be operated more effectively—the cables and microphones could be left in place and the sockets below the No Smoking sign demonstrate some links between the band box, prompt desk and the sound box. Despite this 'band box'

Fig. 3 Players in the band box, 1981. (Joe Cocks Studio Collection. ©Shakespeare Birthplace Trust)

being built the designs for each production varied and, as Ian Reynolds was able to elaborate, the band continued to play from many other spaces as well as onstage. The two front of house boxes next to the proscenium arch, to which there was access from backstage via staircases in the Prompt Side (PS) and OP wings were among the most commonly used front of house band locations.

In 1975 for Terry Hands' season of History plays, two gantries were built, one on either side of the stage as part of Abd'Elkader Farah's set.[32] In other years players have played in the fly galleries which were reached by the same stairs as the front of house boxes, while in 1976 most of the music

---

[32] Abd'Elkader Farah was later known in print as Farah, but to his friends as Abd'El.

for *Much Ado About Nothing* (Barton, music by Walker) was performed in the OP wing, and most of *The Winter's Tale* and *Troilus and Cressida* (both Barton, music by Woolfenden) were performed from the PS wing. Finally, that same year *Romeo and Juliet* (Nunn, music by Oliver) was almost all onstage and for *Comedy of Errors* the band was on a narrow platform projected from the PS wing seated two abreast.[33] The following year (1977) the Histories season continued with the band back on Farah's stage gantries while for *As You Like It* (Nunn, music by Oliver) the band was split on two levels again at the side of the stage and in the slips. Until the end of the 1983 season the band played in these various locations; band box, wings, front of house boxes, gantries or onstage in costume. This demonstrates the flexibility of the players in responding to the director's and designer's vision for each production and the extent to which musical performance at the RSC differed from that in a musical or opera where the players were likely to spend the entire performance in one fixed location. It was also unusual in the extent to which musicians performed onstage.

It was in 1984, not 1974/75 as documented in Fig. 2, that permanent space was created in the back dock, behind the back wall of the stage that lasted until 2007. Having completed the drawing of the sites of the band box Roger Howells went back to his own files and discovered that the permanent elevated band box seen in the diagram in the Back Dock from 1974/75 was in fact not built until the latter part of the 1984 season—though as the players note, there were two gantries for the 1975 season that remained until the permanent band box was installed that probably confused the issue. Howells wrote a memo in late 1984 listing the major stage building works to be undertaken during the winter of 1984/85 which included extending the width of the fore stage and revealing the brickwork of the proscenium arch and the proscenium doors at left and right to audience view. Further hidden pass doors were created and the Cue Board for the Deputy Stage Manager (DSM) was moved to 'a masked-off cubicle at the end of the circle box on the Prompt Side'. His note includes the following addendum:

> As an additional feature, towards the end of the season a ten foot high platform was constructed in the Back Dock to accommodate the band when being amplified off stage, thus freeing Wing and Side Bay areas for scenery storage and allowing limited storage and passage way under the platform. R.H. (Howells 2013–2017)

---

[33] This production was recorded for DVD, but the band didn't appear on stage for the video.

The very tall space of the back dock was split horizontally and a floor put in above head height so that a much more spacious band area was created. The rear of this new area (PS end) was screened off for percussion with a Perspex screen that had doors leading to the main part of the band box and a 'cage' in the percussion area for storage. This was less claustrophobic than the previous band boxes as it was larger, open and high.

There was a grand piano up on the platform and a stairway at either end so that musicians could get on and off stage easily, while not interfering with the traffic of actors and stage managers below. Although this space remained in place it was out of use again towards the end of 1985 as the roof at the back of the theatre was removed to develop the Swan Theatre. The open pit was brought back into use for several musicals including *Kiss Me Kate* in 1987 and *The Wizard of Oz* in 1989, and for several Christmas shows including *Secret Garden* (2000), *Alice in Wonderland* (2001) and again for *Merry Wives the Musical* in 2006. The original plan was that *The Lion, the Witch and the Wardrobe* (1998) should also be performed from the pit, but in the end the band was back in the band box, which was perhaps not ideal for a musical, while *Beauty and the Beast* (2003) was accompanied from the front of house boxes.[34] During this time the band also continued to play in various other locations: Richard Brown describes a production of *Mother Courage* (Davies 1984) starring Judi Dench 'with a lovely, lovely score' by George Fenton, for which the musicians were placed right around the back of the cyclorama at various points. 'They had swivel doors so they had to be placed on the door on the back side so they would be swivelled and suddenly be there instrument in hand. It needed a lot of very slick choreography. There were two numbers in that which I conducted downstage with my back to the [proscenium arch] with a white glove and a pen torch'. This production only played at the Barbican in London, but it demonstrates the integration of musicians into the design and the directorial concept for each production.

The RST closed for a major rebuilding programme from 2007 to 2010 and the Swan was also closed. The band played in the temporary experimental Courtyard Theatre on a raised gallery at the back of the stage during

---

[34] Ironically, given that musicals are more likely to use the pit from where musicians and music director can see the stage, musicals are easier to follow than plays. As noted above, plays require musicians to adapt the timing of music cues live in performance so that it fits speeches, whereas songs, by linking melody, harmony, and rhythm are much easier to follow and although musicians still need to follow changes of tempo and adapt to the stage, the music is more likely to be played through from beginning to end (Brown, R. 2014).

this period of closure, perhaps more like the placement of the band in the indoor theatres after 1608, before returning to the rebuilt theatre in 2011. It seems that very little thought had been given to the placement of the band in the rebuilding programme, and the only place that could be found was once again behind the stage. As Ian Reynolds noted 'one wit remarked that after a hundred million quid we were still freezing our ***** off in exactly the same place as twenty-five years before' (Reynolds 2016a). After the New York residency that year the band was located on the 'paint frame', a narrow gallery on the third floor high up behind the stage, where, with some exceptions, they stayed for the next two seasons, taking over the whole width of the gallery which was a good size and had a reasonable acoustic, though it got very hot. Since then the musicians have lost the first floor backstage 'studio' and have moved even higher up the building to a band room on the fourth floor that unfortunately is not sound proofed. However, the recent productions I've seen have often had the band located in view in triangular blocks known as the 'cheese pieces' because of their shape. They are just inside the auditorium either at ground or circle level on either side of the thrust stage of the new auditorium, or at gallery level upstage centre. These positions give good accessibility to stage and auditorium for live appearances and according to Bruce O'Neil the bands are happy there (O'Neil 2016).

During the residencies in Newcastle-upon-Tyne the band didn't have a permanent home until the 1987 rebuild, but were variously placed under the stage and in a variety of dressing rooms or in the area behind the stage. After the rebuild in 1988 two small cramped, stuffy sub-stage rooms were allocated to the band. Similarly once the Barbican opened there was a virtual recording studio in the basement from where more than 50% of the scores were played. Richard Brown recalls that it was very sad that audiences were often unaware that the music was live at all (Brown, R. 2014).

Despite this extraordinary list of places musicians performed around the buildings, the players record that this was always perceived as being at the service of the production. Players moved from one location to another during many performances, depending on whether they were playing atmospheric music or appearing on stage, and all this was the result of a director's and designer's vision for the piece. This might have had the potential for all sorts of problems with ensemble cohesion as instrumentalists tried to hear each other, see a conductor, or spot a cue, but technical rehearsals were exhaustive and any communication problems were dealt with immediately. A number of different offstage locations might be tried so that the correct effect was created onstage and then headphones, monitors or cue lights were organised to make that location practical for the musicians. In fact, it appears that part of the joy of working at the RSC was the variety of music, instruments, locations and collaborators with whom the musicians came into contact.[35]

Although in my interviews I heard many comments about difficult and cramped conditions, and that space had to be negotiated for with many other departments who were also essential to the success of productions, understanding the larger picture seems to have been a key feature of music production, and collaboration one of its joys.

The Science of Flow

Although speculation about potential consequences of current negotiations between the MU and the RSC resulting from changes to working practices and the reduction in the number of 'permanent' players is interesting, the focus of this study is the past, and it seems that the long and close working relationship of the core group of players, and the many excellent freelance players who returned repeatedly and added to this core team contributed to a spirit of creativity and flow.

'Csikszentmihalyi's theory of flow …proposes that individuals experience a flow state when the challenges of the task are perfectly matched to their own level of skill' (Sawyer 2003, 253/356). Experiencing a state of flow is pleasurable for the participants. It requires a known structure and a certain amount of fear—improvisers refer to it as 'groupmind', 'a state of unselfconscious awareness in which every individual action seems to be the right one and the group works with apparent perfect synchronicity' (Seham 2001 quoted in Sawyer 2003, 257). The performance of music by an ensemble of excellent musicians working together to achieve the effects the composer imagines in co-operation with a music director the group trusts elicits this state of 'groupmind'. It is not surprising therefore that in the spirit of collegiality and in order to maintain the quality of the performance and the high level of cohesion and collaboration the players look after each other's deps, making sure they are prepared for onstage entrances or understand any cuts or changes, are aware of awkward corners, or long pauses in the score or performance. It is this spirit of colle-

---

[35] Richard Brown, Jim Jones, and Ian Reynolds all spoke of variety as one of the key reasons for their enjoyment of working at the RSC.

giality that shines through in all the exchanges with players and music directors; the band was happy and successful because it was able to produce high quality work and felt supported and valued.

There is a psychological explanation for what the musicians describe; as Ian Cross notes in 'Music and communication in music psychology'. When people make music together, they co-ordinate their behaviours in time (Cross 2014). Normally this results in a pulse around which all the participants work, allowing them to anticipate, predict and align their parts with those of others: 'when making music together, participants entrain their attention, actions and sounds with those of other participants' (Ibid.). This is not simply that the musicians align themselves with a music director but that all the musicians work together in creating the body of the music. In this case, though, there is a further wrinkle as players slow down and speed up, sometimes without the aid of a conductor or music director, to make a piece of music fit the length of a speech or scene change that might deviate slightly from performance to performance; and experienced theatre musicians do this together without any overt communication at all (Jones 2016a, b).

The scientific evidence indicates that 'when people entrain their behaviours with one another [...] they are likely to experience an enhanced sense of mutual affiliation with each other'. As Cross summarises it, playing together 'has powerful effects on social bonding' such that 'a sense of collective convergence' is likely to be sustained (Cross 2014). Musicians who play together over a long period are likely to experience a powerful sense of belonging to the group as well as satisfaction and pleasure in the coordination of that music. It seems likely that the group cohesion and the collaborative creativity of the group results, at least partially, from the fact that the group makes music together. This satisfaction arising from the creation of excellent music working with excellent theatre means that other issues may be treated with less concern as long as the group is able to make music effectively.

And there is one further issue; the working environment or playing spaces in which the musicians perform are many and various, offering variety for the players even though the locations may occasionally be less than ideal. As Ian Reynolds remarked:

> Unless there were severe problems of safety or logistics we would have a go at anything. Any RSC musician could regale you with stories of weird and wonderful things done onstage during our careers and being onstage with

some ethnic instrument just got from the music store and playing a cue just learned in the teabreak was all part and parcel. Our flexibility was our greatest survival tool. However, by far and away the most important aspect was that each individual in the contract set-up had a high level of classically trained instrumental technique. (Reynolds 2016a)

To return to the creativity theory with which this chapter began, the quality of the performance that requires the group to perform at the peak of its abilities despite all the pressures adds to the sense of flow and the pleasure of performance.

The question that creativity theorists ask is whether it is possible to identify the single 'ideation unit' provided by one contributor to a group work. Clearly the musical and sound 'units' produced by the players are identifiable in the performance, but the steps through which that result is reached, the flow that generated the ideas, and the process of maintaining that sense of flow through productions and seasons is not so clearly identifiable. The decision to employ a certain group of musicians or to build a band box in a particular location, to employ a particular director or composer, or to ask the musicians to appear onstage creates a situation that leads to a spiralling flow effect of other decisions whose consequences can rarely be traced simply to the one decision. All these are contributory factors when considering the production and performance of music in a collaborative environment where many creative teams interact around the central focus: the performance. The ephemeral nature of the interactions and the importance of good communication among the production team are all difficult to predict, document or define. All the contributors are essential even though their contribution may be un- or under-acknowledged. Productions rely on the high levels of skill of musicians and music directors, the expertise of theatre composers, the development of specialists in sound design and operation, the contribution of actors and the vision of directors.

Conclusion

At the start of this chapter I suggested that the slow pace of evolution and the long periods of employment of many staff contributed to the freedom for creativity to occur. Music psychology predicts that playing together produces 'entrainment' or 'groupmind' but that this relies on the quality of the output and the ability of all members of the team to contribute their different but complementary skills to the production of the shared outcome. Not only have the players become part of a unique collaborative process, but, as well as their very high level of instrumental expertise, they have learnt some very particular skills that include performing onstage; working with actors, directors and composers; adapting music to fit text and stage action; communicating effectively with stage management, directors, and sound departments over technical requirements; and creating a collegial atmosphere by supporting deps and playing in strange locations. Within this framework excellent productions appeared in which music played a key part. However, many interviewees commented on the changes that began to occur as a result of increased digitisation, reduced numbers of long-term contracts, and the growth in the numbers of productions and performances. The framework that had produced an extraordinary collaborative project began to fragment leading to new structures and practices whose consequences are, as yet, somewhat unclear, and to which I will return later. But the people I have only focused on briefly in this chapter are the composers, so it is to them that the next chapter will turn.

Collaborative Composition at the RSC

> *Orpheus' lute was strung with poets' sinews,*
> *Whose golden touch could soften steel and stones,*
> *Make tigers tame and huge leviathans*
> *Forsake unsounded deeps to dance on sands.*
> *Visit by night your lady's chamber-window*
> *With some sweet concert: to their instruments*
> *Tune a deploring dump; the night's dead silence*
> *Will well become such sweet-complaining grievance.*
> (*The Two Gentlemen of Verona*, 3.2.79–82)

Orpheus, in classical mythology, was, with his lute playing, able to charm all living things and even some inanimate objects. He was the singer/songwriter above all others, and seems an appropriate figure to introduce a chapter about the composers of music. In the speech above Proteus uses the reference to Orpheus and his lute to encourage Thurio to take a concert (a consort or group of instrumentalists) and play beneath Sylvia's window so that he might win her heart. Music is able to accomplish such feats in mythology (and in musical theatre). While we don't generally believe music to have such magical abilities now (and not in literary plays) it is already clear from the discussion above that playing music affects the players. While I will not address music's affective powers directly I will outline some of the aesthetic changes that have occurred in the way composers work and the music they produce that creates different experiences for audiences.

The research enquiry in this chapter explores two central questions: how the process of collaboration that lasts at least a year influences the music heard on opening night; and how composition changed over time, revealing developments in production practices, stylistic changes in taste and technological innovations. To address the first part of this enquiry I look in detail at notebooks, prompt copies and scores of a number of plays and periods, comparing some of the processes and strategies with those of the early modern period and with Roland Settle's 1957 description of how to compose for theatre before addressing some of the compositional processes involved in creating a score. Then to address the second part I consider several treatments of a single text—*Macbeth*—that were created at intervals during the period from 1961 to 2015. This strategy is designed to highlight some of the key changes that affected the processes of composition and the aesthetics and functions of theatre music at the RSC. Thus there are two timelines in this chapter; the timeline of a production from the idea of a particular play being mooted to the opening night, and the changes in the ways in which music is written and used at the RSC that occurred between 1961 and 2015. Broadly the findings are that the expediency of the production process often results in a composer's vision being absorbed into the overall collaboration to the extent that it becomes inseparable from other parts of the performance, though there are significant changes in the sound of composition over the longer period of the research.

The Production Timeline

The usual timeline for a production is that decisions about which play to produce and who will be booked as the creative team are taken as much as a year in advance of the opening night (and sometimes even further ahead). Sometimes composers might have very little time to write music, but on many occasions they will begin having conversations with the director at the start of that period, giving plenty of time for development. It is very clear, however, that every experience a composer has with a different director and producer is different, so outlining a single coherent process is doomed to failure. There are some key points that can be pinpointed and some practical similarities in the production timeline that structure the creative process, however.

As noted, composers are likely to have been involved in conversations about the production with the director and possibly the designer from an early stage and often as much as a year before the performance is due to open. Looking at the developing plans or models of the set, and discussing the period and feel of the production will have led her/him to begin a period of research and to make suggestions to the director about musical styles, genres, orchestral timbres and so on. Nigel Hess describes the initial stages of the process as beginning 'months before rehearsal' and from that discussion gradually the ideas are formulated (Hess 2015). Ilona Sekacz refers to the two masters (other than the director) as 'the clock and the calendar' (Sekacz 1994, 261). Although composers might have initial meetings over several months the rehearsal period generally takes six weeks for a play followed by a technical rehearsal of two to three days, two dress rehearsals and a preview period before press night. The entire band is likely to be present for the whole technical rehearsal that may take two or three very long days. In musical theatre and elsewhere it is more common for a pianist and the MD to attend and note any changes that need to be put into band parts before the dress rehearsal, but the attendance of the entire band means that cues, their length and the place of their playing, can be experimented with and any difficulties resolved at this stage, and this is required because of the collaborative, live and onstage presence of musicians. As Sekacz notes of her score for *Troilus and Cressida* (1985) 'During the technical I adjust the lengths and sometimes the qualities of the piano music to suit the action. The head of the sound department sits with me in the auditorium and together we adjust the levels of the tape and the live music' (Sekacz 1994, 265). In this case she had created a sound tape depicting war scenes that would contrast with a piano score that would reference the domestic world. The piano could be played live offstage and mimed by an onstage actor, or be played live onstage. In a final coup de théatre the piano converted into a pianola courtesy of the inventive engineering of head of music, Michael Tubbs; the piano played itself even down to the movement of keys. These are the two time frames within which the composer must work: first having conversations and doing research over several months when they formulate ideas and some write quite a lot of material, and then an intensive rehearsal period during which a lot might change.

The Writing Process

Guy Woolfenden found it difficult to describe the writing process, commenting that after building relationships with the director and designer, and knowing the script and the instrumentation, he simply wrote 'music that seems to fit' (Woolfenden et al. 2013). The directors described their concepts, the designers showed their drawings and the composer offered ideas and concepts in sound. Each responded to the stimulus of the others while eventually also allowing the pace and movement of the actors in rehearsal to influence and alter what was produced in a spiralling and effervescent process of generation and regeneration. Nigel Hess described using the piano with pencil and paper to create lots of different sketches of motifs and ideas that he would go through with the director, discussing the themes, atmospheres and styles, and deciding which versions to take into the rehearsal room to try out with the actors (Hess 2015). During rehearsals and in collaboration with the director he discovered where extra bits of underscore might enhance the dramatic mood or where themes were not working, and would be on hand to make changes. The technical rehearsal is the time when most changes might be made—for example, if a truck took three times longer to move than anticipated—but the very large support group and the experienced live musicians made such late changes perfectly possible, and indeed, normal. Such collaboration, he remarked, contributed to the pleasure of working at the RSC (Hess 2015).

Ilona Sekacz is more systematic in documenting the four stages of her process of composition for the theatre in collaboration with the creative team as: 'talking about it, research and thinking about it, writing it and fitting it to the action' (Sekacz 1994, 261). But the process she describes in her article 'Composing for the Theatre' is only another way composers work. James Jones had spent many years as percussionist for the company before being asked to write the score for the season of plays known as *The Histories* directed by Michael Boyd.[1] He spent the entire six-week rehearsal period of each play in the rehearsal room with the company, improvising live, then scoring the music for the other players and leading the performance as music director from the percussion chair. This is a similar process to that used by Peter Brook and Richard Peaslee for the production of *A Midsummer Night's Dream* in 1970, though Peaslee was not in rehearsal every day. Adrian Lee also devised scores in the rehearsal room with actors

---

[1] *Henry IV* parts 1–2 (2000) and *Richard III* (2001).

and director, a practice that was surprisingly uncommon even when he first worked at the RSC in 1996 (Lee 2017).

Jones, from his experience as a player over many years, described a different composition process, that of Stephen Oliver, as 'last minute and chaotic'. Oliver brought songs and dances into the rehearsal room early so that the actors could learn them, but since the other parts of the score needed to be fitted to text or scene changes, and Oliver had extraordinary facility as a composer, they were often only written at the very last minute (Jones 2016a). Some composers leave more of the score unfinished than others at this stage, and rely on their own invention and the reading skills and flexibility of the musicians so that they can make overnight adaptations to incorporate changes by the next day. The ease of this has, of course, increased in recent years since the widespread use of digital scoring software means that changing a master score allows immediate printing of new and accurate parts. Until the introduction in the 1990s of such software as Sibelius all scores and parts were written by hand and band parts were copied out overnight by music copyists.

Asked which of the composers was most adept at preparing a score for the vagaries of theatrical rehearsal and performance, the musicians mentioned Ilona Sekacz's scores. She carefully incorporated ways of changing the length of music cues on the spot by inserting 'till ready' bars, pauses, word cues that signal when to continue, and musical patterns that could easily be repeated without upsetting the musical structure (Jones 2016a). In Fig. 1 there is an example of one of Sekacz's graphic scores from 1982 (for *King Lear*). This is the storm scene in which the sound of the storm was created by recording voices speaking into the resonating box of a piano, effects were then added and the three tapes played alongside the music (the bottom three lines of the score). Above that in the score are the live sounds of offstage performers also speaking into microphones, keeping time with the semi-improvised instrumental score all of which is dictated by the verbal cues in the action that structure the forward momentum of the piece. The issue here is that the three sound tapes would need to be recorded in advance and the actors would need to rehearse—making adaptations late in rehearsal difficult—but recording on three separate devices meant that any of the sound tapes could be cued or paused at any time throughout the scene. All the other cues are fixed to word cues from the stage as noted in the score and so could be adapted as required by the production live at every performance. This is only one of many developments in scoring that composers have experimented with in order to

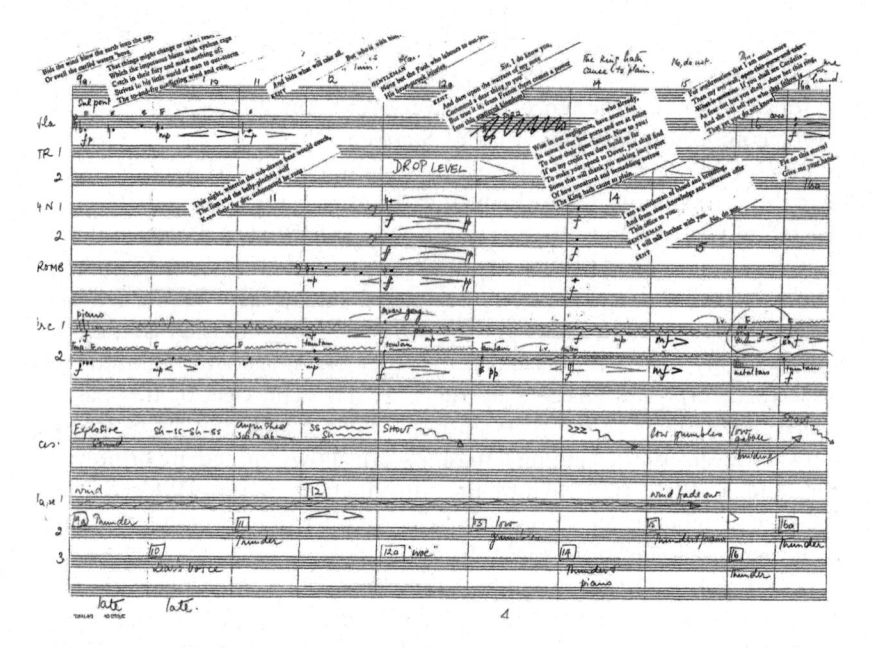

Fig. 1   *King Lear*, 1982. (Music by Ilona Sekacz. By permission of the RSC)

structure and plan a complex sound world, parts of which would be performed live and parts rehearsed and recorded, while yet other parts were subject to improvisation so that the entire piece created an aural world but has enormous flexibility in performance.

Graphic scoring had been developed by contemporary composers from the 1960s onwards, following such luminaries as John Cage, Earle Brown, Morton Feldman and Cornelius Cardew, and offered opportunities for a much higher level of interpretation or even improvisation in performance within fixed parameters. Part of the reason for this development was that it removed the fixity and reproducibility of performance, making each performance unique, but it also altered the hierarchical relationship of composer and musicians allowing greater freedom for musicians to make an original contribution.

There will be more discussion of scoring below, but for now I will return to the process of writing with Gary Yershon who spoke about beginning to develop ideas for each new production in early discussions with the director. For Yershon one of the key decisions was the choice of ensemble, so when director David Thacker asked for a melodic and romantic score for *As You Like It* (Thacker 1992), Yershon's first choice would have been 'a mass of strings [but] there just wasn't the money' (Yershon 2016). Instead the romance was created using a synthesiser for mass strings especially in the masque, but otherwise he used harp and flute. For *Hamlet* (Warchus 1997) the sound world contained a tuba, a euphonium, an alto flute, a guitar and bass guitar; 'it was quite a weird combination of things' (Ibid.). Finding the sound world for Yershon is an important step in creating the designer's world in aural terms since 'instrumental colour can do a lot of the work for you'. He continued: 'you are driven by your colours to create a certain kind of music. It will push you either to work with those colours or to pull against what the instruments naturally do, so it generates a spectrum of possibilities.' He also discussed the amount of time spent in the rehearsal room, partly to teach songs and dances, but also because that kind of interaction with actors and director is part of his creative process; to some extent he 'finds it' in the rehearsal room (Yershon 2016).

Michael Bruce also described the importance of creating the 'sound world' of a production through the choice of instrumentation and through being open to the possibility that the musical concept might shift completely during rehearsals as new information is continually fed into the process. He focuses on creating a sound world that combines 'elements of music and sound design into a cohesive whole… ensuring consistency across all elements' through collaboration in the rehearsal room with the director and especially the sound designer (Bruce 2016, 24).

Within the time frame of pre-production and rehearsal the composer needs to provide music where it will be required by the production, whether because it is called for in the text, or for a scene change, or because it will promote and enhance the director's vision of the work. This is what is sometimes called music or song spotting. Michael Bruce described how, for a production not at the RSC, he and the director 'went through the play and marked the points where music might fit, and noted what each scene change needed to accomplish both dramatically and practically' (Bruce 2016, 30)—a process that all composers go through. Nigel Hess similarly describes very early discussions with the director about where music is going to go and what it is going to do (Hess 2015), something Settle in 1957 had also suggested. Settle also remarked that the prospective composer should consider whether music should 'fade-in or arise suddenly to emphasise a dramatic effect' (Settle 1957, 22). Richard Brown also spoke about the importance of deciding how music started and finished, referring to these as the 'inpoints and outpoints'. In many cases, just like when writing film music, this is so that the entry or exit of music is imperceptible; unless it is desirable for theatrical effect there should be a disruption of the atmosphere as music enters (Brown, R. 2014).

Alongside music spotting, what the production will look like seems to be a key feature for many composers in deciding how the production will sound. Richard Brown, who wrote several scores for the company during his time as Company Music Director at the Barbican, commented on this (Brown, R. 2014), as did Guy Woolfenden, who said:

> I couldn't have begun to work on this play [*Henry V* in 1975] without knowing Terry's ideas [Terry Hands, the director] about the play, and Abdel's. Until Abdel [Abd'El Farah, the designer] had come up with the catwalks at the side of the stage I didn't even know whether we had a place to put musicians. Until Terry had told me how the opening sequences of the play were going to be done—in actors' ordinary clothes, as if at a rehearsal— I couldn't decide how and when to start the music. (Beauman 1976, 46)

Ilona Sekacz describes the collaborative process as one that is 'headed by a director who is responsible for the finished product' (Sekacz 1994, 261). She recounts a filtering process where all ideas are offered to the director by all the contributors, and all the creative personnel abide by his decisions.[2] Like the other composers she notes that the rehearsal process will change the concept to some extent as new discoveries are incorporated into the production, new discoveries that might need to be reflected in the music, but the larger thematic ideas, instrumental colours and musical genres already have been settled upon.

Songs and dances are taught to actors early in the rehearsal process and will change very little, but the length and style of other music cues change during the rehearsal period, and music changes more than most elements during the technical rehearsal as the length of scene changes becomes apparent. Music can continue to change as a result of the dress rehearsal, and even after the play has been performed for audiences during the preview period. As Sekacz says 'scene changes usually get shorter as the stage crew learns the best ways of manipulating the set, and they

---

[2] There were relatively few female directors employed at the RSC at this time, but in this case I refer to 'him' simply because Sekacz focuses in her article on a specific process of collaboration with Howard Davies.

may lengthen again if the audience reacts, say with laughter or applause' (Ibid., 261). Because of this, music directors play a role in working with the composer to adapt and implement the composer's vision of the sound world for the practicalities of theatre production. The amount of input from the music director, and the amount of revision that takes place varies from production to production, composer to composer, depending on experience and availability.

Richard Brown commented on the many functions music carries out simultaneously that are both practical and aesthetic. As he describes it, the songs and battles don't move within a play; the structure of the work always remains the same, but the productions can sound very different and so have a different effect on audiences and performers. It is this originality in each new production that creates variety for the composers, and indeed for the actors, stage management teams and the musicians who might, in a lifetime, work on many productions of the same play. Similarly, even the scene change music that articulates travel from one place to another, such as Verona to Milan in *Two Gentlemen of Verona*, can create completely different atmospheres and begin and end at surprisingly different places.

In sum, the various processes within the timeline include the following: discussions of time and place setting and the vision of what the director wants to achieve with the production; sound and music spotting and discussions of the journey or task each music cue needs to accomplish; whether it needs to be noticed or not and thus how and where it will start and end; decisions about instrumentation that will create the colour palette of the production and are likely to be influenced by the designer as much as the director; and then the adaptations that will occur during rehearsal and production weeks. With all this information composers generate ideas, share them with the director and gradually build up a draft score that continues to evolve even sometimes after the production opens.

I will return to some of these ideas about music's function in "Theatre Music at the RSC" below, but clearly such features are not particular to the work of the RSC, and since many of the composers, directors and musicians are freelancers who work in TV and film, this understanding of the relationship of sound and vision crosses media in the analysis of audio-visual imagery. However, what is particular about the work of the RSC is the long-term collaborative process that allows and supports experimentation during the rehearsal period, and adaptation of the musical score and performance by long-serving and experienced live musicians during the run of the show.

Collaborative Composers

That theatre music is a collaborative art by now goes without saying, but perhaps the closest collaboration is that between composers and music directors. Some freelance composers ask for more interaction and support from the music director, others arrive with, or (on very rare and relatively recent occasions) send in, a complete score or set of cues for the music director to translate as required by the performance. Still others enjoy collaborating with the versatile music directors, sound designers and performers. Whether or not the composer is an active collaborator who attends rehearsal regularly, the music director's job is to translate the score into performance, thus generating a coherent interaction between the composer's music and the director's vision. The music director is always on hand to work with the composer, assisting with arranging the music around the required cues, teaching songs and dances to actors, and leading the musical ensemble in performance. It is generally a very balanced collaborative process. However, Richard Brown recalls a young composer coming in for a show in which Terry Hands wanted the band onstage throughout, but Hands had given the composer the idea that mock medieval effects were required. Unfortunately, when he heard the sounds the composer had written Hands thought the timbres were too distinctive and overpowered the scene. Gradually he cut cue after cue, decimating the score. On the DX7 synthesiser there was a sound that he liked—a calliope sound—that could be used to play the melodies without being so present in the scene. By the time the show opened all the carefully scored material had been cut and the onstage band played just five cues with the rest being played by the MD using that sound. Brown's point is that a composer should not take what the director says too literally but should find a musical way of contributing to the dramaturgy.

Other composers have had similar experiences, according to Bruce O'Neil; finding whole sections of their beautifully scored music cues cut for entirely practical reasons at the first technical rehearsal. In some cases this music has been revived on CDs of the music for shows (O'Neil 2016) since the problem was not the music itself but the timing or the change of direction during rehearsals. Woolfenden always advised that a composer should take great care not to frighten the director by using too many technical musical terms, particularly if the director was not naturally very musical. However, many of the directors understood music and its effects very well such that the director's use of language to describe what he wanted was usually sufficient. An example of this was that Peter Hall simply described *Richard III* (in the Wars of the Roses season of 1963) to Guy Woolfenden as 'Medieval Fascist' and Woolfenden knew exactly what was required (Woolfenden 2018).

A different type of experience is described by O'Neil as the process of working with Laura Marling's songs for *As You Like It* (Aberg 2013), a composer who was not present for the rehearsals. He incorporated themes from the songs into the show as incidental music, and although he described this as a specific and unusual case it is not unprecedented that a composer would write songs or themes and hand them over for the MD to arrange as incidental music. In particular, O'Neil notes that it was the model in Frank Benson's day in the 20s, 30s and 40s when notable composers were music directors of productions, and they were adept at arranging and orchestrating so it was unnecessary for the composer to carry out these roles. In the case of *As You Like It* O'Neil used the raw material he had been given, which he then developed and adapted for the climactic moments in the play during rehearsals. As he recalls, '[Marling] wrote enough material that had enough variety within it' so that he could use chord sequences, textures or melodies elsewhere. 'The most radical thing I did was combine two different songs that happened to work nicely slotting together' (O'Neil 2016); a wedding dance and an anthemic tune were combined at the climax at the end of the play thus serving the play and the director's vision. This is a rare occurrence of a well-known singer songwriter being engaged, who probably had a good effect on the box office, but who was not used to theatrical compositional practices. It is to the credit of the music director that the transformation of the seasons required to progress the play's context was as effectively accomplished as it was, though, of course, the musical style and the popularity of the songs also brought a new and fresh sound to the production. Occasionally the director is also recorded as the composer as in the case of Peter Brook in *Titus Andronicus* and *The Tempest* (Lindley 2006, 111), but in general the practices outlined above hold.

These anecdotes demonstrate something of the fluidity of boundaries between arranging, orchestrating and composing and the overlap in the roles of music director and composer. Clearly composers who hand over a score or group of pieces have a different relationship to the theatrical style and concept of the piece from those who are in rehearsal developing and adapting the music throughout, but given the expertise of the music director the productions can be equally successful. It is just another of those fluid collaborative relationships that add variety and keep the process of creating the music for a production interesting.

Composing Theatre Music

Having discussed the practicalities of the production timeline for composers it is now time to consider the writing process itself. Quite an interesting picture emerges from Ronald Settle who wrote about the practice of composing music for theatre in 1957. Settle's work provides a starting point against which to understand the changes that were about to take place. He begins by highlighting the similarity in the work of a composer seeing a film he is about to score and the music director of a theatre reading a play or seeing it in rehearsal and deciding what music should be used. That many of the later composers for the RSC wrote for all media only serves to support such correlations—if anything the interactions between media only become stronger.

One of the issues Settle raises is that of whether to use existing music when creating an original theatre music score. At the time of his writing this was the common practice: 'the music plot must necessarily be chosen from existing compositions and, although there is an almost unlimited stock available, some inaptness in the choice of incidental music occurs not infrequently in the theatres to-day' (Settle 1957, 19). Over the previous quarter century there had been an incredible growth in musical activity in the film industry, sound radio, television and gramophone recordings, all of which had improved the quality of the materials available. Settle's concern was that the cumulative effect of this growth was that audiences had a keener perception of music and a wider range of repertoire, and it was to this repertoire that musicians of the period turned when creating music for theatre. He advised composers to choose music that is 'congenial to the general mood of the scene', and which is 'comparatively rarely heard as hackneyed works are apt to draw attention to themselves by appealing to the auditory sense—music should be heard rather than listened to' (Settle 1957, 22). This reinforces the idea that well-known music has a stronger sense of presence than the 'unheard' music for which composers of theatre music often strive.

Settle suggests that 'gramophone records are invariably the most popular and effective means of using incidental music' and for bridging the blackout of scene or costume changes (and it is clear he is talking about specially made recordings played on a panatrope—about which there will be an explanation in the next chapter), but for anything longer it is better to 'put up the house lights to half and have some live music played by the orchestra'. Both, he says, are potentially disruptive, since the switching on and off of orchestra lights is as distracting as the intrusion of a recording. This is interesting given the discussion in the previous chapter about the move to the use of live music and musicians in the 1960s after a period when recorded music during performance had been the regular practice, with live music only at intervals.

His instructions for composers are that: music should indicate and be consistent with the period of the production; that the music should be written by one composer if possible to ensure uniformity; that in the tragedies the emotional aspect of the music should be the point of focus rather than historical authenticity; that for incidental music live and recorded sources should not be mixed; that consideration should be given to where the music was to be played and by whom; and that scene change music should not clash with other music in the play such as songs (Settle 1957, 70). The early practice at the RSC appears to conform in most respects to this strategy with the employment of a single composer for each production working alongside the director assisting in the creation of a unified vision for the production and very little use of pre-existing music except when a particular effect is required.

In the 1960s and 1970s the early music movement spread throughout Europe and the USA, and can be witnessed in the desire for 'authentic' productions at Stratford in the 1950s and 1960s (Wilson 2011, 135). Performers and researchers were interested in exploring what the performance of music of earlier periods might have sounded like by playing the works on instruments of the period, but towards the end of the twentieth century there was a further development. 'Historically informed performance' (HIP) combined the attempt to apply the stylistic and technical aspects of performance and the use of instruments of the period based on detailed research so that the production might recreate the approach, manner and style of the era when the work was conceived. This practice was followed at Shakespeare's Globe Theatre that opened in 1997 where Claire van Kampen, having researched musical practices in the Renaissance period worked with players of early musical instruments 'to marry modern reconstructions of Elizabethan and Jacobean music to Shakespeare's texts for performance in the Globe using only reconstructed period instruments without amplification or electronic aids' (van Kampen 2008, 80). In the 1960s, when composers were employed to write new music for productions at Stratford, it was sometimes influenced by, or in the style of, Elizabethan ayres, catches, ballads and songs. This was not the only research into the early modern period at Stratford—composers could employ players of early music instruments and during the 1960s and 1970s period instruments were quite frequently incorporated conforming to expectations of authentic music practice. A variety of early musical instruments were played by David Munrow in the 1960s and later by many of the RSC musicians who learned the nearest instrument to their modern instrument on the spot so as to expand the instrumental range and timbre of the band (Woolfenden et al. 2013). Munrow was employed in the RSC band between 1965 and 1967 and recalls that he

> played bassoon at first, but the musical director at the time, Guy Woolfenden, encouraged [him] to perform on the instruments of Shakespeare's time as well. Woolfenden remembered how Munrow would scribble down notes [for the composer] about the tonal qualities and compasses of instruments such as the crumhorn, shawm and rauschpfeife—with comments such as "let me get my breath back after playing this one...." (Munrow Website)

Although the modern Shakespeare's Globe Theatre has included Elizabethan productions using period instruments and ensembles, incorporating songs and instrumental music from Elizabethan sources, the musical language, the musical instruments and the musical delivery might all appear somewhat alien to audiences accustomed to a very different sound world from that of the indoor and outdoor Elizabethan and Jacobean theatres. Even at Shakespeare's Globe the historical recreations, while fruitful as experiments in recreating the acoustic environment of the plays, cannot reproduce the reception and signification audiences brought to productions of the period—though they are undoubtedly atmospheric and popular. The Royal Shakespeare Company in the proscenium theatre of the 1960s represented an aesthetically and politically different world view from that on the thrust stages of the early modern period, even as it attempted to incorporate the kinds of musical signification that were being documented by researchers.[3]

---

[3] These include Jorgenson, Paul *Shakespeare's Military World* Berkeley: University of California Press, 1956; Long, John H. *Shakespeare's Use of Music: A Study of Music and its Performance in the Original Productions of Seven Comedies*. Gainesville: University of Florida Press, 1955; Manifold, John S. *The Music in English Drama, from Shakespeare to Purcell*. London: Rockcliff, 1956; Noble, Richard *Shakespeare's Use of Song: With the Text of the Principal Songs*. Oxford: Oxford University Press, 1923; Seng, Peter J. *The Vocal Songs in the Plays of Shakespeare*. Cambridge: Harvard University Press, 1967; Sternfeld, F. W. *Music in Shakespearean Tragedy*. London Routledge and Kegan Paul, 1963.

In very broad terms at the inception of the Royal Shakespeare Company in 1961 composers were exploring to some extent the ideals of 'authenticity'; drawing on published research, exploring extant materials and incorporating early instruments into a particular type of signification that might not have any real claim on 'authenticity', but followed a line of practice supported by research enquiry. But that was only one aspect of the diverse practices employed by many different composers, some of whom were interested in the latest innovations in non-tonal or electronic music. In the course of the following 55 years, ideas, ideologies, practices and technologies have changed, and contemporary practice has been documented by Michael Bruce in his recent practical guide *Writing Music for the Stage* (2016). He notes that 'Shakespeare's work ... more than any other plays in the classical canon, can inspire and withstand bold new interpretations' (Bruce 2016, 19). Such choices will never be arbitrary and will always involve great imagination to make them work, requiring research, discussion and collaboration. Surprisingly, though, throughout all these developments and adaptations much of the signification remains fairly consistent even as the sound worlds and the historical and geographical settings of the works have been transformed. The process of developing the score for a new production has not altered much either.

Two Gentlemen of Verona

The Two Gentlemen of Verona is a comedy written right at the start of Shakespeare's career (between 1589 and 1593).[4] It contains just one song ('To Sylvia') which is the song Proteus encourages Thurio to sing under Sylvia's window in the speech at the start of this chapter, though on this occasion music is 'out of tune' and 'false' because it is a faithless man who has composed the song. More importantly it requires the scene to be set first in Verona and then in Milan, offering opportunities for shifts of musical genre. I am going to turn to three productions from 1991, 2004 and 2014 to document some of the possibilities for musicalising that shift of location.

The 1991 production directed by David Thacker had music by Guy Woolfenden but the score incorporated 1930s music by Cole Porter and George Gershwin played by an onstage band. This production is particu-

---

[4] It is thought to be his first play. See Wells and Taylor (1997), Carroll (2004), and Warren (2008) as well as various anthologies including Wells et al. (2005).

larly interesting because of the decision to incorporate existing music—a decision taken by the director who had already planned the production around this idea.[5] This was a rare event at the RSC perhaps because it is entirely possible to create music 'in the style of' that doesn't draw attention to itself in quite the same way as using well-known music does. There is an immediate recognition among audiences not just of the time or place but of the specific song, and playing the melody of a well-known song also calls up the lyrics that are then associated with the new context and new meanings are created. Such intertextual associations can be productive for comedy or irony, but using music or song that has associations always does something more than using music whose style or genre creates associations or signifies without such direct resonances and references.

In the early modern period the music for productions was assembled from a number of sources (Lindley 2006, 111) and Shakespeare's lyrics were fitted to popular tunes in some cases, while in others extant songs were inserted in their entirety. This practice is clear since the names of the tunes that were used are sometimes included in the quarto or folio texts or in other documents that researchers have been able to locate. Christopher R. Wilson, for example, notes the stage direction 'catch'[6] in *Twelfth Night* then discusses the clues in the text that might indicate which ones might have been appropriate, but concludes 'it is not possible to determine which was used nor is it essential' (Wilson 2011). It is not only for the songs and dances that music was recycled, however, and although not all these tunes have been identified, it appears that the practice of introducing familiar music is widely acknowledged by scholars. Indeed, it 'persisted through the nineteenth and early twentieth centuries so that, for example, Arne's eighteenth-century settings of *Tempest* songs continued to be used at least until the 1930s' (Lindley 2006, 111). Mendelssohn's incidental music for *A Midsummer Night's Dream* (op. 61, 1842)[7] was ubiquitous until well into the twentieth century.[8]

The familiarity of the music is thought to have contributed to the reception and affect of the production as a whole on an audience who

---

[5] Woolfenden had requested to write the score for this production because the play was quite rarely performed and it was the only one of Shakespeare's plays for which he had not yet composed a score (Woolfenden 2018).

[6] A catch was a popular part-song.

[7] He incorporated a concert overture from 1826 (op. 21) into this score.

[8] Parts of the score were re-orchestrated to accompany Max Reinhardt's film of the play (1935), which will only have increased the familiarity of the music and its link to the play.

understood the contexts of the works and their conventional associations. In a newly commissioned score the familiarity of a piece of music is missing, but its genre, style, instrumentation, harmonic construction and timbre all communicate information that provides a context for the scene. This gives the director great flexibility in promoting new visions or readings of the work for contemporary audiences, while the opportunity of using existing and well-known music is particularly useful for ironic or comic effect or specific commentary.

Fiona Buffini's touring production of *Two Gentlemen* (2004) opened in The Swan and was also set in the 1930s. This time, with music by Conor Linehan, it contrasted a 'dull countryside' with 'swinging and sophisticated Milan' (Billington 2004), offering opportunities for music and dance to be added so that the musical contrasts separated these worlds. Most recently (2014) Simon Godwin directed a production for the RST with music by Michael Bruce that retained the Italian setting but in a deliberately undefined contemporary period.[9] For this production Bruce was asked to add a new song and dance sequence at the start of Act 2, Sc. iv, partly to emphasise the difference between the sleepy rural Verona and the spectacle of Milan. Bruce found a translation of a Shakespearean sonnet in seventeenth-century Italian whose lyrics added a European flavour to the 'energised Eurobeat musical influence' that he had written for the scene (Bruce 2016, 130–1) so that the song sounded both authentic to a historical Italy, didn't introduce any non-Shakespearean text, and had a fresh, modern musical sound.

I've mentioned these productions to give a sense of the way three productions of the same play, all set in Italy, are enhanced by totally different musical worlds. Michel Chion, in his book about film music, *Audio-Vision*, talks about the audio-visual illusion that he describes as 'added value' (Chion 1990, 5). He explains this as:

> The expressive and informative value with which a sound enriches a given image so as to create the definite impression, in the immediate or remembered experience one has of it, that this information or expression "naturally" comes from what is seen, and is already contained in the image itself. Added value is what gives the (eminently incorrect) impression that sound is unnecessary, that sound merely duplicates a meaning which in reality it brings about, either all on its own or by discrepancies between it and the image. (Ibid.)

---

[9] This production was filmed as part of the RSC Live season and is available on DVD produced by Opus Arte: 1168D.

It is clear that decisions about locations are generally made by the director who has a vision for which themes s/he wants to explore in a production, but that after the initial meeting with the director the composer conducts research to discover interesting ways of evoking an appropriate time and place in musical language that appears 'natural' but adds value. Meanwhile Richard Brown describes the importance of scene change music as 'not only papering over the cracks but at the same time advancing mood' and potentially 'surprising the audience'. A scene change takes the audience on a journey from one world to the next; it is a liminal moment of transition, but it is also required to retain or create an atmosphere, while at other times creating texture or tension. The diverse potentials of music are observable through comparison of the styles of these three productions. There are the intertextual references of the Porter and Gershwin songs, the sophisticated Milanese jazz or the energised Eurobeat disco, all of which add flavour and texture to articulate the difference between Verona and Milan. These choices say something about the cool wit, the elegant sophistication, or the head-banging urban modernity the directors wanted to evoke in Milan, which reflects on the characters of the young men as they are drawn in to the Milanese scene in 1991, 2004 and 2016. This can be summed up in the phrase 'music always does something'—while its signification may not be precise it has an impact that must always be considered.

Macbeth

I'm now going to consider in much more detail a number of productions of *Macbeth*, a play that is one of the most significant in the canon. It was written later in Shakespeare's life, in about 1606 (Wells et al. 2005). It is a military play with many opportunities for signalling, atmospheric writing and thunder. According to Christopher Wilson, in the early modern theatre music and instruments had two principal functions, to accompany entrances and exits and to add symbolic significance (Wilson 2011, 123), but there were also plenty of other musical opportunities related to the play's production such as soundings of the trumpet to announce the performance itself, music between the acts and possibly a 'Concluding song, dance, flourish or other music' (Manifold 1956, 22). Clearly there was a lot of music, though not all of the potential opportunities were taken at all performances.[10] More important for the discussion of *Macbeth* are the sounds of military signals. Trumpets are the most commonly mentioned instruments in the outdoor theatre since they 'not only signalled the start of a play but were frequently and conventionally employed, with or without the accompaniment of drums, in their dual function of signalling the entry of kings, emperors, and others of high status, and imitating the sounds of war' (Lindley 2006, 96). So while there is some debate over the placement of musicians in the indoor and outdoor theatres and the number and skill of instrumental players, and there is even more debate about the actual music played, the types of instruments and the levels of professionalism of those that played in the indoor and outdoor theatres, there seems no doubt at all that a significant amount of music, led by trumpets and drums, was a common accompaniment to theatrical performances.

Trumpets and drums featured in military plays or battle scenes, since historically trumpets were used to signal instructions to cavalry soldiers in battle—drums were used similarly by the infantry (Wilson 2011, 124). It is hard to know how often such calls were actually used in the Shakespeare canon as the Folio texts were often assembled and published after the event by a book-keeper from the theatre company who recorded the practice. Whether or not music cues appear in the Quarto text they may have been played as normal practice—too normal to document—especially since many are referred to in speech (Lindley 2006, 116). So the documented incidental music cues may be only a small proportion of the occasions on which music was actually played. However, with the proviso that the incidences of music recorded in the texts may not be accurate or complete, the documented occasions provide the starting point for this discussion.

Macbeth 1962[11]

Roberto Gerhard (who will be discussed in more depth in the next chapter), after having composed scores for RST productions by Peter Brook, Peter Hall and George Devine, was employed to write the score for Donald McWhinnie's production of *Macbeth* in 1962, perhaps because the two were

---

[10] In fact Lindley also questions whether the 'jig' that is often cited as the afterpiece was always as bawdy and satirical as some suppose. He provides evidence that some performances may have been followed by dances that were not jigs especially after the departure from the company of William Kemp in 1599, and in particular suggests that the evidence is sufficiently scant that a complete picture cannot be accurately provided.

[11] This production was analysed using literary sources as well as the score.

acquainted through the BBC Radiophonic Workshop that had been established in 1958. The BBC Radiophonic Workshop was inspired by developments in avant-garde electro-acoustic music (by composers such as Pierre Schaeffer and Edgar Varèse in France, Karlheinz Stockhausen in Germany, or the New York school of John Cage, Earl Brown, Christian Wolff, David Tudor and Morton Feldman in the USA) and a studio was built within the BBC. There a popular kind of electronic music was developed for use on radio or television as jingles, signature tunes (most notably for the realisation of Ron Grainer's signature tune for *Doctor Who* by Delia Derbyshire) and incidental music (including for *Doctor Who*). Gerhard's score (along with his score for *Coriolanus* [1959]), is 'perhaps the most unusual among [his] scores for Stratford, due to its utter lack of melodic character' (Llano 2013, 127). It is created using clusters and quasi-electronic timbral qualities, shrill sonorities and piano glissandi (which must be played using 'nail-files over strings' in the style of John Cage's prepared pianos) (Ibid.). A Majorcan ximbomba, which produces a nasal noise when rubbed by a wet hand, is incorporated in the Witches' scene as well as 'clusters on both hands of the piano, which saturate the harmony' producing a decidedly unmelodic score. This created a sound world that may have been an imitation of the sonic and timbral qualities of electronic music, though the effect of the culturally alien ximbomba is difficult to judge. When using it Gerhard 'reproduced the regular metre that characterizes its use in popular celebrations' thus drawing together high and low culture, but also creating an alien sound world for the witches in the Stratford context. The production was revived in 1964 and Gerhard also recycled two of the music cues, the 'Witches Scene' and 'Banquo's Ghost', for a BBC production. I mention this production to draw connections with the electro-acoustic avant-garde and innovations in percussive and timbral writing (that arose from the innovations of Stravinsky and the 12-tone or serial composers, Schoenberg, etc.). It is clear that from the start composers were writing music that was both varied and innovative incorporating the very latest sonic experiments into theatre production.

Macbeth 1967[12]

Since its inception the RSC had used the New Penguin Classic versions of the texts with stage directions for its early productions. The earliest prompt

---

[12] For analysis I relied on scores, prompt book, and production notes at the Shakespeare Birthplace Trust archive in Stratford and the electronic tape in the Delia Derbyshire collection at John Rylands Library, Manchester University.

scripts contain the pages from these texts glued to lined paper so that the actual stage directions and lighting cues could be lined up with the spoken cue lines, and it is clear from the marginalia in some of Guy Woolfenden's earliest scripts and cue sheets that they formed the basis for the distribution of music cues (the music spotting). The moves and cues of all are written in pencil on the lined paper opposite the cue, with 'standby' and 'go' points identified with numbers. Clearly the cueing, the complexity of technical equipment and the number of departments involved was still relatively small, to the extent that although the band was sometimes given a green light for an entrance or a cue, in the main they responded to cues in the same way that actors do. This can be seen in Fig. 1 of "Musical Collaborations at the RSC"—the Trumpet book for *Henry V* above. It is only later that the cueing of music for productions is documented in increasing detail.

The 1967 production of *Macbeth* was directed by Peter Hall with music composed by Guy Woolfenden. By the time of this production Woolfenden had been at the RSC for five years and had composed music for over 25 productions including *The Wars of the Roses*, *Hamlet* and *Henry V*. In the 1967 season he also composed music for *Coriolanus*, *The Taming of the Shrew*, *Romeo and Juliet* and Tourneur's *The Revenger's Tragedy*. This continuity of practice, where he learnt theatre composition from Leppard and before him Drinkwater by playing their scores, might suggest that Woolfenden's own compositions perhaps exemplify the core expectations for theatre music at the RSC at the time, combining originality of content with a defined aesthetic and generic style. On the other hand, he had been at the RSC when Gerhard's score for *Macbeth* was performed, had known him whilst at Cambridge, during which time Woolfenden regularly visited Gerhard's home to help make and record unusual sounds on his French horn or the piano or any other instrument to hand (Woolfenden 2018). It was to this more experimental world that he now turned for sounds to complement his score.

Delia Derbyshire had originally read maths at Girton College, Cambridge, before transferring to music history where she met Woolfenden who was reading music at Christ's, and with whom she shared a relationship of mutual respect.[13] Derbyshire and Brian Hodgson already worked at the BBC Radiophonic Workshop when Peter Zinovieff, a Canadian

---

[13] David G. Butler undertook a major research project to digitise Derbyshire's archive now based at John Rylands library, Manchester University, and reports this based on analysis of archival materials.

Broadcasting Corporation employee, was introduced to its facilities. Two years later Unit Delta Plus was formed by the trio, though Derbyshire and Hodgson continued to work for the BBC too (Niebur 2010, 131). The new company produced music and sound for theatre, commercial and popular entertainment outside the restrictions of the BBC. Unit Delta Plus disbanded in 1967 as Zinovieff wanted to continue his serious compositions while Hodgson and Derbyshire continued to work on electronic music scores for film and TV (Woolfenden 2018).

Possibly on the advice of David Collison of Theatre Projects Woolfenden approached Derbyshire for sounds to complement his score (Woolfenden 2018). According to Jane Woolfenden it was a happy collaboration with regular visits to Deodar Road, Putney were Zinovieff lived and had his electronic studio. This was clearly a collaborative project since the credit for music for this production was shared with Unit Delta Plus Electronic Music. That the credit was shared at all was in itself innovative as sound was not then a separate discipline, meanwhile involving live musicians onstage to play other parts of the score was also still in its infancy. This score, that combined recorded music and electronic sounds with live instrumental performance, was quite experimental, following Woolfenden's own experiment in electronic sound recording for *Henry V*. It perhaps also set the tone for the development of greater collaborations with sound designers in the future and flies in the face of Settle's advice not to mix live and recorded sound (Settle 1957, 70).

Macbeth is notable for opening with thunder and lightning rather than music. Altogether the text contains at least 20 instances of sound or music with the greatest number in Act 5 from Sc. ii onwards; the battle at Dunsinane is 'punctuated and orchestrated by incidental music' (Lindley 2006, 113). Each army enters with 'drum and colours', there are 'Alarums' in Scene vii that signal the exit of various generals and the continuation of the battle, a flourish is played in Scene viii to sound the retreat, and a final one signals the status of the new King of Scotland, Malcolm—thus ending the play with trumpets. Earlier in the play a sennet announced Macbeth's accession to the throne, and hautboys and torches accompanied Duncan to Macbeth's castle. J.S. Manifold notes that this is rather ironic since the association of hautboys with hospitality would be well-known, and is used here as Macbeth welcomes King Duncan while plotting his murder (1956). It is the music for battle that is predominantly played live by the brass and drummers of the wind band who appear onstage with the armies. The importance of these cues, however, is that they are incorporated into the scripts used at the RSC and signal where live music was likely to occur since it functioned as a signal with the diegetic world of the plays.

The 1967 production used music at all the places in the script where music or sound is mentioned. Figure 2 shows the relationship between script, music cues, sound cues and score since it contains the cue number, the page number in the Penguin classic, whether the cue was to be played on one of the tape decks or live and a description of the sound. I will return to the sounds in this list later, but want to draw attention to some of the live events first.

Cue 2a is an 'Alarum', a term that appears in the published text and which is usually the sound of drums but occasionally bells or other noises that are most common in the history plays in connection with battles (Naylor 159). The Alarum might be described as loud, low, short, within, or 'with excursions' (parties of men running about) but it always occurred during a fight. Gervase Markham, in *The Souldier's Accidence* (1635), described 'alarums' as one of the most important signals drummers should know 'which sounded, every man (like Lightning) flyes upon his enemie, and gives proof of his valour' (Lindley 2006, 114). Marches, too, are instructions from drummers to the assembled soldiers, but such aural signifiers also compensate for a lack of bodies onstage as a play's army marches off, filling the stage with noise as a tiny group of actors and drummers represents an army marching to war.

'Flourish', as in Cue 5, (also sometimes 'flourish of trumpets' or 'flourish of cornets'), is a far less precise code for what we might now describe as a fanfare (Naylor 1965, 161). It signalled the entrance or exit of a king, queen or a distinguished person, though it occasionally marked the end of a scene, a victory, or a proclamation by a king. It can be confusing though, since a flourish can also give warning of the approach of play-actors, as at the entrance of Pyramus and Thisbe in *A Midsummer Night's Dream* and the arrival of the players in *The Taming of the Shrew* (Manifold 1956, 13). Certainly short trumpet calls can be used on all these occasions, which the contemporary composer manipulates or alters to make sense to a contemporary audience. Sometimes flourishes are extended into sennets—as in this case in Cue 14—which is played by a group of trumpets and is longer than a flourish or fanfare (Manifold 1956, 28) as it accompanies processions of royal or important persons (Naylor 1965, 172). The reality is that

M A C B E T H   - Cue-list

Cue Page Deck Description
TXXEXX

1	53	A	Thunder/wet noise
1a	53	B	Thunder/familiars ("meet with Macbeth")
2	53	B	Thunder/wet ("filthy air")
2a	53	live	Alarum
3	56	live	Drum exit
3a	56		Thunder/wet noise
4	57	live	Drum
4a	59	A	Thunder/familiars
5	62	live	Flourish
6	65	live	Flourish
7	67	A	Martletts
8	69	live	Procession
8a	69	A	Door slam
8b	69	B	Banquet noise
8c	70	A	Door open and close
9	74		Bell
10	74		Owl shriek
10b	75	A	Crickets
11	77/8		Knockings
12	81	A	Alarum bell
13	54	A	Tolling bell

I N T E R V A L

14	86	live	Sennet
14a	94	A	Horses
15	95	live	Sennet
16	97	A	Banquo chill
17	99	A	Banquo chill
18	104	A	Wet thunder
19	A.B.C	B	Bubbles
20	106	live	Drum/knocks
21	107	B	

Stage Management.

Fig. 2 *Macbeth*, 1967. Cue list for sound and music. (Music by Guy Woolfenden. By permission of the RSC)

modern audiences might not understand the nuances of these terms, but would recognise a fanfare, a march or a processional alongside the dramatic action they accompany.

Tuckets on the other hand are distinctive signals that operated as character motifs that were usually played on one or more trumpets, but to confuse the issue they are sometimes recorded simply as 'trumpets' as in Cue 34. They are distinctive calls that identify an individual person of rank so that preparations can be made for that person's arrival (Manifold 1956, 27–8). The important fact is that trumpets heralded entrances of dignitaries and sometimes players, but they could additionally be related to a specific character and be used as an ongoing motif. While such signification is much less common in modern life, and a text or phone call presages an arrival, pageantry still relies on trumpet fanfares, and by linking a fanfare with a distinctive motif at a character's entrance a modern composer may attach the characteristics of the fanfare to the character who has entered.

Other stage directions not in this list or this play refer to cornets. A cornet was an open horn with finger holes that produced a softer tone than the trumpet. It was used in the indoor and private theatres where the noise of trumpets might be overwhelming (Wilson 2011, 123). Equally hautboys, which are related to shawms, are reeded instruments (forerunners of the oboe family), that were used for quieter moments or in the indoor theatres, and always implied a certain special importance in the music, perhaps connected to a royal banquet, a masque or a procession of dignitaries (Naylor 1965, 169). The witches have a dance in Act 4, Sc. i that contains the supernatural vision of the eight kings that will follow Banquo's line: having seen this Macbeth realises that although he is now king he will not establish a dynasty. This magic or hallucination is accompanied by hautboys whose use signals the other-worldly (Lindley 2006, 137). Alternatively, one might conceptualise the show of eight kings as a kind of masque or entertainment for Macbeth which would also account for the use of hautboys as signifying instruments (Manifold 1956, 61).

A score of 45 cues appears at first sight to be a relatively extensive score—but the live band plays in only 16 of the cues, the rest being taped sound effects. Although a full score was produced the band parts were written by hand in individual part books so that they could be clipped on instruments in the manner of a marching band. These part books have only the first name of the player on the outside demonstrating the permanence and familiarity of the music team. In addition there seems to be a fair amount of doubling. Robin Weatherall, for example, is the percussionist who in this score plays military tenor drum, antique hand drum, side drum and tabor, but also has the trumpet fanfares in his band part—a pattern we will see again in Brook's *Dream*. The reverse doubling is provided by Derek Oldfield, clearly a brass player who plays Horn in F and Fibrhorn in F, but who also plays a drum cue with hard sticks (Cue 31). Robert Pritchard (named as Bob in the band parts) also appears to be playing both drums and brass. Edward Watson (Ted) seems only to have a part for Cue 8, and though he is listed as playing soprano saxophone the score calls for shawm in Bflat—the nearest equivalent to the hautboy.

'Bob's' band part gives instructions about which of the two costumes to wear for which cues. He has all the verbal cues written in including which entrances and exits to use and where to stand, so he was probably leading the marching band and may even have been acting as a formal or informal music director for the performances. The band began the show at Prompt Side (PS), where they played Cue 2A wearing 'red costumes with fur cloaks'. The prompt script gives the same information—that the band assembles PS from where they 'Play on Witches' and 'Drums during witches scene as called for in script'. They then enter on the cue 'hover through the fog and filthy air' and march forward onto the stage where they start to play at the sound of thunder. The group of bandsmen stay onstage until the end of scene ii and exit by the same route during the blackout. The band parts are also marked up in pencil with information about how long they have until the next cue. After Cue 14—a sennet that is played live (for which the band is dressed in white costumes)—it is noted that there are seven pages (of the script) before the next cue, and after Cue 15 (another sennet) the band has at least 3/4 hour to change back into their red costumes.

The first flourish for the band, Cue 5, is marked *Andante Maestoso*, and while the patterns of each of the five players is individually quite rhythmically square on the beat, the interaction between the parts generates quite complex rhythms making an interesting and complex fanfare, while the open harmonies and the *Maestoso Pace* suggest the calm and peaceful state of Duncan's rule. Cue 6 is an extended version of Cue 5 that adds a more rhythmically complex and harmonically interesting answering phrase. The longest individual cue is number 8 (led by the shawm), which is written as 10 bars of music, but has first and second time bars and a *Dal Segno* so that it can be lengthened and shortened to suit the action. The band plays it as a processional *Alla Marcia Moderato* as they march across the stage following a green cue light to lead Duncan and his entourage to Macbeth's castle. The prompt script contains a diagram of where the musicians end up at the OP side of the stage. This is Act 1, Sc. vii where the playscript calls for 'Hautboys and torches. Enter, and pass over the stage, a Sewer, and divers Servants with dishes and service. Then enter Macbeth'. The shawm melody is syncopated and circular using a small range of notes and similar rhythmic and melodic patterns at different parts of the bar. This creates an unsettling sense of hearing a pulse that is always slightly deferred or uncertain, while the melodic use of the augmented fourth (the tritone or devil's interval) and the timbre of the shawm all contribute to a slightly unsettling entrance to Macbeth's castle that fits perfectly with the Macbeths' intentions for Duncan after the evening banquet.

The longest section for the band is from Cue 29 to the end of the performance. Cues 29–32 are for drums alone as the armies assemble and battle is waged (Act 5. Scs iv, v and vi). Then at Cue 34 the band must 'Enter silent' at the cue 'make all our trumpets speak give them all breath—those ….harbingers of blood and death'. They play the cue then go into the PS wing as soon as they can, where they stay for a series of tape cues during the battle scene, during which they also play alarums and flourishes (36, 37, 38, 39A, 42) and then enter from PS with 'Robin drumming' and stay on through Cue 45 (marked 'heroically' this is the same music as Cue 5 where it is described as a flourish) that is played at the cue 'so thanks to all at once who we invite to see us crowned at Scone'. This flourish conforms to Manifold's list of musical items which calls for such music at the end of Act V.

Since there is no need to trim or replace candles between acts the show is performed in two halves, and consequently there is no requirement for music between each of the five acts, though there are sounds or music at each of these 'Act' moments. The first half of the show ends with a tolling bell at the end of Act 2, Sc. iv and the second begins with a live sennet at Act 3, Sc. i, the second half ends with two iterations of the flourish that was Cue 5 when played first for Duncan, repeated here as his son Malcolm takes his place on the throne, uniting the two in the reinstatement of the 'rightful' line of kingship and resolving the disruption of Macbeth's actions. All the live music cues are functional for military signalling or fanfares, though clearly they also have other effects. They are scored in full though the cues themselves are very brief, and conform to conventional tonal harmony with some rhythmic and harmonic connections to early modern or 'authentic' music.

The recorded cues that were more frequent and pervasive than the live musical moments were recorded on two tape decks (A and B) and were created by Derbyshire.[14] Examples of sound cues include Thunder / Wet noise (Cue 1), Banquet noise (Cue 8b), Owl Shriek (Cue 10), First, second and third apparitions (Cues 21–23) and some music cues that are clearly recorded are Witches' Dance (Cue 26) and Calm Peaceful music (Cue 27 and 27a). There is also a sequence of 'Tension-building' and 'Tape fight' in the last Act. The sound effects fit the list in the request from Woolfenden to Derbyshire and the prompt book cues, and create an unusual atmospheric world that contrasts with the alarums, fanfares, sennets and flourishes played live by the musicians. For example the first sound cue contains three artificially generated crashes and a rumble to represent thunder. A whistling wind rises and falls and a bubbling sound continues within this polyphonic texture. This is described in the cue sheet as Thunder/Wet noise and perhaps suggests a blasted heath for Macbeth to meet the witches as well as a bubbling cauldron. This combination of sounds—wind, bubbles and crashes—is repeated in various iterations at frequent points throughout the score, underpinning the continuity of this other world.

Niebur notes that around this time Derbyshire was finding it increasingly difficult to spend sufficient time creating new sounds for her compositions (Niebur 2010, 135), such that some of the sounds in this score were in fact reused from 'an earlier BBC production (which had nothing to do with *Macbeth*!) although the vast majority of the sounds created for the RSC *Macbeth* were original' (Butler 2016). The artificiality of these sounds, separate from the live music, communicates a sense of the uncanny, the metaphysical that reflects the distorted world of magic that overwhelms the Macbeths. The metallic clang of a door (Cue 8a) is dull and heavy with reverb so that the sound fades slowly, while the screech of an owl is highly amplified with piercing high frequencies and a long reverberation. Even the alarm bell rung to spread news of Duncan's murder is penetrating because of the way the frequencies and processing are manipulated. Only the 'calm peaceful music' differs from these loud and otherworldly sounds. This is created by overlaying voices singing a simple Latin chant, again using heavy reverb to give the effect of stillness within an echoing church. Between these sound cues the live sounds of military

[14] There is a copy of a reel-to-reel tape in the John Rylands Library at Manchester University that appears to be a draft of Tape A for this production.

direction must have seemed somewhat pedestrian depending on their relative volumes. Overall, however, the practice here seems to conform in large part to what is called for in the stage directions and predicted by the researchers into early modern theatre practices, with the addition of the uncanny noises created for the electronic score. Two completely different sound worlds are created—the live sounds of the innocent characters with links to religious music to signify the 'rightful' monarchical line as god-given, and the distorted, processed electronics of the witches and those they infect with murderous intent.

The most significant features of this production are the presence of musicians onstage, and the degree of conformity to the stage directions and what was known of the instrumentation and style of Shakespearean practice in the live music alongside the heavily processed electronically generated sounds. This creates an aural and atmospheric distinction between the rightful line and the disrupted chaotic world arising from the metaphysical temptations of the witches.

Macbeth 1976[15]

The 1976 production of *Macbeth* directed by Trevor Nunn at The Other Place also had music composed by Guy Woolfenden, but there are no musicians listed in the programme. Because of the smaller space and the requirement for musicians in the main theatre it appears that all the music was pre-recorded and the number of cues is significantly reduced. There are only 11 'sound cues' noted in the music score which still combines both sound and music under the aegis of the music department.

The first cue is an atmospheric clap of thunder at the start of the show before the entrance of the witches and the second cue is not until 11 pages later, when Macbeth, having been made Thane of Cawdor, heads home to his castle to prepare for the arrival of King Duncan. The third cue occurs when hautboys and torches are called for before Duncan's entry into Macbeth's castle, and is repeated as the fourth cue before the dinner at the castle that evening. The next cue marks the entrance of Banquo to Macbeth's Coronation ('thou hast it now: King, Cawdor, Glamis, all'). The sixth as the murderers leave to kill Banquo and the royal party enters

---

[15] This production was recorded for television and is available on DVD starring Ian McKellen and Judi Dench. *Macbeth* (Fremantle Media: FHED 1776). For analysis I also looked at the score and prompt book.

for the banquet. The seventh marks the return of the murderer with blood on his face and anticipates Macbeth's visions. The eighth provides the introduction to the witches' final scene. The ninth, at the end of the sleepwalking scene, plays the drums and colours for Macbeth and his army. The tenth does the same for Malcolm, Seyward, Macduff and their army hidden in branches of Birnam's wood. The final cue responds to the call to 'make all our trumpets speak' as Macduff engages in the battle.

For this production there is a substantial deviation from the requirements of the published text and substantially fewer music cues. This represents a low point in the performance of musicians, that perhaps results from the introduction of a second theatre with no space for a band and no extra available musicians. Given that before the arrival of Peter Hall the wind band had recorded all cues and only played interval music this is not as unexpected a strategy as it perhaps appears from a contemporary perspective, and it is interesting to note what were considered the key cue points for this pared down musical score. There is, too, a lack of dynamism resulting from the absence of the music's ability to alter pace and create atmosphere.

Macbeth 1986[16]

In 1986 Adrian Noble directed a production with a music/sound score by Geoffrey Burgon and sound by John Leonard. Geoffrey Burgon had composed concert music, television music and recordings. Most well-known among his scores were the incidental music and theme tunes for the television series *Tinker, Tailor, Soldier, Spy; Testament of Youth; Brideshead Revisited;* and the film *The Life of Brian*. As with many productions from the late 1970s onwards, composers were employed who brought a vast experience of incidental music from other media rather than, or as well as, classical composition.

The music for this production uses tonal harmony and predominantly brass and drums (two horns, trombone, two percussionists) for the military signalling. In this case, however, there is the addition of a taped voice—the singer Suzanne Flowers—adding atmosphere especially during the witches' scenes and when those scenes are remembered and discussed. The flourishes or fanfares contain the patter of a semiquaver motif played

---

[16] For this analysis I watched the audio-visual recording and looked at the score and prompt book.

by the two horns a minor third apart moving over the interval of a third which creates a sense of unity in the score. The opportunity is taken at the dinner to introduce two period dances, a Jig and a Galliard, that provide a contrast between the mood of Macbeth and his wife and the other participants celebrating the military victory.

The instructions to the band have become much more detailed following the action onstage, and the information in the prompt script about the music and its cueing is also much more detailed, while the majority of stage directions from the Penguin version are no longer included in the typescript. However, this score is still written formally in full score from which the band parts are copied. The score uses the rhythmic structures, notation and terminology of classical composition, referencing the dances and airs of the early modern period alongside the familiar opportunities for fanfares and drumming. Altogether this seems like a step back from the earlier innovations in composition to a very traditional approach despite the fact that this is the first of this group of productions to have a sound designer credited. Perhaps, therefore, the innovations were occurring elsewhere at this time.

Macbeth 1999[17]

The 1999 production marks a substantial shift in approach that is closer to the early distorted sound worlds of Gerhard and Derbyshire than the more recent past. The music is much more integrated within scenes and is no longer confined to the places where the old stage directions stood, or even to scene changes. Instead the musical and sound world of this adaptation is much more pervasive than in any of the previous productions of this play, though it has some correlation with the integration attempts of Sekacz in the *King Lear* score in Fig. 1 above. Adrian Lee began his career in association with an experimental/intercultural theatre group at Goldsmiths, University of London, conducting research into the music of Indonesia. He collaborated with theatre ensembles in Madhya Pradesh and Karnataka and musicians from other traditions to develop an eclectic mix of world music styles. By the time he worked at the RSC he had devised music for several Young Vic productions and worked at the Royal National Theatre with Robert Lepage and on the stage adaptation of

---

[17] For analysis I watched the archived AV recording, looked at the musicians' script/score and the prompt book of the production.

Rushdie's *Haroun and the Sea of Stories* (1998) where his original sound worlds were greeted with critical acclaim and popular satisfaction. This eclectic mix of world music styles, timbres and instruments, including those from the Middle East and Southeast Asia, replaced the Western wind band instrumentation previous composers of *Macbeth* had used. This was a radically different sound world, signifying practice and scoring system. World music practices thus provide another innovation resulting from the interactions between contemporary classical music and theatre music.

For this production there is almost no written score in the formal sense, but cues annotated in a copy of the script as can be seen in Fig. 3.

The cues, which were played by Lee himself (on percussion, keyboards and harp) and Joji Hirota (percussion), are for cymbals, bell sounds and drums including ujimé, chinton, autoharp, tubular bells, gongs, bowed bowls and cymbals. In the 1970s the Penguin Classic text had disappeared to be replaced by a typescript of the text with very few stage directions, a fact that appears to have given composers licence to imagine the sound world and spot the music cues inventively throughout the performance. Music and sound are no longer the province of the music department alone, but are the product of collaborations between, in this case, Lee and sound designer John A. Leonard for Aura. The result is a composite atmospheric sound score in which it is difficult to differentiate who is creating which sounds. This score is perhaps more redolent of the type of nontonal world Roberto Gerhard attempted to create in his 1962 score, or Derbyshire with her shrieks and gurgles in 1967—though there is no suggestion that Lee would have been aware of that. It also builds on the improvisatory devised processes that Sekacz experimented with in the 1980s (Fig. 1 above) in linking musical motifs, stings and longer percussive cues to the script and action rather than to a rhythmically and harmonically structured formal score. I'm suggesting that developments in contemporary and electronic music and acoustics were influencing theatre music and that the freedom from the need to create sound effects or to symbolically represent stage actions, as well as the removal of tonal harmony had long since begun to allow music to take a different and sometimes more psychological or commentating role.

As can be seen in Fig. 3, the first scene, the entrance of the witches, begins with bowed cymbals and bowls accompanied by a rolled chinton followed by a gong. The notes of the bowls, G sharp, A and C sharp over an F sharp pedal are somewhat dissonant, but the timbre of the bowed

PART ONE
THE WAR

Black out
TV

ACT ONE

Scene One

Thunder and lightning.
Enter THREE WITCHES

1ST WITCH   When shall we three meet again?
              In thunder, lightning, or in rain?

2ND WITCH   When the hurly-burly's done,
              When the battle's lost and won.

3RD WITCH   That will be ere the set of sun.

1ST WITCH   Where the place?

2ND WITCH   Upon the heath.

3RD WITCH   There to meet with Macbeth.

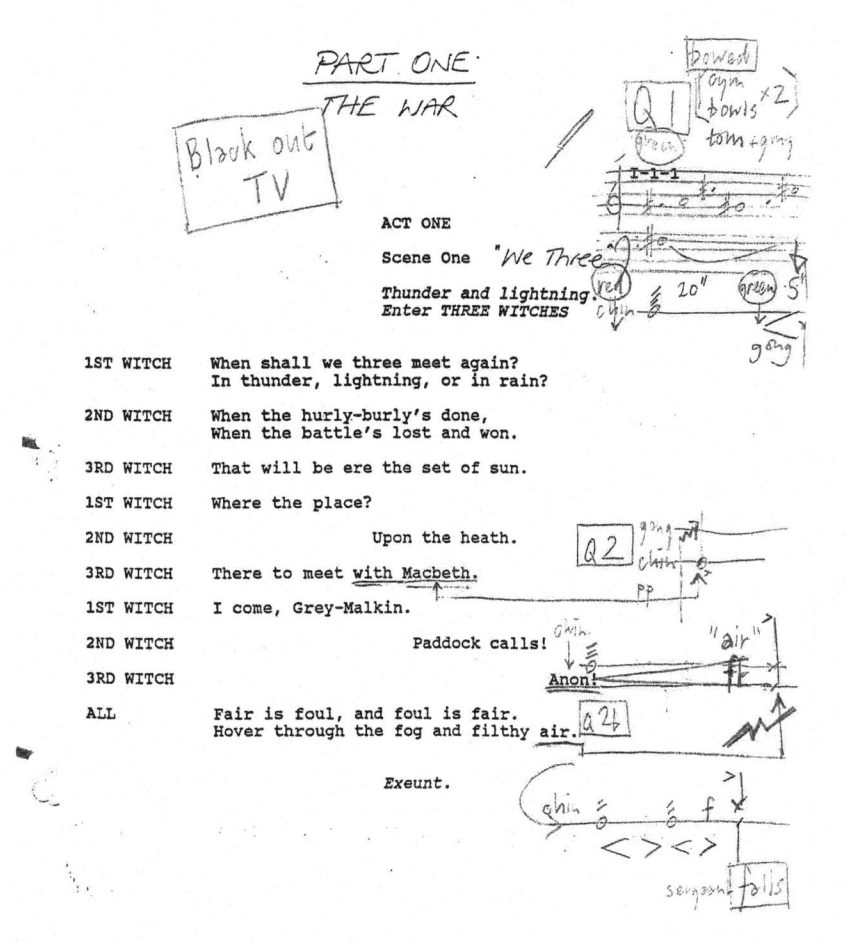

1ST WITCH   I come, Grey-Malkin.

2ND WITCH   Paddock calls!

3RD WITCH   Anon!

ALL   Fair is foul, and foul is fair.
              Hover through the fog and filthy air.

                              Exeunt.

Fig. 3 *Macbeth*, 1999. Annotated script Act 1, Sc. i. (Music by Adrian Lee. By permission of the RSC)

bowls and cymbals, that is metallic and piercing, creates a haunted and unsettling atmosphere. As well as such atmospheric cues, the musicians add percussive comments that punctuate the scene. For example, after the third witch says that she will 'meet with Macbeth', there is a punctuation from a gong that is struck lightly and rolled so that the sound increases in volume followed by a very quiet thud on the chinton; a premonition of doom. After the next spoken word from the second witch 'Anon' a quiet roll on the chinton begins that continues under the final couplet of the scene and concludes with a fortissimo crash after the final phrase, heightening tension and drawing attention to the portent of the words. This is followed by further drumming for the scene change until the sergeant in the next scene falls with an accompanied crash.

This type of detailed musical or sound commentary that is interjected between words is particularly apparent when Macbeth first imagines seeing a dagger and later when he sees the vision of the murdered Banquo. These hallucinations are performed by dissonant metallic screams that illustrate the pain of his disordered brain. Sometimes the connection between sound and image is direct and clear, at other times in the score the disjunction between Macbeth's vision of the world and an external reality are less directly marked in musical sound. This disjunction doesn't only apply to Macbeth, though; when Lady Macbeth hears knocking the sounds are sometimes realistic and at other times the effect is of a heavy slow drum march or a slow beating heart. These sounds are interchanged to confuse the sense of what is and is not real for her.

In the final fight between Macbeth and Macduff the sound of the dagger (the same sound as used when Macbeth hallucinated a dagger—a diminished seventh on the bowed bowls), and other sound images on visual cues during the combat (a 6th and a 4th) are used to signal Macbeth's hallucinations, the final one of which distracts him so that he can be stabbed to the sound of a wind gong hit and allowed to ring. This type of articulation of physical action in sound has a comic history in music for cartoons and clown comedy, and appears in film thrillers. Here the percussive and piercing timbre of the sounds removes the comic element but has the effect of highlighting actions within a controlled and balanced sound score. Such 'mickey-mousing' intensifies tension and articulates or draws attention to a specific action in a very detailed and integrated response to the narrative.

In addition to the atmospheric sounds produced live by the two players there is recorded vocal music sung in Latin that locates the performance in the early Western Christian tradition. This music is modal, has the texture of plain chant and is used first to signify Duncan's rightful kingship at his first entrance (Cue 8b). Then a *Te Deum* is sung to replace the sennet at Macbeth's coronation (Cue 19). *Veni Creatus* is sung to underscore the murder of Lady Macduff and her children, providing a stark contrast between the murderous actions and the peaceful religious music. The chant is repeated at the end of Malcolm and Macduff's scene in England, thus drawing a musical connection to strengthen the textual relationship between these scenes. Male voices sing a requiem to signify Malcolm's success and Macbeth's death, and in between these choral signifiers of the religious context the other-worldly sounds, shrieks, bangs and rhythmic excitement signifies a world out of joint with musical harmony and Christian order.[18]

What this score achieves is a new type of signification that focuses on the psychological and metaphysical; signalling Macbeth's and Lady Macbeth's states of mind rather than the physical activities of military conflicts and the actions of entrance and exit, though there is a significant amount of military drumming too. Interestingly the final fight takes place in silence apart from the hallucinatory effects and so draws attention to the psychology of paranoia that leads to Macbeth's downfall rather than the excitement of fighting. And even as the dissonant hallucinations signal Macbeth's psychological unease and his downfall, the drumming to celebrate Malcolm's coronation as the new king of Scotland is accompanied by a sting from the gong and sustained bowed cymbal presaging more violence yet to come before Fleance will be crowned. The apparent resolution signalled by the religious/ceremonial music at Malcolm's success is undermined suggesting that the story has not completed and that order has not prevailed.

Macbeth 2011[19]

The final production of the group—the 2011 production directed by Michael Boyd—has music by Craig Armstrong played by three female cellists who can be seen in Fig. 4 seated in view throughout the performance. They are located on a balcony above the main playing space, upstage centre, from where, like a Greek chorus they observe and comment musically on Macbeth's progress. Playing only a few music cues they overlook a derelict space, a broken-down hall laid waste by the battle, where frescoes have been destroyed, rubble is lying around, and gaping holes in the walls provide entrances and exits. The cello music derives

---

[18] This use of Latin vocal music was prefigured in Trevor Nunn's 1974 production with music by Guy Woolfenden for which choral music was recorded by the choir and organist at New College, Oxford.

[19] At the time of this research the music score was not available in the archive, so this analysis relies on the AV recording and the prompt book.

Fig. 4 *Macbeth*, 2011. Onstage cellists. (Photo by Ellie Kurtz. ©RSC)

from Armstrong's *Slow Movement* (1994) and was first used in Michael Boyd's production of *Macbeth* at The Tron, Glasgow in 1985, where Armstrong was composer in residence. It was subsequently also used in Baz Luhrman's film *Romeo and Juliet* (1996) and exists as a concert piece in its own right (Sandland 2015).

The production contains a series of sound and music cues as well as the cello music played onstage, all noted in an extremely detailed prompt book and all amplified and reverberant; there are knocks, muffled thuds, bells, heartbeats, wing flaps, wind and drone sounds. As dolls drop from the rig there are muffled thuds, later the sound of a neck breaking, a door slam and the sound of a door knock explodes, and silence is interrupted by swifts beating their wings. The children, who play the witches while hanging high above the stage, are heavily miked so that the effect of their voices is of an eerie, reverberant and oppressive sound world where the slightest whisper will resound, causing ripples across the theatre space and the world of the play. In this world, nothing can be secret because everything echoes. Alongside this the music the cellists play is not designed to signify in a straightforward way, for example, signifying a time or place, that the king will enter, or to underscore a fight with high energy, but to create a world out of joint and entirely separate from reality. In this case, the three cellists create a much more abstract musical world, a sample of which is available on YouTube.[20] Their music derives from the structures of neo-tonalism as developed by Terry Riley, Michael Nyman, Philip Glass, Steve Reich and later John Adams and Henryk Górecki; yet another innovation from the so-called classical world that has worked its way into film and now theatre music. As the players are visible throughout the play they also contribute to the theatricality of the event, because while the music they play is highly charged emotionally their presence and its relation to the coolness of neo-tonalism is not directly illustrative and so somewhat disruptive of immersion in the world of the play.

---

[20] https://www.youtube.com/watch?v=mdIMzdm_neM [Accessed 30.09.15]. This trailer demonstrates the musical world of the cellos, but this speech is not accompanied except by a hum and sound effects in the play. Part of 2.11 of the onstage action is at: https://www.youtube.com/watch?v=WAojuVbKQtg [Accessed 30.09.15]. This scene gives access to the volume and reverberation of the sound effects and the speech and is accompanied by a very low hum. The scene is followed by a cello cue. A longer section of the music is available on Armstrong's website at: http://www.musicsalesclassical.com/composer/listen/Craig-Armstrong [Accessed 19.10.15].

This performance begins in silence as soldiers enter through the broken walls and windows and tell the tale of the battle. The witches' scene follows, beginning as the children are dropped in from above. Hanging high in the air they sing 'Agnus dei, qui tollis peccata mundi, miserere, miserere' (Lamb of God, who takes away the sins of the world, have mercy, have mercy). The cellists begin to play as the children speak, amplified and with high levels of reverberation. The cellos begin very quietly, with open chords and no vibrato. In later scenes the cellos are more impassioned with vibrato and rising phrases as a lyrical and sustained texture grows. At other times the score requires that they bounce their bows on the strings to produce a more rhythmic, and percussive texture. As Banquo is attacked a solo note sounds followed by a rising phrase, slow and sustained. Such lyrical and harmonious music continues to juxtapose the action throughout the murder and as the actor playing Banquo gets up and leaves. The theatricality of the cellists' presence is mirrored in this action; the play is acted out by players and the accompanying music makes a ritual of the acting out rather than signifying either threat or fight. The music becomes much richer with a loud drone or undertow as masked dancers are flown in who dance at a different tempo from that being played by the cellos, which remains slow. Music and stage action are thus separated in their tempi, rhythms, energy and signification, forming a complex composite that is out of joint with the play's narrative but not with its enactment as ritual activity or re-creation.

As well as the children/witches asking for mercy using text from the Latin mass at the start of the production, the coronation of Macbeth begins with the priest performing a ritual for the dead accompanied by his intonation of the *Pie Jesu* in the counter tenor range accompanied by the cellos that become increasingly loud and dissonant. 'Pie Jesu, Qui tollis peccata mundi, Dona eis requiem' (Pious Jesus, Who takes away the sins of the world, give them rest). Here the voice itself is 'queered' in this range, just as the use of children to represent the witches queers the idea of innocence and experience. Then as the coronation moves forward the phrases of the *Kyrie* (Lord have mercy) become more ornamented and the scene concludes with the *Sanctus* (Holy, Holy, Lord God of hosts). Elements of the Catholic Requiem mass continue the sense that the performance as a whole has a ritual function, reinforced by the presence of the cellists and the performance of material that is, at times, semiotically unrelated to the narrative action.

The battle scene is accompanied but not illustrated by music on the cellos. When Macbeth is certain that he cannot be defeated unless Birnam

Wood comes to Dunsinane the cellos play a low sustained note with falling sighs above it, a motif that develops into a melody that becomes almost romantic before stopping dead at the sound of a scream. As the wood begins to move a more rhythmic close harmony cello motif begins, low in pitch with small glissandi and tremolo, and bells signal the start of the battle. The ability of stringed instruments to slide into and out of consonance is used here to depict an uncertainty, a lack of solidity in the world. The pitch rises as Macduff enters and the slow sustained tones continue throughout the fight between Macbeth and Macduff until a bell signals a stop and the explanation that Macduff is not born of woman occurs in silence. The two combatants fight on in silence and it is not until Macduff has killed Macbeth and sees the image of his dead children and wife hailing him as king that high harmonics begin again without vibrato.

This production has elements in common with the 1999 production. The music has an identity separate from the former illustration of military activities. In the empty aftermath of battle music is used to suggest something of the atmospheric and psychological drama rather than the physical world, sound cues are used when it is necessary to illustrate physical actions such as for military cues, thunder, knocking and so on, but amplified to a high level and with noticeably unnatural levels of reverberation. Here the sound, music and musicians contribute to the articulation of performance as ritual through the demonstration of theatricality and the separation of musical and visual signification.

Conclusion

The narrative of these productions demonstrates something of the development of musical signification between 1962 and 2011. At the start of the period composers often conformed to the stage directions of the script, and they were limited by the employment of the wind band and Western tonal harmony, though even at the start some composers incorporated the percussive use of dissonance developed by Stravinsky and Schoenberg. Alongside this it was still important for music to act as signifier for military signalling and noise effects. By the 1990s composers were using a greater variety of instruments and timbres and had sometimes moved away from tonal harmony and formal scoring to produce a more complex and pervasive sound world that was integrated into the playtext and a director's vision of the production in a much more detailed and collaborative interaction. Rather than having a signifying function within the military framework of the play, music began to complement sound, which took on more of the illustrative functions, so that composers were freed to be able to comment on the action, to signify something of the psychological state of characters, to generate mood, to signal a different type of disjunction within the world of the play and the theatre space and to contribute to theatricality and the ritual of performance. In fact it appears that the RSC moved though several clear stages of development reflecting different attitudes to tradition, innovation and technological development.

Hall ran the company in the 1960s, a period of cultural ferment when innovations in sound technology affected both pop and classical music and may have led to some of the innovations in electronic sound at the RSC. That Hall and Woolfenden were young men leading a new company through the counter-cultural revolution may also have affected their attitude to innovation and experimentation. It is interesting that the rather more conservative years occurred when Nunn and Hands led the company in the middle period when Margaret Thatcher was in power and money was tight. It may be that the ethos shifted and the company became slightly more risk averse at these times. Even though composers were employed from outside the company there may be a correlation between a greater reliance on familiarity and what was safe at this time. During the later period there appears to be a greater confidence in experimentation, much higher levels of devised and improvised composition (even though such practices really began with Brook in 1970) alongside an interest in the psychology of drama under the artistic directorships of Noble and Boyd. Perhaps this demonstrates a maturing of the company and a period of financial stability as a result of the greater commercial success of a number of productions (including *Les Misérables*). The increased interest in world music, neo-tonal and repetitive harmonies, and devised processes that derive from non-Western music also appears during the period of intense globalisation as neo-liberalism released world trade. It would be inappropriate to correlate the musical innovations with such external factors based on such a small sample, but it is nonetheless interesting to speculate about the changing tastes of the company within the changing politics and fashions in the UK at the time alongside the growth and maturation of the company itself.

These productions of *Macbeth* demonstrate a remarkable consistency and continuity within the processes of writing and production but an enormous diversity in the ways in which developments in contemporary classical and popular music have been incorporated. The development of sound design has freed music from being bound up in signification of character and action, rather surprising in this action-packed historic and military story, but perhaps the presence of stage action and the increased interaction with sound effects has released music to a greater diversity of roles. This disjunction may say something about the particular directors and composers, the production concepts and the rehearsal processes of the productions discussed above, and it is inappropriate to generalise on the basis of such a small number of productions, but it does raise the possibility that music's roles are potentially greater and more diverse than many assessments of its functions, that focus predominantly on signification in relation to text, allow.

Not only is there much more music now, the majority of which is played live in interaction with sound design, but the way scores are notated has altered too. At the start of the period a composer would have to write a fixed score that was generally scored in full for the wind band and the cues recorded. This created fixity but was also much easier for players to read and perform. The next step was that band members appearing on the stage needed to have much more sense of individual responsibility and responsiveness to the stage action as they began to adapt to the vagaries of spoken dialogue or scenery removal, to entrances and exits, costume changes and characterisation, even though the actual notes and rhythms being played were still fixed. Much more fundamental, though, was the introduction of more flexible scoring that was adaptable to the needs of the stage. Ilona Sekacz's score for *King Lear* in Fig. 1 and Adrian Lee's score in Fig. 3 demonstrate different approaches to the integration of text and music that also require rather more input from the band members as improvisers. As technology allows a fully scored work to be adapted much more quickly it is possible that a greater degree of direction from composer to player will return, but the nature of the integration of music into the dramatic text that reflects a fluid and cinematic level of atmospheric writing is certainly a feature of many current productions.

In the next chapter, and before moving forward with an assessment of the functions of theatre music and sound, I will explore some of the developments in sound technology and sound design that transformed what musicians were able to sound like, but also what sound designers were able to achieve. As the sound department developed so too did the nature of the collaboration and the hierarchical relationship between the two departments.

Electronics, Sound and Fury at the RSC

> *Be not afeard; the isle is full of noises,*
> *Sounds and sweet airs, that give delight and hurt not.*
> *Sometimes a thousand twangling instruments*
> *Will hum about mine ears, and sometime voices*
> *That, if I then had waked after long sleep,*
> *Will make me sleep again: and then, in dreaming,*
> *The clouds methought would open and show riches*
> *Ready to drop upon me that, when I waked,*
> *I cried to dream again.*
> (*The Tempest*, 3.2.135–43)

The thousand twangling instruments of which Caliban speaks in *The Tempest* include hearing Ariel, invisible, playing on a tabor and pipe. The tune they hear might be the same tune they are singing; a surprise that seems magical to them and signifies for them something of the spell-binding and other-worldly place they are in. And that is where this chapter focuses; on the noises of the island, its sounds and sweet airs humming about our ears in the island of the auditorium. Many such sounds go unnoticed even as they manipulate atmospheres, events or locations, and involve or replace music.

As discussed in "Collaborative Composition at the RSC" above, Michel Chion describes 'added value' as the way in which a sound enriches the image in a way that appears to be 'natural' or a duplication, when in

© The Author(s) 2018
M. Taylor, *Theatre Music and Sound at the RSC*, Palgrave Studies in British Musical Theatre,
https://doi.org/10.1007/978-3-319-95222-2_4

fact the sound brings about a meaning through its combination with the visual imagery (Chion 1990, 5). As discovered in the different productions of *Macbeth* analysed in the previous chapter each musical score added information and expression to the visual and narrative world such that the world seemed coherent, the meanings clear, the expression 'natural'. Sound works with music to create this aural experience of theatre, and indeed may have the effect of producing greater immersion in the experience than music, since music is sometimes extraneous, whereas sound ordinarily encompasses the re-creation of natural sounds to simulate an environment. Be that as it may, sound came under the auspices of the music department at the start of the period of this study. The development of a discrete and separate art form in sound design is another part of the history of theatre music at the RSC, so it is to the development of sound design as an inseparable partner of music composition that this chapter will turn. Although I will mention lighting as a sister technology to sound design in terms of infrastructure, this chapter focuses on the relationships between sound and music since both contribute to the immersive aural experience of theatre. As Ross Brown explains, 'in musicology but also in everyday aesthetic experience, musical and ... sonic environments are becoming blurred categories—hybrids or mash-ups' (Brown 2010, 2). This environment of sound transfers into the theatre where different parts are controlled by sound designers and composers working in collaboration to create an overall aesthetic concept that supports the director's vision and the audience's emotional engagement and understanding. There is, of course, also extraneous sound, though I do not address that directly in this book. As the tools and practices of creativity in sound design have undergone a process of transformation following from the development of new technologies, so too, new listening practices and expectations of the immersive experience of theatre have emerged. Clearly such tools and practices don't apply only to Shakespearean performance, and I will refer to musicals as well as plays at the RSC in what follows, but this chapter documents the changes in working practices and personnel resulting from the developing sound technologies available in the RSC theatres. The aim is to explore how the relationship between sound and music departments, personnel and aural environments has altered since the middle of the twentieth century and what possibilities that creates for directors, composers and sound designers.

Music and instruments were played in Shakespeare's theatre as part of a noisy outdoor theatre world combining sound and noise, intrinsic and extrinsic to the action, with bells, chimes, guns and thunder frequently required, as well as the sounds of nature with birds singing and dogs barking.[1] Thunderous noise may have been made by opening the wooden trap door at The Globe, while battle noises were made using guns and canons, one of which accidentally set fire to the building in 1613 (Curtin 2016, 154). The mechanical devices of early theatre sound demonstrate the extent to which what audiences imagine they hear may be different from what they are actually hearing. In Act V, Sc. iv of *Coriolanus*, for example, the messenger mentions 'the trumpets, sackbuts, psalteries and fifes, Tabors, and cymbals and the shouting Romans, make the sun dance' whereas the stage directions call only for Trumpets and hautboys, drums and shouting. As Smith explains this demonstrates how language often framed the performance and reception of sound. However, before discussing the interaction of sound and vision we will first consider the development of theatrical sound.

Ross Brown traces a line of continuity from early modern theatre practices through the sound and fury of melodrama to the twentieth century when the Victorian theatre combined sound machines with the early days of gramophone recordings. At this point he notes three sonic worlds: the 'real' world of actors' voices and auditorium noise; the 'live' world of sound effects created in real time by thundersheets, doorbells and coconut shells; and the electro-acoustic world of recordings that were conventionally accepted as 'realistic' but not 'real' or 'live' (Brown 2010, 31). This combination or mixed ecology of sounds is still an effective description of the artifice of theatre that might also be described as combining the acoustic and electro-acoustic (Ibid.), though of course it doesn't include music. One aspect of this discussion, therefore, is the relationship between the live, the real, the realistic and the musical through the use of immediate and mediated technologies.

When the RSC was inaugurated music was played from recordings alongside the newly revived appearance of musicians and actors onstage, with very few sound effects being created live. There was not a sound department as such, but operators from the stage management team whose job included the amplification of musicians in their many and diverse locations. Gradually sound operation became a separate activity, and then a fully-fledged sound department emerged, responsible for

---

[1] Bruce Smith describes the sound world of the early modern theatre in *The Acoustic World of Early Modern England—Attending to the O-Factor* (1999).

sound design as well as engineering and operation. Alongside the development of sound design as a specialist area in its own right, sound technologies have evolved; microphones became more sophisticated with wireless technology, new instruments including synthesisers and samplers appeared linked by Musical Instrument Digital Interface (MIDI) interfaces, sound desks changed from analogue to digital and then to computer controlled systems, and speakers became smaller and cheaper, able to be placed in many locations. All this affected what could be produced either live or recorded.

As digital technology developed, theatre music has been transformed. Not only can sound effects be cued by specialist sound operators using sampling keyboards, but music's timbres can overlap with sound effects, moving away from the tonal harmony and orchestral sounds of motivically unified and developed scores. The separation of realistic 'natural' sounds from the 'artistry' of music disappeared as a result of MIDI keyboards and many innovations in keyboard technology. Musicians are now able to play scores containing the sorts of sounds Delia Derbyshire had recorded for the 1967 production of *Macbeth* while sound designers can create aural environments and sound effects using the same or similar technology, so that the soundscape produced by the combination of music and sound departments remains coherent even as the overall effects have been transformed. As Michael Bruce suggests, 'Often, a sound designer will add sound effects on top of the music after you have provided it, sometimes leading into the set-up of a scene or to counterbalance the music cue with something firmly planted in the reality of the scene change' (Bruce 2016, 217), thus mixing the 'realistic' and the musical in a complex aural dramaturgy. It is now often impossible to separate these sound worlds especially if they are delivered through the same PA[2] systems, but an audience would not want or need to separate them; they work together to create the aural environment. Within this environment a performance is perceived as 'realistic' subject to the suspension of disbelief of audiences and the coherency of the production and performances, and the borders between sound and music, albeit now in separate departments, are once again indistinguishable for the listener. These developments provide the starting point for an exploration of the interactions of music and sound design using live and mediated technology in the unique environment of the RSC in three sections: the kit; the operators; and the designers. The questions this chapter ultimately explores are how the development of MIDI and subsequent

[2] PA is the widely used term for the public address system comprising amplifiers and speakers used in theatres, cinemas, "and elsewhere".

music/sound technologies altered the practice of sound and music composition and operation, and what the consequence of such developments are for collaboration and aesthetics.

The Kit

Before the invention or incorporation into theatres of recording technology an array of mechanical devices was used to produce acoustic sound effects operated live and by hand including thunder-runs, rumble carts, thunder sheets and thunder drums, avalanche machines, wind machines, rain boxes and drums, crashes, gunshots, explosions, creaks, groans, growls and roars, footsteps, trains and carriages. These noise machines were the earliest theatre sound technologies played live and designed to provide realistic effects (from within the theatre building itself). This section tells the story of the development of infrastructure at the RSC from the early days when it consisted of the mediated sound effects and music from panatropes[3] alongside the live voices of actors and some of the mechanical devices listed above through to the introduction of computer operated systems that enabled control of an entire soundscape.

Barry Jackson, who was artistic director of the Memorial Theatre from 1945 to 1948, had dispensed with live musicians in the pit and instead commissioned recorded music in order to cut costs and to remove the problem of accommodating an orchestra. This decision led to a dispute with the MU and a fine being imposed on the theatre, but facilitated an increase in the stage size and an alteration in its shape. The band, or orchestra as it was called at the time, remained employed and continued to contribute pre-show and interval music and concert performances. The newly commissioned music for each show was recorded and played on panatropes, though from the mid-1950s reel-to-reel tape was also used in a slow process of evolution from disc to tape (Kendall 1981 in Llano 2013, 109 n.9).

David Collison describes his first experience of operating a panatrope in 1954 at the Arts Theatre in London, a machine he describes as 'a large metal coffin with two 78 r.p.m. turntables and pick-up arms equipped with groove-locating devices' (Collison 2008, x). The difficulty was in

---

[3] This was a device for playing discs on which sound effects and music were recorded and played back in theatres. Its operation will be discussed in more detail below.

dropping the needle into exactly the right groove at the correct moment, cued by a green light from stage management, while simultaneously setting up another cue on another record on the other turntable, or adding a new sound on top of one that was running. Various cuebars and other cueing devices were created that improved the accuracy of dropping the needle at the correct point (Ibid., 130–1). The other issue with the discs on the panatropes was that copies needed to be made every few weeks to retain the quality of sound reproduction. Reel-to-reel tape machines gradually replaced the panatropes; they were much easier to record on, made operation easier because leader tape was inserted into the tape at the start of each cue so that the cue could be lined up to start almost immediately the button was pressed, and cut-off tape could be inserted to stop the machine automatically at the precise moment the cue ended. However, in developing a new production these machines were much less flexible because all the layers of a sound recording had to be agreed on and the length decided before the recording was made, whereas with the panatropes a series of separate effects could be mixed live from recordings on separate discs. Collison remarks that at first the panatropes continued to be used for the early stages of a production because of the flexibility they offered, but once the lengths and effects were agreed on and the production had settled down tapes were made and replaced the discs. This development of sound and music was mirrored in theatres around the country with tape recorders beginning to replace turntables by around 1952 (Kaye and Lebrecht 2009, 7), but panatropes continued to be used until well into the 1960s.[4]

In fact Collison wonders whether the demise of specially composed background music at most theatres other than the RSC, rather than resulting from the MU's tightening of rules for recording music, may have at least partially resulted from the inflexibility of the tape machine. This reduced creative experimentation until the digital sampler, with its instant access and memory, emerged and the production of soundscapes became an innovative and creative task once again. As he concludes, 'since my days struggling with the panatrope at the Arts Theatre club in the 1950s, the technique for creating sound effects seems to have come round full circle.

---

[4] The earliest mention of a panatrope is the launch in 1927 of the Brunswick Panatrope, but the device that was developed in the UK by Simon Sound just before the Second World War and followed by many other versions and editions became so ubiquitous that the word 'pan' itself was later used to mean a sound cue (Collison 2008, 84 and 127).

What has changed is the method. Back then, digital technology would have been the stuff of science fiction' (Collison 2008, 259).

In the 1960s, following the inauguration of the RSC, the first job of the sound staff was the mixing of live sound in the auditorium—a mix that at that time included recorded sound effects and music from the panatropes and reel-to-reel tape recorders alongside the live acoustic voices of actors and instruments of onstage musicians. In the 1950s at Stratford the lighting department and operating room had been moved to the back of the dress circle into what had originally been the royal box, and new Strand electric boards were installed. Peter Hall became artistic director in 1959 and one of his improvements was the introduction of new sound technologies, developed in conjunction with refurbishments to the theatre, but that still meant that two tape machines were mounted in a 'homemade sound control panel … that was situated on a perch above the prompt corner' (Howells 2013–17), with volume controls and speaker switching as can be seen in Fig. 1. From this point of operation it is obvious there was neither sight of the stage nor a realistic chance of balancing

Fig. 1 Michael White and the Revox in PS Wing of RST, 1959. (Courtesy of the RSC)

the sound. Instead sound was cued by a system of lights and sound levels were set in advance and had to be adhered to.

At the Aldwych things were slightly better. From 1962 the sound operator was in a stalls box on the Prompt Side (PS) at the front of the auditorium. Lighting (LX) was operated from the Opposite Prompt (OP) side in another box with a shaded panel. The boxes were converted into booths, but even for sound there was no opening window so 'although [Sonia Higgins—the operator] could see the stage, she could not actually hear what she was doing' (Collison 2016). This was a problem that continued for many productions and in all theatres especially at Stratford until surprisingly recently, with the exception, according to John Leonard, of musicals, when the sound desk was moved into the auditorium (Leonard 2016).

It was during the 1961 season that, for the production of *Ondine* starring Leslie Caron, Collison invented a tape-delay system to create an echo effect. Peter Hall wanted the voice of Leslie Caron and the other water sprites to sound 'other-worldly' so Collison

> rigged some microphones and fed them into a tape recorder and out again to a loudspeaker way up on the fly floor. When recording, the distance between the record head and the playback head produced an echo – enhanced by the distant loudspeaker. This is known as "tape echo." (Collison 2016)

This system was accidentally switched on during a rehearsal when the musicians were playing a fanfare live onstage, and it added to the sound quality to the extent that 'a duplicate system was set up in the theatre at Stratford-Upon-Avon and "switch on echo mikes" became a standard feature on the sound plot for all on-stage music' that was 'used for live music for some years' (Collison 2008, 167). John Leonard explained that this was still in operation in the mid-70s when he joined the company: 'there used to be a dedicated tape machine that ran 7.5 inches per second with a full reel of tape on it that just did tape echo from a pair of mics on the side of the stage', though by this time this was 'very old hat', and he wanted the company to invest in rather more modern technology (Leonard 2016).

In 1972 there was a major rebuild of the Stratford auditorium for the Roman Season directed by Trevor Nunn and designed by Christopher Morley. The stage and auditorium were reconfigured, and in the course of the building work additional boxes were built at all levels, the stage was mechanised with lifts and rakes, the lighting controls, that were already in a box at the back of the auditorium, were brought forward within the lighting box and a new board was installed. At the same time the issue of interference with the audience experience was addressed; the problem had been that conversations between the DSM[5] in the prompt corner and the lighting operator on headphones in the box would disturb audience members sitting close by. By introducing a window at the front of the box, lighting technicians speaking to stage management or other departments over headphones were less audible and distracting to the audience, and a foldback speaker from the stage to the box meant that the operator could hear the show live. Verbal cues from stage management were relayed over headphones, and cueing directly from the stage was increasingly used before the introduction of computerised systems after 1994. This all meant that the lighting operator could be much more flexible in cueing, taking visual and verbal cues from actors as well as responding to the cues from stage management.

During the 1972 rebuild, two void areas on either side of the lighting box were brought into operation. An old projection cubicle on auditorium right was given a larger window and was often used as the director's or assistant's box; it allowed directors and assistants to enter and leave, having watched and made notes about part or all of a performance, without disturbing the audience. Auditorium left provided another void that had a tiny high window, and it was to here that the sound operator was moved; a move that was no help at all in allowing the sound operators to hear the balance of sounds in the auditorium. A sliding window was introduced later, but even then sound operation was difficult for an operator who needed to hear the mix of sounds and the balance of music and speech or sound and music that the audience was hearing. According to John Leonard, the sound mix heard through the foldback speaker in the box was completely different to that heard by the audience. He recalls that there was 'a tiny and completely useless window' in the old box, and the effect was the same at the Barbican, where 'there was a sign above the window that said, "It doesn't sound like that in here"'. Leonard records that sound mixing at the time was a lot like 'painting by numbers, which I didn't find particularly successful at all. Because the equipment, the consoles, were so big, you couldn't have them in the auditorium; they had to be in the control room, which was a bit of a nuisance' (Leonard 2016). Jeremy Dunn recalls that in The Swan there was also a glass

---

[5] DSM is the widely used term for a Deputy Stage Manager who is responsible for noting all moves and changes in a prompt script and cueing actors, lighting, sound, "and all other" technical staff during the performance.

covered box, the window of which was 'accidentally' broken during the recent redevelopment, and that the sound desk in the main house has been in the stalls since he arrived. Michael Bruce, working at the RSC as a composer more recently comments that the presence of an audience alters the sound balance because 'human bodies soak up sound', noting that 'It usually takes a couple of preview performances to plot an exact level for all music cues' not only because of the bodies but because of the 'general hubbub that audiences make' (Bruce 2016, 219–20). This is the problem sound operators and designers faced, trying to mix to settings decided at a technical or dress rehearsal knowing that the sound would be different in practice every night.

The problems of sound design and operation were exacerbated in the late 1970s, because, as Leonard records, this was a time when money was short and sound was considered relatively low on the list of priorities for investment. When he arrived at Stratford from the Bristol Old Vic in 1975 most of the equipment was less modern than he had been used to, including, for example, an old Electrosonics console that had toured the world with Peter Brook's *Dream* before being installed at The Other Place (Leonard 2016). Leo Leibovici also remembers that 'It was pretty clunky. It wasn't helped at The Other Place by the fact it was mechanically clunky, so the people could hear all the tapes going on and off' (Leibovici 2016). Leonard and Collison both recall that in order to make the console work properly they needed 'to hit it from time to time because the cards that did most of the work would come loose in their sockets. You'd give it a belt on the side and it would go back in again'. Although all interviewees remember a high level of collaboration and sophistication in the work itself, there are repeated references to the 'decrepit' equipment at this time, especially but not exclusively at The Other Place. However, by the start of the new century a different picture had emerged of substantial investment that I will return to below.

During the mid-1970s the band often played in their dedicated bandbox with multiple microphones permanently sited so that the sound operator could mix them live to a stereo auditorium system, but Leonard reports that 'we adjusted, half the time not being able to hear what the hell was going on ourselves' (Leonard 2016). There were two problems therefore: the band was in one box unable to adjust their sound balance—a balance they needed to hear to play well; the sound operators were in another box unable to hear what the audience could hear to adjust accordingly. Figure 2 shows an operator in an isolated box in 1981 hearing the show through foldback speakers on the wall to his right. On the positive

Fig. 2 Trevor Pearce in the sound box, 1981. (Joe Cocks Studio Collection. ©Shakespeare Birthplace Trust)

side, by this time sound operation had become a specific and important job, so the next stage was for the sound desk to be moved out into the open at the back of the stalls, though this occurred only for musicals. For the production of Guy Woolfenden's musical adaptation of *The Comedy of Errors* in 1976/77 at the Aldwych the desk was moved into the auditorium. For *Les Misérables* (1985) the team commandeered a mix position at the front of the first circle at the Barbican. This practice set a precedent followed for subsequent musicals, though it was only possible for the mix position to be moved downstairs to a central position at the back of the stalls after the latest refurbishment at Stratford (Leonard 2016).

Bill Graham was head of sound when Leonard joined the sound department in London from Bristol Old Vic in 1978, having already worked as a freelance at the RSC on three shows in the mid-'70s. After Graham left

Leonard was appointed Head of Sound for all the RSC theatres in 1980, and it was then that he devised a memory routing system controlled by a simple home computer; the first such system designed for theatre sounds in the UK, but which was not incorporated by the RSC at that time (Collison 2008, 195). Leonard records that his desire to update equipment and computerise systems, which was not possible because of lack of funding, was one of the reasons he left the RSC in 1987. However, he remarked much more optimistically that it is a better organisation now that the focus is clearer 'and they're not desperately trying to do everything all the time' (Leonard 2016).

The Barbican theatre opened in 1982 with a specification that had been agreed many years earlier—a situation that resulted from about seven years of delays because of building problems. Leonard became Head of Sound during the much delayed build, but the budgets and designs had already been agreed by his predecessor and contracts placed. The City of London, who was the client for the building, was resistant to incurring additional costs, but had allowed the mixing desk size to be increased and a memory routing system introduced at a late stage of development (Collison 2008, 202). Nevertheless Leonard notes that by the time of the move into the building the equipment had been in storage for five or six years, most of it was by then antiquated and 'quite a lot of things blew up as soon as you plugged them in' (Leonard 2016).

Lighting and sound contracts had been awarded to Rank Strand Electric, but only a few months after the theatre's opening the company closed its sound department, leaving the RSC staff with no technical support. By this time it had also become normal elsewhere to operate shows with heavy sound requirements from the auditorium whereas the Barbican's huge desk could not be moved out of the box. Leonard attempted to persuade the RSC to invest in his proposal for a digitally controlled mixer, but to no avail, though other companies made this investment, as did the RSC somewhat later (Collison 2008, 202). The production of a large-scale commercial musical in 1985, *Les Misérables*, was what forced the management to invest in sound equipment and design, and increase the resources allocated to sound. Even when Leonard returned to the RSC much later he felt that the theatre was behind the times in terms of the investment in sound equipment and capacity (Leonard 2016). He acknowledged that this resulted from lack of funding from the Arts Council especially during the 1980s and 1990s, though a somewhat different picture is painted by the current Head of Sound who regards the introduction of Lottery funding in 1994 as the turning point in investment.

In the mid-1980s synthesisers began to become readily available and stable enough for live use in theatres; they opened up the possibilities of generating electronically created sounds and sound effects using MIDI technology to link electronic musical instruments directly to sound systems. These were totally new sounds that could now be programmed on synthesisers, and their introduction was an enormous step towards blurring the boundaries between sound and music. At about the same time samplers arrived that allowed musicians to link the new polyphonic digital keyboards, and in fact any digital instrument, to 'samples' of real instruments that had been recorded and saved. The sampler effectively downloaded the recorded sound and played it through the instrument at whatever pitch was played. A dog barking could now be played on a keyboard at a pitch or even in a melody or chord, while electric guitars or any electronic instruments (flutes, clarinets, etc.) could also produce the sounds if connected to the sampler via MIDI. Even a complete orchestra or string section could now be sounded by one polyphonic instrument. The realism of a 'musical instrument' sound was still somewhat problematic, though, as the timbres and overtones of the instrument were inexactly reproduced on the early synthesisers producing sounds that were clearly 'synthesised' rather than orchestral sounds. However, these new sounds were incorporated into scores and sound effects. Meanwhile the early samples were only effective over a small pitch range so were not very realistic, while phrasing and musical inflections were difficult to recreate on a different family of instruments. A keyboard, for example, is not able to produce the effect of breathiness produced on a wind instrument, or mirror the attack of bowing on a stringed instrument. The advantages were that complex musical clusters were now enabled that combined the melody and harmony of music with the recorded sounds and noises of soundscape, and sampling made it possible that either musicians or sound operators were able to play the new instrumental sounds or sound effects as and when required (Collison 2008, 103).[6] This technology was employed by sound designers and technicians and revolutionised the way in which music was performed and recorded (Kaye and Lebrecht 2009, 9). MiniDiscs, compact discs, DATs and samplers began replacing reel-to-

[6] For a comprehensive chronology of key inventions from 1820 up to 1994 see Collison 2008, 66–104.

reel and cassette tape in the mid-1980s and 1990s, and by the 1990s most sounds were recorded directly onto computers where audio editing and processing was made much simpler by the graphic depictions on the screen. At the same time the production of music scores was also facilitated through music composition software.

One of the issues with the early synthesisers was that the settings for sounds were quite complex, and had to be annotated and then input into the synthesiser to reproduce the same sound each night. Gradually it became more straightforward as the technology developed, but even in 1998 the checking before a performance of the set-up of the various keyboards for *The Lion, The Witch and the Wardrobe* and *The Winter's Tale* was important and onerous. The set-up process for the Korg and Clavinova keyboards (each of which had a raft of different onboard and disc loaded sounds available) is shown in Fig. 3.

Although at first these technologies were prohibitively expensive, the prices soon reduced as items moved into the mainstream market and achieved economies of scale. These computer assisted samplers and playback systems increased the amount of storage space and the ability to manipulate, reproduce and trigger all kinds of sounds with greater accuracy and complexity. In many theatres the sound designer was responsible for providing all elements of sound and music, but at the RSC the commitment to live music whether played on acoustic instruments or these new digital tools, was maintained alongside an increasing focus on sound design.

In the case of the actual operation, sound effects can be triggered more accurately using digital technology because there is no leader tape or hiss to worry about, so that when the DSM gives a cue, or when the sound operator takes a visual cue the sound effect fires immediately.

> How much better is it that with modern technology when you press for the sound effect or the microphone to come in, it comes in and it doesn't hiss? That the amplifier is a modern amplifier that's working properly, and isn't for instance a valve amplifier …that would take ten minutes to warm up properly? (Dunn 2016)

The combination of computer technology and a detailed written cue list makes it possible that in an emergency a new operator can manage the show without knowing it hugely well.

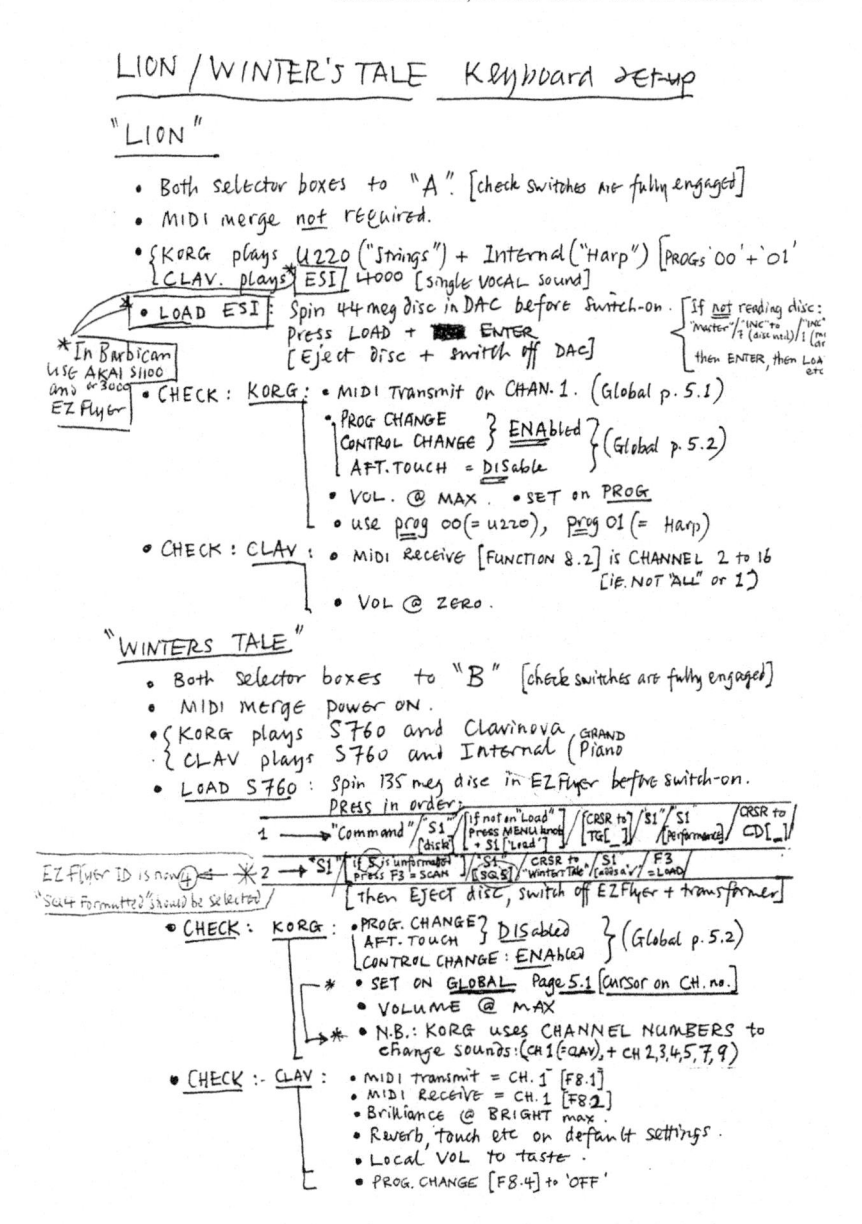

Fig. 3 *The Winter's Tale* and *The Lion, The Witch and The Wardrobe*, 1998. Keyboard settings. (Music by Ilona Sekacz. By permission of the RSC)

Moving into the twenty-first century one of the main innovations has been the creation of 'soundscapes'. R. Murray Shafer claims to have coined the term soundscape to refer to the sonic environment in which we live, comprised of the natural environment and the sounds of civilisation (1994, cover note). Soundscapes in theatre are not only created by recording natural sounds but can be created by actors' voices or musical instruments that establish an environment within which performance exists. All these ideas of soundscape as environmental or acoustic sound that accompanies and structures performances and lives are formulated from the same root. The term offers the sense of something environmental, continuing and evocative that provides an atmospheric context.[7]

Jeremy Dunn, the current Head of Sound, noted that the increasing importance of soundscape in sound design results from the fact that technology is cheaper so there is more of it. When he arrived in Stratford there were six speakers at the back of the auditorium. Now, after the recent renovations there are 56 speakers 'wrapping round the auditorium'. He described how, going back even further, when John Leonard started in the theatre there was very little sound reinforcement in the auditorium, but that a speaker would be placed, for example, for a dog, upstage left, and even moving a speaker relied on the company having extra cable. Once lottery funding was introduced there was much more investment in such technology, the most useful of which gives the designer the ability to work at a laptop in the stalls where they can hear the show, and remotely control the 96 channel sound desk and reverb units. However, Dunn was very clear that John Leonard, Paul Slocombe, Charlie Hall and all his predecessors had invested in very good quality equipment of the time, some of which is still in use. They made wise choices when they invested, so that even though the company now has state of the art equipment some of the older kit is still used for touring or to put an effect into a prop. More importantly for the arguments in this chapter, the new technologies have made possible a new range of sounds and a new approach to mixing the live, the musical, and the mediated sounds to create the combined aural world or 'soundscape' for each production.

---

[7] The suffix 'scape' can mean form, shape, scene, or view, or a specific type of space. The overall term soundscape is used throughout this book to refer to the creation of a background atmospheric context, whether environmental or musical, acoustic or electronic, within which theatrical performance is perceived.

The Operators

Separate teams of sound and lighting designers and operators were gradually introduced in theatres around the country—lighting preceded sound by a considerable margin—each growing into complete departments as technology developed and productions grew more complex. But despite this growth sound remained the poor relation of lighting. Examples of the oversight of sound include a publication onstage Planning and Equipment published in 1949 that devoted just one paragraph to sound effects, consisting largely of the requirement for the provision of a plug socket, while an American *Guide to the Planning and Construction of Proscenium and Open Stage Theatres* covered sound in seven bullet points (Collison 2008, viii). Ross Brown has compiled a list of all the literature on theatre sound design up to 2001—many of which are 'how-to' books; a list that comprises just ten books in the English language dating from 1936 to 2001 (Brown 2010, 14). This situation is changing rapidly, but does illustrate the nascent state of sound operation and design at the start of the period of this study.

In 1961 Peter Hall invited David Collison to create sound effects for a number of productions including *The Cherry Orchard*, *Ondine*, and *As You Like It*.[8] In all there were five productions, four of them at the new London base, The Aldwych, and when *As You Like It* was televised by the BBC Collison noticed that he had received a sound credit (Collison 2008, 167); it is likely, therefore, that he was the first credited sound designer employed at the RSC and possibly in British theatre.[9] For the production of *As You Like It* during that season he created a 'deep-in-the-woods atmosphere with bird song' (Collison 2008, 167). As he remarks, it may now seem mundane to create that kind of environmental sound by installing speakers around the auditorium, but at the time it was noted by a critic since it was such a novelty.

For Brook's production of *King Lear* (1962) no music is mentioned in the programme, but Roger Howells remembers that at the Aldwych and

---

[8] Before this Collison had worked with Peter Hall on productions in the West End. First was *Waiting for Godot* at the Arts Theatre Club in 1956 and later *Brouhaha* in 1959, the success of which meant that he was later called on to work at the RSC when Peter Hall became artistic director there.

[9] Ross Brown contests that Collison's first credit as sound designer was, in fact, in 1959 for the repertory season at The Lyric, Hammersmith (Brown 2010, 34).

on the tour to Paris the following year (1963) he was responsible for operating the electronic sound. Helen Cole King notes in 2008 that this is the only Brook production to date devoid of music, but that the overall sound design created

> a recurring clash and jostle through which the play's harshness is voiced. Clinking armour and chains, the thudding of boots and wood, creaking leather, as well as the vibrating rusted metal sheets used in the storm scene are all designed to do some violence to the ear, as well as to the eye. (King 2008, 418)

Lear's voice in this production became a 'voice of thunder' that battled with the electronically produced and live sounds of the storm. Howells recalls that for the 1963–1964 tour of *Comedy of Errors* and *King Lear* to Eastern Europe, Russia and New York, several musicians travelled with the company since the former had a band onstage throughout, hidden under the stairs of the set, playing Peter Wishart's score. Those same musicians helped make the sound effects for *King Lear*. Sound and music were already overlaid to create a combined effect and were taken for granted as part of all performances with the musicians joining stage management in working thundersheets, rain machines and the wind machine as well as playing music.

When Collison began work at the RSC in 1963 part of his job was to record the group of RSC musicians in a house owned by the RSC near the river. He vividly recalls that 'It had no heating and it was very damp. The musicians had trouble playing because their fingers and their instruments were so cold' (Collison 2016). Later in the 1970s, when Collison was running Theatre Projects (a sound company which had a small studio in Neals Yard, Covent Garden) he continued to record all the recorded music cues for the RSC (and also all the recorded music for the new National Theatre Company). This was made possible by the contract negotiated with the MU in 1962 (as discussed in "Musical Collaborations at the RSC"). However, this was not the end of the story as far as recording music was concerned. The special arrangement for using recorded music at the RST and the National Theatre was renegotiated in the 70s; taped music continued to be used, but within very limited strictures required by the MU as part of its 'Keep Music Live' campaign. In around 1973 or 1974 Woolfenden was conducting a session at a studio in London when he was stopped by the MU representative who had noticed that the music was going to be played in the theatre and actors were going to sing live to the recording. One of the session musicians refused to continue the session because 'according to union rules, a singer had to be present when recording a backing-track' and the session had to stop. Around the same time, Collison's company also had a problem with a trumpeter who tried to stop a recording session for the Mermaid Theatre for the composer Richard Willing-Denton. Bernard Miles had previously obtained permission for the recording so it went ahead, but that was when music recording for theatre really came to an end at least in that studio—in about 1973 or early 1974 (Collison 2016).

The antithesis of that story is told by John Leonard who recalls

> a memorable occasion when we were doing *Coriolanus* (Hands, 1977) in London with Alan Howard and one of the percussionists was asked to do a particular sound effect live from the balcony where they were sitting up on either side of the stage. A voice replied saying "I'm a musician; I am not a sound effects generator." (Leonard 2016)

This is in stark contrast to the experience of everyone collaborating on the *King Lear* tour mentioned above, and demonstrates some of the tensions as the sound department was established and the MU's 'Keep Music Live' programme took effect.

Although in the early 1960s at Stratford stage management operated sound and lighting and jobs were shared between the team based on their individual experience rather than according to a hierarchical structure very soon a 'young chap' (Collison 2016) was employed specifically to operate the sound within the stage management team; this was probably Julian Beech who Howells and Leonard both recall at the RSC. Collison notes that in 1963 he was pleased that 'Although each play was full of recorded music and effects, my task was made easier by the fact that the company now had a member of the stage management team solely responsible for operating the equipment'. Roger Howells operated sound at the Aldwych for some productions during his tenure as stage manager there, but it was at the Aldwych that a permanent sound operator was first employed, Sonia Higgins. Leo Leibovici also worked in the sound department at the Aldwych from about 1971 or 1972, and by that time a separate sound department was well established, however in studio productions both at Stratford and in London tape machines were still being operated by a DSM.

The next substantial change occurred with the opening of The Other Place in 1974. With two theatres at Stratford it became apparent that the music and sound departments couldn't cope with all the demands being made by directors in all the theatres. At Stratford

> the two theatres shared the same pool of musicians and The Other Place was supposed to run at no extra cost to the RSC because the Arts Council didn't want to fund a studio theatre. So the idea was that we use people who would otherwise not be doing anything that night. It wasn't actually true but that's the way it worked. (Leibovici 2016)

Leibovici recalls that many of the musicians didn't like The Other Place much as it was 'just an old tin shed' with a control gallery from which lights and sounds were operated, and the musicians were often squeezed into those cramped conditions. Michael Tubbs enjoyed working there, though, and often arranged and performed the music onstage, and Reynolds noted (in "Musical Collaborations at the RSC") the independence musicians enjoyed at that theatre. These were the more modern productions that sometimes employed several musicians onstage for plays such as *Baal* (Brecht, Dir. Jones, 1979) and musicals like *Piaf* (Gems, Dir. Davies, 1978). Leibovici operated lighting often matching his cues with Tubbs so that lighting and music were co-ordinated, while the stage manager cued what was necessary and operated sound. It was here that sound designers had the opportunity to be more creative, and the team became much closer in performance because of the physical proximity. 'It was a completely different relationship between the technicians and the actors from the main house [...] you were literally thrown together' (Leibovici 2016).

Another part of the task of the sound department was to 'mic up the band if required, because usually they did [require it], because normally the band was not onstage. They were in their nook somewhere or behind the scenes or whatever' (Leibovici 2016). So the sound department would make sure they had the right microphones, bring them in and set them up with appropriate amplification and speakers around all the theatres so that the composers and musicians were happy whichever theatre they were working in. The operators mixed the band live as well as operating the sound effects, balancing the acoustic onstage instruments, the mediated music from the box and sound effects with the live voices of the actors. In general the sound mix would begin with the composer and sound designer sitting in the stalls and commenting on the way the band mix sounded and relaying that to the operator in the box who needed to note the settings without being able to hear the sound live. 'In the end' Leonard remarked,

I think we reached a very good arrangement and they [the music department] realised that the sound department could help them making things sound better, getting different equipment in, using different techniques, advising them on certain things that they probably didn't know about. (Leonard 2016)

In 2016 Jeremy Dunn spoke very persuasively about the fact that one of the most important innovations resulting from computerisation was the ability for operators 'to be more right more of the time' (Dunn 2016).[10] His experience of the company covers a wide period overseeing and working in the two main theatres, the smaller theatres, as well as touring and latterly overseeing the entire operation. As he describes it, the two main roles of sound operators are to mix audio for performance and to change over between different performances in the repertory season. In his early years in the late 1980s and early 1990s this meant that every setting on the desk had to be written down and reset for each performance. A 40 channel desk might be 3 metres by 1.2 metres deep. Resetting meant setting the gain, EQ,[11] faders and so on in the correct position, a task that was both monotonous and time-consuming. Sometimes there were mistakes. The desk shown in Fig. 4 is a smaller board in The Swan, but even so it is clearly a detailed task to check each setting. With computerised systems 'we go EDIT, show: OTHELLO, LOAD. That's going to be more right—what's not to like about being more right?' For musicians this also represents a huge improvement as rather than having someone in a sound desk at the other end of the theatre mixing the sound they are hearing from the stage they now have little individual 'Aviom' foldback systems. Through this system each player has the ability to control their own foldback in real time and each player can have a different foldback mix. That system has only been in operation since about 2013, but before that, and since 2000, the music director had all the feeds and could control what each player received, so that if a player was struggling with a particular audibility problem it could be fixed much more locally and swiftly.

---

[10] Dunn first worked at the RSC in 1989, worked at the Barbican, took some time out when the RSC withdrew from the Barbican, before returning to Stratford as sound manager in 2000, a job whose title changed to Head of RSC Sound in 2004 and in which he remains.

[11] EQ stands for equalizer. Equalisation is the process by which sound is altered so that different frequencies (such as the bass or treble) are relatively more noticeable in the balance.

Fig. 4 Setting up the sound desk upstairs in The Swan's top gallery, 1990. (Malcolm Davies Collection. ©Shakespeare Birthplace Trust)

The other main task of the sound operators was miking actors' voices and musical instruments. This is not just so that audiences and performers can hear a good balanced sound, but it allows the sound designers to add effects. For example, if the musicians are onstage but playing underneath a balcony it would be more 'realistic' for the sound to contain a little reverb, so a microphone will be added to pick up their sound and the sound designer can add that effect; an effect that changes the real into the realistic.

Voices have been miked very rarely since the 1970s. At that time there were only four legal frequencies for radio mics and the kit was expensive to hire, so it was only the musicals that used any sort of reinforcement until after *Les Misérables*. The first musical to use mics was probably *Comedy of Errors* (1976) for which the band was lightly amplified and there might have been one or two radio mics that were considered a huge extravagance (Leonard 2016; Woolfenden 2018). However, miking was used to create special effects particularly for characters who needed to sound other-worldly or magical. Even now, Adrian Curtin records that 'contemporary theatre sound design for Shakespeare does not necessarily entail "high-tech" doctoring of the actors' voice or the performance soundscape' (Curtin 2016, 156), except for 'actors playing supernatural characters ....or for outdoor productions that have high levels of ambient noise' (Ibid., 158). On the other hand mics give the sound department the opportunity to enhance and help actors especially when singing. Leibovici remembers how the sound department gave Jane Lapotaire 'lots of foldback so that she felt confident about her singing' during the production of *Piaf* by Pam Gems in 1978, but in fact the team avoided 'poshing it up too much[12] because that wasn't the point' (Leibovici 2016). The designers were giving her confidence through foldback sound levels but mixing differently in the auditorium. Even now every attempt is made to deliver any necessary amplification of voices as unobtrusively as possible.

The size of the sound department has fluctuated enormously during this period. Jeremy Dunn records that during his time at the theatre there was generally a staff of about nine but that when there were lots of tours going out in the late 1980s and 1990s it had gone up to twenty-five. On the other hand retrenchment following the withdrawal from the Barbican reduced the staff team, and again during the refurbishment from about 2004 it went down to just five. Depending on the number of houses, shows and tours the number of staff members rises and falls, and as sound operators go out on tour with a show someone else is employed to backfill at Stratford.

The period has seen a prodigious professionalisation in sound operation. What began as a task of operation by stage managers has developed into the complete control of the sound world by a designer or operator from a laptop in the auditorium. From there routing through processors to speakers can now be managed live during the technical rehearsal. The range of sounds being mixed has altered too, from pre-recorded sound and music feeding into the auditorium speakers to a complex mix of live and recorded music and sound alongside the acoustic or processed onstage voices. Music and sound departments have become entwined and interdependent, with musicians reliant on sound operators to hear their mix and to balance their auditorium sound, but sound department reliant on the musicians and composers for the creation and production of music and the sound world of a performance. Here, in a similar fashion to the collaborations noted in "Musical Collaborations at the RSC", the consequences of the

---

[12] Making it sound too refined.

longstanding relationships become evident as the departments collaborate to achieve the best results for the production and the greatest satisfaction for the team members.

The Designers

As noted above, David Collison was the first sound designer employed at the RSC, but even before he arrived bringing a new approach to sound in the theatre, the more experimental music had already begun to move away from tonal harmony, incorporating a textural and dissonant sound world. In fact, from the late 1940s the fact that music was to be played on tape opened up certain possibilities for composers that altered the potential types of music that might accompany plays. While some productions strove for a romantic or folk inspired attempt at perceived 'authenticity', there was a simultaneous exploration of the latest developments in experimental music, including sound clusters, dissonance and polytonality. Such experimental and innovative music might have been difficult to play live at every performance, whereas the possibility of repeating a take to achieve perfection in a recording studio altered what composers could write. The use of experimental music to accompany theatre appears to have been stimulated partly through the employment of Roberto Gerhard, a Spaniard who had studied with Schoenberg, exiled to the UK from the Franco regime, who had been living in Cambridge since 1939. He was a musical experimentalist who explored the nature of composition, form and structure using a unique combination of folk music, serial techniques and electronics. He wrote nine scores for the Memorial Theatre between 1947 and 62, eight Shakespeare plays and music for a production of Chekhov's *The Cherry Orchard*, all of which were commissioned despite what he perceived to be the misgivings of the British establishment about his incorporation of the experiments of the Austro-German avant-garde. The incidental music he wrote for the theatre was in fact an experimental area even within his own output; the challenge of theatre provided him with the potential to compose music 'in which he could first implement certain daring ideas and procedures, such as the use of electronic music' (Llano 2013, 108). Although these scores were played by the orchestra and recorded for performances, the sound world they engaged with moved away from tonal harmony and explored novel sonic effects.

Roberto Gerhard's 1947 score for Peter Brook's production of *Romeo and Juliet* incorporated motivic representations of the two households and a polytonal tension that might represent the antagonism between the two families. This prefigures the type of dramaturgy that will be discussed in the next chapter, but here the incorporation of polytonality is important because it introduces a musical language that is innovative and textural, defying the constrictions of romantic harmony or melodic simplicity.[13] In his second commission, for *Cymbeline* (Michael Benthall, 1949), Gerhard developed ideas about thematic and motivic unity in a score that was equally dissonant and polytonal though still within a recognisably orchestral sound world. His composition for *The Taming of the Shrew* (George Devine, 1953) consists of just 14 brief cues, all except the wedding music being scene change music, but even here, in a score that seems to have little function beyond disguising scene changes, his writing is conceived as a unified and organic musical structure. Thus the music, which departs from any attempt to represent geographical or historical context, retains a sense of formal and timbral unity while exploring new sound worlds, languages and textures.

Some reviewers, who rarely notice or mention music, commented that Gerhard's score for *King Lear* (Devine, 1955)[14] was the second most distinctive element but only because the music was felt to be too conspicuous; only Noguchi's set design received more comment. This was one of the first theatre scores to use electronic music in Britain (a successor to Gerhard's own score for Bridget Boland's *The Prisoner* that premiered at The Globe Theatre in 1954) and closely following the first compositions specifically created to explore the possibilities of electronic tape technology, such as Boulez's *Deux Études* (1951–1952) and Stockhausen's *Studien I & II* (1953–1954). Notably, it preceded the establishment of the BBC's Radiophonic Workshop in 1958 (Llano 2013, 120), where the techniques of sound generation, as well as oscillation, looping, distortion and other forms of processing were incorporated into incidental music, theme tunes and jingles for mainstream listening on radio and television. It is worth noting that the press publicity material announcing the opening of the Radiophonic Workshop noted that the techniques were used to provide an additional dimension for radio and television productions, and that such effects were not able to be produced by either music or conventional sound effects at that time (Niebur 2010, 62). This is a feature that

---

[13] Much more detailed analysis of all Gerhard's scores for the RSC is contained in Llano 2013.

[14] For this score Gerhard was paid twice the average fee of £125 even though, as is common practice in live theatre, a number of cues were cut in the final stages of rehearsal.

underpins the arguments of this chapter—that technological developments have blurred the distinction between sound effects and music, the work of composers and sound designers, or in the case of the Radiophonic Workshop, technicians. Some composers, however, were creating dissonant and percussive music with instruments at the same time that the Radiophonic Workshop began to experiment with alternative methods for extending the world of sound and the potential of noise music.

Gerhard's score for *King Lear* (Devine, 1955) was designed to achieve the same timeless, 'universal' quality as the designs that Devine had conceptualised for the production, which abandoned the declamatory speaking style in favour of a much simpler 'realistic' approach to the text. In line with this Gerhard tried to avoid the signification of historical or geographical location so that the 'place' of performance was neutralised (as much as is possible given that music always has an effect) and attention focused on the simple delivery of the spoken word.

In the same season Peter Brook directed *Titus Andronicus* with a score by another young experimental composer, William Blezard, who created a sound track 'inspired by the experimental "musique concrète" being composed at that time'. J.C. Trewin describes how Blezard recorded ashtrays, pots, pans, pencils on Venetian glass phials and wire baskets used as harps for the raw sounds out of which he constructed the score. For the funeral march two microphones were placed inside and underneath the piano so that a recording could be made of the sound resulting from stamping on the pedal and making the strings shudder. This was then manipulated to lower the pitch and slow the sound waves and make a gigantic effect. Sound had become a decisive feature in the primitive cruelty of the play (King 2008, 418).

In his next score *Pericles* (Richardson), that followed in 1958, Gerhard departed from his earlier use of dissonant harmonies and sound clusters, and, instead, used open fifths and triadic chords with pentatonic melodies and static harmonies. These types of scales and intervals remove the directionality and tensions of tonal harmony, which are replaced by static atmospheres and timbres, somewhat in line with Claude Debussy's impressionist practices. Once again there is the removal of the signification of time and place in favour of an atmospheric approach which opens the possibility of a less specific and more 'universal' reading of the text.

Peter Hall arrived at the Festival Theatre and became its artistic director in 1959, when new sound equipment was procured for the theatre in conjunction with other refurbishments. As Gerhard noted, up to then he had always worked with 'shoe-string equipment' without audio or visual control, automatic switching devices or modulators, gain or envelope control.[15] For his production of *Coriolanus* (Hall 1959) Gerhard composed 53 short cues most of which provided fanfares and 'noises' for the battle scenes and cries from the crowds, blurring the distinction between what might later be the responsibility of sound design and composition. The score used minimal orchestral resources, concentrating on a small brass ensemble and percussion. All cues were pre-recorded and performed from the Panatrope, a device that was now being exploited to the full to achieve what was then regarded as 'scenic realism'. This was a departure for Gerhard from the more complex polytonal or dissonant but lyrical writing in his previous scores, towards the production of sounds and the consideration of 'noise' as music following the innovations of John Cage.

Finally in 1962 Brook directed *King Lear* which, as noted elsewhere, expressed nature's harshness and man's cruelty through the medium of sound, even though this was not a 'musical' score but one created entirely in sound (King 2008, 418), while Gerhard wrote the score for *Macbeth* discussed in "Collaborative Composition at the RSC". The work of experimental composers like Gerhard and Blezard, as well as the imagination of directors like Brook, Devine and Hall, is important for this discussion because it exemplifies the way sound and technology grew out of musical innovation and towards the creative generation of sound and music as a unified and fully conceptualised part of the production. In those 15 years theatre music had moved away from a Mendelssohnian orchestral timbre and romantic use of tonal harmony into the modern world where dissonance, polytonality and percussive sound clusters began to be used to create atmosphere and to signal the dissonant worlds within the plays.

Guy Woolfenden was already at Stratford when these scores were performed, and, although his own music remained within a British tradition, incorporating folk rhythms, fluctuating tempi and tonal harmony within polyphonic patterns that the players commented had a uniquely 'British' sound, Gerhard's, Blezard's and Brook's work may have influenced Woolfenden's experimentation with electronically generated sound effects. His score for *Macbeth* (1967), described in "Collaborative Composition at the RSC" above, incorporated an electronically generated sound effects score created by Unit Delta Plus alongside his composition of live music but this score was not Woolfenden's first experiment with creating a sound effects tape.

---

[15] A letter from Gerhard to the British Council, quoted in Llano 2013, 126.

In a letter to David Collison to mark his 70th birthday Guy Woolfenden recalled that 'my recurring memory of working with you ... in the early days of that wonderful company, is what fun it all was'. He continues to describe scraping the 'rough bass strings of an old Steinway grand with a half-crown coin, to make "sword noises" for Peter Hall's *The Wars of the Roses*' (1963). He cut his finger in the process and remarks to Collison that 'it was cruel of you to record my cries of pain—but you were correct to point out that they were unrecognisable when played twice as fast and tarted up with a lavish dollop of echo'.[16] Collison recalls that in fact the scratching sound was 'played backwards so that the percussive elements were at the end' (Collison 2016). This is important because it demonstrates not only the way sound effects were being generated from acoustic sources using the techniques developed in the musique concrète studios of Pierre Schaeffer in France[17] but also the easy collaboration between professionals even before the formal creation of a sound department.

For the production of *Henry V* (Barton, 1966) another sound tape was made by Collison and Woolfenden; the list of cues and their assignment to one of three Decks is in Fig. 5. The season had included all the historical plays in sequence, so by the time the team arrived at Henry V they felt that they had already used every possible trick to represent a battle. A decision was made to recreate the battle of Harfleur in semi-darkness with sound alone rather than, once again, 'having a few actors thrashing about unconvincingly on the stage' (Collison 2016). Woolfenden and Collison gathered together the ingredients for a 'realistic' depiction that included a sword noise which 'was a particularly unpleasant and penetrating metallic sound made by bowing with violin bows on cymbals'. Collison produced a selection of arrow swishes from a bamboo cane repeated in a tight sequence. This was mixed with a copy of the 'standard arrow noise' from Olivier's film of *Henry V*, produced through the inauthentic twanging of an elastic band round the needle of an old fashioned gramophone player. Screams, shouts and other crowd effects were made by actors and Woolfenden composed some French and English trumpet calls and flourishes (Collison 1976, 83–4).

---

[16] A copy of this letter was provided to the author by David Collison from his private collection.

[17] Tape compositions were created by manipulating recordings of natural sounds and voices, and later manipulating sounds created using electronics and early synthesisers, at the RTF in Paris, then in the Groupe de Recherches de Musique Concrète. This was followed in the UK in the early 60s by the inauguration of the BBC's Radiophonic Workshop (RTF was the national broadcaster of France at the time—earlier named RDF and later ORTF. It was here Pierre Schaeffer first experimented with sound technology).

ELECTRONICS, SOUND AND FURY AT THE RSC   121

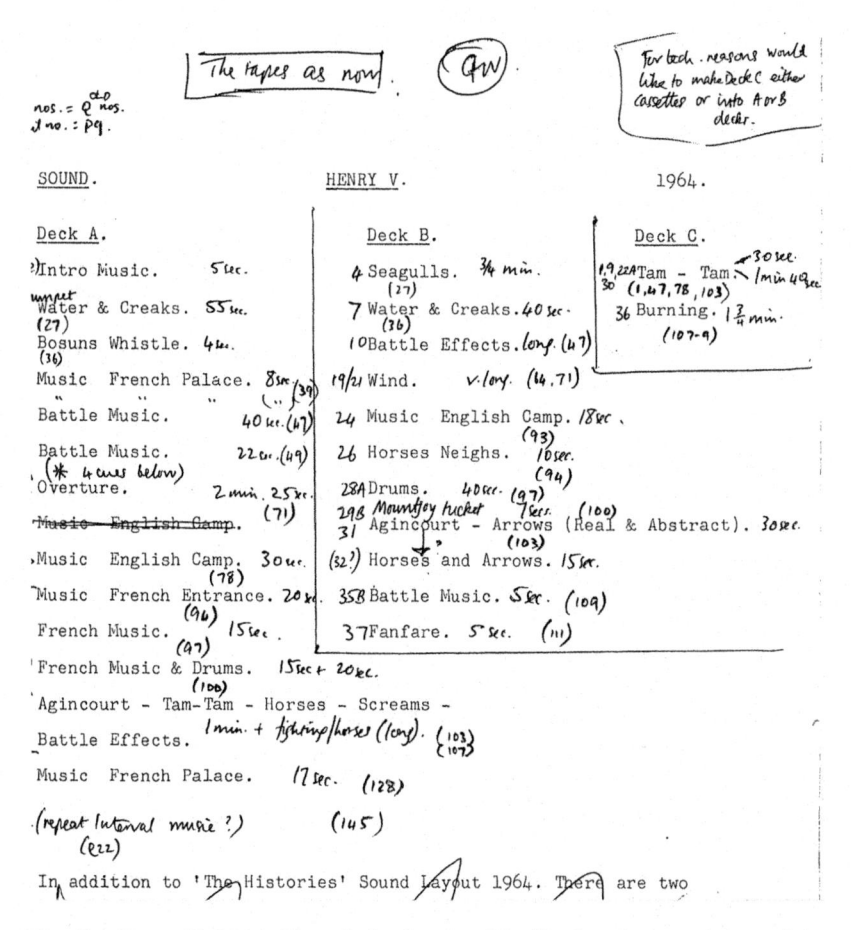

Fig. 5 *Henry V*, 1966. (Sound plot by Guy Woolfenden. By permission of the RSC)

Woolfenden recalled that the battle needed to start and finish 'realistically', but the middle needed to reach a vicious climax of horses, bugles, arrows, shouts and the clash of arms over the increasingly screeching sword noise accomplished through layering sounds and editing the sequence. Even beyond this something extra was required to create tension. The pair decided that during the previous speech an underscoring sound should begin so that the battle seemed to grow organically from the speech, linking the whole sequence together. To achieve this, they recorded continuous bowing on a tam-tam; when continuously bowed the instrument vibrates such that the sound increases in pitch and intensity. Finally, after the great climax of the sound tape the metallic sound was faded again leaving a 'realistic' battle among the actors onstage and the focus returned to the action. Collison continues the story:

> The background to the effect we called the "undertow" was Guy bowing on a tam-tam with the sound starting in the mid-range and building higher and higher until it was a screeching crescendo. To this we added other metallic sounds including noises to mirror the previous more realistic arrow effects. Where we wanted basic battle horn calls – not formal fanfares – I recorded Guy blowing various instruments including a trumpet mouthpiece pushed into a piece of rubber tubing with a large kitchen funnel pushed into the other end. It was a convincing horn, but then he said he would like to try a more muted sound. This he achieved by placing the funnel on top of his head. When I looked up from the tape recorder and saw this ridiculous sight, I could not carry on for laughing. (Collison 2016)

The battle used four tape machines with carefully timed tapes that the sound operator had to pause and restart, changing volume and speaker settings throughout the sequence (Collison 1976, 83). It appears to have been quite a tour-de-force as a music/sound strategy, and its operator was required to perform with incredible focus and accuracy every night. This battle scene was so successful that the sound tape was reused for the same battle in the 1974 production directed by Terry Hands (Beauman 1976, 51), although Woolfenden records it as 40 seconds long and Collison as four minutes long. Woolfenden described the moment as follows: 'the stage is completely bare, except for the Chorus—one man alone at the back of that huge stage. And what I hope it does is give the audience an aural stimulus, so that their visual imaginations begin to work, and they begin actually to see the horror of that battle' (Beauman 1976, 51).

This example demonstrates a really successful collaboration between sound and music to create a design concept for the battle. This is important because when sound design began in the 1960s and early 1970s in America, most sound designers were composers and might create such combined music and sound combinations, whereas in the UK most sound designers were not composers. This meant that in most cases at the RSC composers worked with sound designers, each supporting the other and potentially inspiring greater creativity. Some composers very quickly developed a certain degree of technical knowledge, while others were less technically adept. Equally, some directors were more interested in what might be possible in developing a fully conceptualised sound world than others. It is only in the twenty-first century that composer/sound designers such as Adam Cork, Richard Hammerton and Ben and Max Ringham have led the way in the UK in combining the roles of composer and sound designer. On the other hand, Michael Bruce, for example, remarks that 'there are those who can do this but personally I still believe that theatre, being a collaborative art form, can benefit from the added expertise that comes from two pools of experience' (Bruce 2016, 213).

By complete contrast, in the early days of live music the job of sound operators was simply to create or organise the recording of sound effects and to facilitate the production of music by the live musicians. Leo Leibovici remembers that in the 1970s 'at Stratford we set up a small studio [to …] produce any sound effects that were required in those days. Initially it was pretty primitive—it was tentatively copying BBC [sound effects] discs … and splicing [them] together' (Leibovici 2016). Nonetheless, both Leibovici and Leonard note that sound design was already developing around the country and both mention the director Howard Davies as being an innovator in what he required of sound, while Leibovici records that 'John [Leonard] was extremely innovative; ahead of his time at that point'. Leonard had been running the sound department, responsible for all the sound and music in three theatres (the Theatre Royal, the studio and the little theatre) and doing four-weekly repertory while at Bristol Old Vic in the early 1970s.[18] By the time he arrived at the RSC he had become used to developing productions very quickly, learning his trade through experimentation rather than formal training, and he had become adept at music editing, adapting pieces of music, playing them backwards or looping them to create effects. It is here that sound design and the work of electronic music studios overlap, and the influence of musique concrète and the radiophonic workshop are felt even before the widespread use of synthesisers and samplers.

Once sound effects began to be recorded the recordists discovered that although time and effort went into trying to record the 'real' sounds, the sounds were often not sufficiently 'realistic' and a finished sound track

---

[18] There he worked with Edward Williams who was a proponent of electronic music and a great user of the EMS VCS3—the prime British synthesiser in the '60s and '70s, used by all the major pop groups. Williams went on to write the music for David Attenborough's BBC television series *Life on Earth* (Leonard 2016).

contained about 75% of fabricated sounds that might have been partially drawn from the available discs of 'library effects'. So, for example, an 'enemy cannonball' was created from

> a sharp crack and splinter of wood recorded in the studio, edited on to a rasping-scrape made by dragging a wooden crate filled with heavy weights along a concrete floor, edited onto general crashes and thumps. The finished effect, lasting only about three seconds, gives the impression of a heavy lump of metal bursting through the wooden side of a ship and crashing along the deck. A few shouts and screams complete the picture. (Collison 2008, 90)

This demonstrates the extent to which the creation of sound is not necessarily 'real' even if it appears to be 'realistic' for audiences who can take meaning from it. Jeremy Dunn, in the twenty-first century, notes that the effect of a gunshot using a real gun is so loud that audiences are shocked and laugh, so that it is often more productive to use a fake gunshot whose volume can be controlled so that the tension of the scene can be maintained (Dunn 2016). There is a recognisable 'shink' sound that audiences expect when a sword is sheathed (Dunn 2016), even though a metal sword being housed in a leather scabbard would make no audible sound an audience might hear. Equally when Lady Macbeth picks up daggers covered in blood there is usually some sound:

> possibly just an element within the music, it might actually be a high violin note, it might be a bowed vibe, it may be a bowed cymbal perhaps. There are the daggers and the assumption is that's the noise it makes when you deliver daggers....that's fabulous in my mind because it helps you to tell the story. (Dunn 2016)

But as he makes clear, this use of sound appears to be pre-conditioned by film sound and music rather than reality.

As electronic generation of sound became much more widespread in the 1980s synthesisers and samplers were regularly incorporated into scores, especially by composers who worked across the fields of theatre, film and television music. Ilona Sekacz was one of the regular composers at the RSC most interested in the generation of new sounds. She was also incredibly collaborative; 'she wanted everybody to be involved. Although the end result was very much hers, you would sometimes suggest ways that things could change or you could help her out in doing things'

(Leonard 2016). She was responsible for incorporating a Fairlight CMI (a digital sampling keyboard developed by Peter Vogel and Kim Ryrie in 1979) at Stratford for a production of *Twelfth Night* (Caird) in 1983 (Brown, R. 2015). The Fairlight was a kind of early sampler that had a big choir effect that Sekacz wanted for the production. Leonard records that 'we spent the entire budget on renting one for one day'. They employed a Polish programmer called J.J. Jeczalik to programme the machine at the Barbican and Leonard notes that 'That was the first time I'd worked with what is effectively a sampler rather than a synthesiser'. In 1987 for a show at The Other Place called *Indigo* (Heidi Thomas, Director, 1987) Sekacz asked for a Synclavier, and the music credit for the show was shared between her and Leonard. She was among the first to make substantial use of synthesisers not to replace orchestral instruments but to generate complex electronic and atmospheric sound worlds.

George Fenton also incorporated music samplers and synthesisers into his scores, while other composers such as Stephen Oliver and Guy Woolfenden tended to continue writing predominantly for orchestral instruments for much longer. John Woolf who later became director of music at the RSC collaborated with Leonard on producing sound and music because of his interest in the sounds that could now be produced. Although 'not particularly technically savvy, we [produced] things like squelchy mud stuff [...] that he could play' (Leonard 2016). The main problem in this development was suspicion from both musicians and the MU that the use of synthesisers and samplers might remove the need for live players. This created some friction from time to time, especially when the sounds could not be created in any way other than by synthesisers or electronics, but in general most of the musicians and sound team enjoyed the creative possibilities generated as music technology completely transformed the nature of sound composition and design.

A Midsummer Night's Dream (1994)[19]

Sekacz's music for *A Midsummer Night's Dream* created an atmospheric soundscape through the incorporation of electronic sounds into a traditional score. The 1994 production, directed by Adrian Noble, is a production whose design references Brook's version with added colour and surrealism, but whose performance focused on comedy rather than the

---

[19] This analysis relies on the AV recording, the score and prompt book.

dark sexuality of Brook's reading. Ilona Sekacz had already written over 30 productions for the RSC as well as significant amounts of television music, radio, film, an opera and a ballet. As usual most reviews made little or no mention of music, but Rhoda Koenig commented that 'the, as usual, excellent music of Ilona Sekacz contributes pomp without pomposity and a sense of mystery that owes nothing to cliché' (1994), though Katherine Duncan-Jones refers to 'woodland folk and souped-up Mendelssohn' (1994), while Nick Curtis in the *Evening Standard* suggests that 'Ilona Sekacz's music recalls Max Reinhardt more than Peter Brook' (Curtis 1995).

This is a strange group of reviews, suggesting and denying cliché, though they all agree that the sound world is romantic, while the timbres and musical content are new. Although seven musicians are employed, flute, clarinet, two horns, percussion and two keyboard players, it is the keyboards that feature most in this score because of the other-worldly sounds they can create. Complex polyphonic sounds are used to signify the magical fantasy space of the midsummer fairyland. These sounds were programmed by Michael Tubbs using an Emax and a Korg synthesiser so that the score included bell wave, life magic, flying, technobass, afterlife and brass. In addition there are some very specific sounds created by Tubbs for this production including 'Ilona's Botts' and 'Ilona's Peril', the latter used at the end of the mechanicals' first scene as Puck and the Fairies enter.[20] Many of these sound combinations give a much longer resonance after the depression of a key than had been possible on a keyboard before. Indeed, they allow notes to sustain beyond the breath control of the most accomplished woodwind player, while the polyphony of this second generation of synthesisers meant that a sound could incorporate built in running patterns, arpeggiated figures, reverberation, tinkling bells or tremolo effects in the background of a sound from a single pressing of a key. This makes these keyboards ideal for underscore because, rather than the articulation of a melody which might interrupt or detract from the speech, a sustained effect is maintained while the texture remains constantly shifting to create an atmosphere that is not 'realistic', but heightened, to represent the 'noises and sweet airs' of the metaphysical world. The challenge such sounds pose is that they become clichés themselves, as happened with the

---

[20] Information derived from the cue sheets and production records at the Birthplace Trust Archive.

patches[21] of the first generation of synthesisers, such as the Yamaha DX7 whose sounds became instantly recognised as DX7 imitations of orchestral timbres.

This generation of polyphonic synthesisers allowed a much greater diversity of innovative electronic sounds to be created very simply, and the user-friendly samplers that appeared at around the same time meant that orchestral sounds could be imitated much more effectively. One strategy used by orchestrators and composers was to employ one or more live instruments with keyboard support creating the effect of a 'family' of that instrument. Thus one violin could now sound like a string section because of the layering of a lead violin that contributed bowing patterns and phrasing as well as melody and timbre. The support provided by a keyboard string sound thickened the chords within the same instrumental colour, while the limitations of keyboard attack, decay and bowed phrasing were masked by the leading live instrument.

Nevertheless, in a nod to the romantic past, the woodwind feature in many of the musical cues in the fairy world. Meanwhile the horns add weight and depth in a number of cues and feature most obviously in the hunting calls and fanfares that are used principally in the world of the Athenians—all of which are supported by brass or wind sounds on the keyboards. Fanfares introduce Theseus and Hippolyta when they enter the wood and announce the entry of the prologue and procession of players for the performance of the tragedy of Pyramus and Thisbe. In this way the musical signification draws on earlier traditions, but it is overlaid with a different type of atmospheric fantasy, and the orchestral soundscape is enhanced by the multiplication of instruments made possible through electronic keyboards. The score is traditional in its use of triple time and compound metres for fairy songs and dances, but less traditional in its underscoring of speeches with slow moving harmonies using complex breathy and spacey timbres. In fact it is the introduction of these types of timbres that triggered a greater amount of underscoring of speech because these new sounds were less intrusive and their volume was entirely controllable. The signalling of the application of flower juice and its effect using wind sounds and light bells is consistent with earlier practice, but the

---

[21] A 'patch' is the name given to an electronically created sound resulting from a particular combination of waves, frequencies, onsets, and so on and programmed into a synthesiser. Each synthesiser had 'banks' (A, B, C, and D in the case of the DX7), containing over 100 patches that were accessed by a combination of switches above the keyboard.

lack of tonal specificity in the magic world, created through a combination of electronic and acoustic timbres, is reminiscent of the impressionistic later scores of Gerhard.

One of the key questions for the director and Head of Sound in the 1990s and the new century is the decision about who to recruit to create sound designs. Employing external sound designers brings in new ideas and innovations, but using the internal staff means that more time can be spent developing the ideas in-house and it raises staff morale because of the opportunity it gives people to express their artistic ambition. These are the same issues faced by the music staff and discussed in "Musical Collaborations at the RSC" above. The balance of those two strategies in the sound department is currently at about 50/50 and that is seen as being the most beneficial. At the time of my interview with Jeremy Dunn in August 2016, Andy Franks and Dunn himself were creating the sound design for the new production of *The Tempest* that had been in development for about a year. This show (that will be referred to again in the concluding chapter) was particularly technological because Ariel was performed by a live actor in a body suit that could trigger a computer generated holographic avatar. The avatar would appear projected onstage at times, sometimes with and sometimes without the actor's simultaneous appearance. Given this extraordinary evocation of visual magic, the sound designers began to explore the idea of a soundscape that would run throughout the play with composer Paul Englishby. The idea was that the soundscape would be created by a combination of three keyboards and sound effects and would reflect the idea that the island is a fantasy world full of strange noises and magic. The use of keyboards was chosen over recorded sound effects because it allowed the soundscape to change key to the appropriate pitch ready to cue the singer in advance of the performance of songs. The sound team were also responsible for manipulating the sound of Ariel's singing using a combination of reverb and pitch correction. At the time of writing the team hadn't decided whether the manipulation effects might be triggered by musicians or sound operators. That type of collaboration, as discussed in "Musical Collaborations at the RSC", is a feature of the work of a company where the staff team have the opportunity for much longer and more detailed interactions.[22]

---

[22] This production was screened as part of the RSC Live season in autumn 2016, and released on DVD in 2017. Opus Arte 1249D.

The final innovation—which continues the discussion of the blurring of boundaries between sound and music—is the employment of the small group of composers who are also sound designers such as Ben and Max Ringham. As Dunn explained, 'when it's a small show one of them will create the combined music and sound for the performance, whereas for bigger tasks they arrive together with one working with the sound team and the other with the music team so that the whole project is unified' (Dunn 2016).

As Ian Reynolds mentioned, it was another composer/sound designer, Adam Cork, who was primarily responsible for introducing pre-generated computer tracks known as 'click tracks' to the modern RSC in 2005. Some of the music, voices or effects are recorded onto a track and the musicians and/or singers play and sing live with the track, thus combining the acoustic and the mediated. The MD and rhythm section of the band has a click played to them on headphones; this track locates the live music alongside the recorded music, so that the live sounds follow the pre-recorded music without any slippage or clashing. This combination of live and recorded sound has the effect of thickening and making the overall effect much fuller, more polyphonic, more textured and altogether more interesting (Dunn 2016). The following year click tracks were used for *The Tempest* in the main house, especially for the ball scene 'which was just so complicated [...] with all this pre-recorded stuff going on' (Reynolds 2016b).

Click tracks have been around for many years as the technology was initially used at the start of sound films; one of the earliest live theatre examples was a click track used in 'Hey There' in *The Pyjama Game* (1973 revival) (Yershon 2016), and I recall using them regularly in commercial British pantomime from the early 1990s. At the RSC it was a longstanding practice until the mid-1960s for music to be recorded with performers singing live, though such recordings didn't rely on a click track. These tracks became more widely used in association with synthesisers and samplers when a click could be generated and recorded onto one track and the live or recorded music synchronised to it, and their use blossomed further with computer technology. But given the importance of live music at the modern RSC click tracks were a relatively late introduction.

There are two issues, however. One is that the MU has, in the past, treated such recordings with a certain amount of suspicion; if there was any suggestion that the click track and its associated recordings would replace conventional instruments or cost musicians' jobs it would be banned. However, click tracks have become more technologically stable and have also been treated with increasing flexibility by the MU and others in recent years, and have been used very widely in musical theatre and pantomime since the 1990s to supplement and enhance rather than replace live music. The other, potentially more concerning issue is that the flexibility that had been built into the long-term collaborations of musicians and performers is entirely removed. Once the click track is activated everyone is locked into the timings that have been pre-recorded and there is no longer space for stretching out a speech or for a scene change over-running.

This, however, is the modern theatre, and increasing computerisation in all areas places these constrictions on creativity even as it promotes diverse sound combinations. It is common practice among musicians when playing together to adapt to slight tempo changes especially when accompanying speech, and indeed it is rare that a live performance will adhere to a strict tempo without a computer generated time stamp, but the practice at the RSC is exceptional in that it requires the players to move as a body, sometimes without a conductor, altering the timing of underscore or accompaniment to fit the speech of actors. Click tracks thus represented another big change for the musicians who were used to listening to each other, picking up each other's body language, anticipating and adapting with the actors. Instead, when playing with a click track they were required to play along with what was effectively a metronomic click, and this was controversial—even leading to discussions about what kind of sound click was best and how to adapt the style of playing to the beat of the music and the click of the track (Dunn 2016).

On the other hand, the diversity of sounds and the level of orchestral and vocal complexity have been revolutionised by this technology—it is just not always very musician-friendly. Of course, way back during the production of Henry V in 1974 the actors' voices were supplemented as they sang along to their own pre-recorded voices, and such recordings have been used to supplement live voices ever since, especially when, for example, actors were singing as they left the stage. This happened in the 2013 version of *As You Like It* (Aberg) with music by Laura Marling, whose curtain call was supplemented by a recording of the company so that the sound was boosted for a 'knees-up' to end the show (O'Neil 2016). The scale—the amount of recording and the incorporation of sound/music rather than just voices into the tracks—has changed radically since the turn of the twenty-first century, however, to the discomfort of some musicians. But, just as synthesisers and samplers changed the nature of sound in the 1970s and 1980s, computers have transformed the complexity of the scores that can be produced by a small number of instruments and a company of actors who may not be expert singers.

All this is in direct contrast to the flexibility that has been created by the ability of sound designers and operators to play, alter and adapt sound effects directly from computers at the moment they are required, freeing them from reliance on pre-recorded tapes and discs. The number of shows being produced makes this level of fast flexibility absolutely imperative in maintaining the high standard of music and sound in every single performance of every single production by the RSC at Stratford and around the world, but might reduce the sense of empowerment and independence of musicians and operators on the ground.

Conclusion

Since the 1950s, when John Cage revolutionised the arts with the idea that all sound might be considered as music, the separation of sound and music has been nothing but a retrogressive programme of hanging onto a disappearing classical past. As Gary Yershon remarked, 'the coming together of sound design, especially since the concept of soundscape as articulated in the 1970s....moved towards understanding the liberation of texture as a legitimate expressive tool away from melody and ... paralleling a move in art where the figure lost its place' (Yershon 2016). Like the figure in art, so too the individualising function of melody comes and goes, but what this combination of sound design and music opens up is the musicalisation of live space. There is still a negotiation between jobs, with composers and MDs working with actors on songs and dances and with musicians on style and performance, while sound designers cope with the technicalities of engineering and acoustics, but the end product is a combined activation of the sound world that often cannot be differentiated by department. Jeremy Dunn noted with pleasure an occasion when director Gregory Doran criticised a particular cue but couldn't tell if it was music or sound. He noted that 'it was great that [even the director] didn't know which one it was' because they must have been working effectively together. Dunn owned up to the fault, but was pleased that the overall combination was so seamless that the aural world provided an effective context for performance.

From the perspective of musicians this is perhaps a slightly different story as their contribution becomes more fixed and less free, independent or improvisatory, but this comment also reflects a company that produces many more productions such that the capacity for collaboration at all levels is reduced (Dunn 2016). Nonetheless I was informed about the recent recording of actors' improvisations for the 2016 production of *King Lear* (Dir. Doran, Music Sekacz) and the collaboration that was taking place between sound, music and the Imagination Studios for the forthcoming production of *The Tempest*. It appears that from time to time the space for independent creativity shifts as a result of different technological opportunities and different compositional strategies. Sound designers and operators in the stalls are enabled to be more creative in mixing the sound they hear, while musicians in a sound box have control over their own output and what they hear but not what audiences hear. More fundamentally, some of the independence to take cues and interact with actors is necessarily removed in a more technologically controlled sound environment. Nonetheless collaboration in the performance continues, and in the end the satisfaction for all is that the combined acoustic and mediated sound worlds produce a coherent and inseparable environment that activates the world of the play. The live voices, the 'realistic' sound effects, the real onstage performance by musicians and the mediated offstage music and sound are all mixed so that the overall effect, the combined ecology of sound, is both an effective reflection of the artifice of theatre and perceived as a realistic and coherent world by audiences.

Theatre Music at the RSC

> *Since once I sat upon a promontory,*
> *And heard a mermaid on a dolphin's back*
> *Uttering such dulcet and harmonious breath,*
> *That the rude sea grew civil at her song,*
> *And certain stars shot madly from their spheres*
> *To hear the sea-maid's music.*
> Oberon: *A Midsummer Night's Dream* Act 2, Sc. i.

As Oberon describes in *A Midsummer Night's Dream* the effects of music can be transformative; in this verse it civilised the rude sea and caused stars to change their orbits. While such metaphysical effects are beyond the scope of my experience there is no doubt that music does have effects on audiences, effects that composers use to expand the audio-visual performance. Michel Chion noted that while music seems simply to confirm what appears in the visual world, in fact it shapes the perception of the visual. As a result of the collaborative process undertaken by composer, MD, director, designer and performers, and in light of the material circumstances of production, it becomes almost impossible to separate the audible from the visual or identify the source of an idea from its interdisciplinary articulation. There is a flow of ideas among the collaborative team which results in an interaction between sound and visual imagery in performance, and an equally complex process of interpretation of the combined imagery among audiences. A timp roll can become a storm because of the narrative; without the narrative it is a timp roll. Perhaps in *Macbeth* or one of the other tragedies or history plays it might simultaneously denote a storm arriving and create an atmosphere of foreboding, and it may also presage a fight or battle. The potential ways of reading the narrative are altered as a result, but only through intertextual reference to a wider musical and theatrical context. This might be, for example, a reference to how thunder in gothic horror films and even in literature often predicts both a stormy night and horrific occurrences. These sonic symbols are part of our cultural heritage and feed into the way sound imagery communicates. Audiences understand such sound imagery subconsciously because of its ubiquity in theatre, film and television over many years.

Equally, the decision to employ a certain group of musicians or to place the musicians on or off stage, in or out of sight creates a situation that leads to a spiralling flow effect of other decisions whose consequences on the narrative, on the performance and on audiences can rarely be traced simply to the one decision. Such decisions affect the perception of liveness and the framing of the performance as 'realistic' or 'theatrical'. They rely on the availability of musicians, the provision of space, the presence of amplification and so on as discussed in the chapters above, and ultimately these decisions feed into the overall theatrical experience. The problem is that this complexity in the collaborative creative process complicates the analysis of why decisions were made and how music was 'intended' to function in performance in interaction with the visual and narrative elements. Though the stimulus for an idea is unclear that does not mean that the performance results cannot be assessed and the factors that brought them into being suggested.

As a result of the survey of productions of *Macbeth* over five decades presented in "Collaborative Composition at the RSC" above, and consideration of the relationship with sound design in "Electronics, Sound and Fury at the RSC", this chapter analyses in more detail some of the ways music functions in productions of Shakespeare plays at the RSC. The way music is used is unlikely to be unique to the RSC or to Shakespeare plays, it has developed from nineteenth century melodrama and been transferred between film, television and theatre by composers and directors working across media. As a starting point, then, since many of the creative team work across media one of the particular questions this chapter focuses on is the consideration of music's liveness in a live theatre context—how is it different from film music? The steps towards this goal begin with questions such as: what are the specific effects music is able to achieve at the micro to macro level (i.e. in a single moment or as an overarching dramaturgy) in conjunction with live action? How does music alter the levels of tension and emotion and affect the performance of actors? What is the effect of musicians performing onstage for actors and audience? Can music and the performance of musicians frame a performance such that a different level of theatricality is revealed? Does this alter the way audiences interact with the narrative and the performance?

The discussion that follows assesses the ways in which the visual elements interact with the aural elements and analyses how music functions in the performance as a whole. It explores music in individual moments and as an overarching dramaturgical driver, and negotiates the way sound, music and musicians contribute to the theatricality and performativity of the event. Some of these aspects arise in music accompanying a recorded source (such as film and television) but there are particular features that pertain to the live performance that I will draw out.

The problem, of course, is that it is almost impossible to separate some aspects that apply to all media from those that only apply to live performance, so although the discussions that follow will explore the ways in which music contributes to the total experience of live performance it will necessarily encompass many of the features that apply to recorded performance. I will use examples from the RSC's Shakespeare plays and attempt to draw out the ways in which theatre music's functions cannot simply be conflated with the ways in which film music contributes to film.

Moreover, one of the things I discovered in attempting to articulate what music can achieve is that each music score, and even each music cue, is likely to have more than one function. This means that any attempt to categorise music's functions in isolation is impossible. None of the functions of music is mutually exclusive; music often seems to do more than one thing at any one moment, and doubtless the functions I choose to explore below are not the only things music does in an audio-visual interaction. Rather, in order to draw attention to certain features that I have found most interesting and that have raised questions for me, I have arbitrarily established some parameters for discussion. Though these parameters result from the survey above and my conversations with composers, they are only one way of approaching the task of accounting for the importance of music and sound in this body of work.

Ultimately I will propose that theatre music (because of certain dynamics of liveness, togetherness, performativity) differs from film music in certain key respects despite sharing many of the same conventions. Owing to the fact that the RSC has a very specific environment of working practices (freedom to experiment with 400-year-old texts, with a repertoire that is regularly reproduced, with a stable and collaborative group of continuously employed people, and in the privilege of a funded model), the way in which theatre music has developed at the RSC to become a dynamic dramaturgical aspect of productions is unique. The liveness of the event, the collaboration and responsiveness between performers, and the involvement of the audience in the energy and interpretation of the event all feed back into the creation of a shared musico-theatrical experience. It is possible that this practice has established a toolkit for theatre music that is an exemplar for theatres elsewhere.

Exploring the Context of Theatre and Film Music Studies

One way of thinking about music's functions—what it does—has been to focus on the moments in a play when sound or music is required; for entrances and exits, to cover scene changes, for underscore or at the finale. Another way of analysing music in theatre has been to consider the production of meaning where musical signification is added to the dramatic signification and a composite meaning proposed. In this case the analysis relates to the potential meanings music contributes to the narrative and can be analysed using a representational or semiotic analysis of music's functions focusing on the narrative. Thus music can signal mood or create atmosphere and contribute to the overall drama using well-known signifiers, but these effects tend to be immediate and local. These are not the only ways of thinking about music's functions, however. Guy Woolfenden describes two types of music in 'nearly every Shakespeare play that I write music for'. These are 'music *of* the play, and music *about* the play. The first category is simple—it's music that is called for directly in the text by one of the characters [...]. The second category [...] is perhaps closer to film music, it helps to set up a certain mood that is right for a particular scene or moment' (Beauman 1976, 49). The first of these is known as 'diegetic music' in studies of film music, the second 'non-diegetic music', but these worlds are not always easily separated in practice. The diegetic music that is called for in the play might include drum signals, processional marches and fanfares that could be played live by onstage musicians but these musical moments have other effects than the simple signalling function: the drums don't simply signal the marching tempo. Also significant are the type of drum, the pace of the march, the attack of the drummer and the rhythm and style of the drumming. What if, for example, Macbeth's army was played on to a rock drum break and Macduff's to a kick-line style drum riff? Clearly this is drumming for an entrance that signals an arrival, perhaps covers a scene change, and is played by onstage musicians as diegetic performance, but it would also transform our perception of those characters and the atmosphere of the moment.

Meanwhile the latter, the non-diegetic, includes scene change and atmospheric music as well as the accompaniment of songs and dances played from the band box or another offstage location from whence music has the potential to create an immersive sense of involvement in the stage world. When this type of music is played onstage there is a visual complexity and revelation of theatricality that some directors enjoy and choose to employ. Particularly in film, the opportunity of blurring the distinctions between these fields, by perhaps panning to musicians or a radio during a scene only after the music has given the impression of being incidental, is often used quite knowingly and deliberately. It is clear that both of these types of music are simultaneously causing other effects and are not always easily distinguishable, though they offer many complex possibilities for composers, sound designers and directors to explore.

The gap between these ways of categorising music, those described by placement in the performance and those understood in relation to diegesis, is also symptomatic of the failure to negotiate the multiplicity of contexts and functions simultaneously. Music that has a theatrical function also contributes to dramatic effect; it can signal mood or create atmosphere *and* contribute to meaning whether or not it is used at a scene change or accompanies a song, and whether or not it is played onstage or off, heard by the characters or not. Gorbman develops her thinking about film music when she discusses the idea of ***mutual implication*** which is to say that 'whatever music is applied to a film segment will *do something*, will have an effect... because the reader/spectator automatically imposes meaning on such combinations' (Gorbman 1987, 15). She describes music in film as having the following effects: temporal, spatial, dramatic, structural, denotative and connotative. Some of these categories will be revisited below (if not always directly referred to), but there are some fundamental differences when applying these ideas to the theatre space because of the immediacy of the performer/audience contract and the live interaction between them. Moreover, there will always remain the difficulty of categorisation of any kind given the fluidity of the relationships between sound and vision and the ephemerality of live performance.

In the sections below, atmospheric and contextual music will to some extent be considered music *of* the play, contributing to the illusion and involvement in the dramatic world, while conceptual music explores the larger scale structures of a production and the director's vision. It is possible these types of musical performance contribute to the perception of immersion in the theatre event, while diegetic music and theatrical music are likely to break the illusion of integration and move into areas of theatricality. It will become clear in the discussions and examples below, however, that these are not hard and fast rules and that all these functions have the potential for overlap and interaction.

Creating Atmosphere

The idea of a binary codification of music's functions in relation to whether or not it parallels the visual imagery or whether or not it is 'called for' within the action seems, already, to be somewhat limited as is the understanding of its roles based on the place in performance it is used. However, there are some useful ideas within such a framework that Michel Chion identified in film music. He described as 'empathetic' music that 'can directly express its participation in the feeling or atmosphere of a scene, by taking on the scene's rhythm, tone, and phrasing' through cultural codes for sadness, happiness, movement and so on. He contrasted this with 'anempathetic' music that progresses 'in a steady, undaunted and ineluctable manner' exhibiting 'conspicuous indifference to the situation' (Chion 1990, 8). An example might be that the atmospheric sound of birds in a wood might not fade when the king dies if the disparity between the permanence of the natural environment and the end of life is sought—an anempathetic effect—whereas the choice to fade or darken the sound effect would be more empathetic. Both of these are atmospheric but whereas the former might tend to construct a coherent experience with the visual elements such that audiences are immersed, the latter, even when not consciously heard, may produce a different, more complex effect. I will return to that idea later, but first I will explore how music creates atmosphere in the theatre space and what the consequences of this are for performers and audiences—whether that is frenetic energy, tension, calmness or unease.

As Gabor Csepregi describes it, 'in a theatre we notice a change as the lights are turned off and people suddenly cease to talk with each other. To be sure, the sounds or lights do not modify the material aspects of these spaces; they merely evoke a momentary and latent significance that we experience as atmosphere' (Csepregi 2004, 170). Similar effects occur as the pit orchestra tunes up or the music begins. Music or sound as it begins or ends the performance establishes something about the world of performance—it creates expectation of the event about to occur and signals something of the performance world that will emerge. The expectation encourages audiences to stretch themselves, making an effort to attend (Home-Cook 2015, 1).[1]

Atmospheres have affective qualities that touch and move us, that we may resist or to which we might yield, but we are constantly exposed to atmospheres as a feature of our embodied consciousness (Ibid., 170), and they are evoked by the other senses as well as sound. The result of an atmosphere is an 'emotional essence' or 'style' that we read into the visual object that exists within the atmosphere (Merleau-Ponty 2002, 281). Gernot Böhme has written extensively about atmospheres, most recently about the aesthetics of atmospheres in stage design, exploring the question of whether an atmosphere is an objective or subjective phenomenon (2013). Atmospheres, he decides, are indeterminate and intangible and yet they communicate a feeling that is shared among audiences, they are outside us and yet create a feeling within us. As such, Böhme regards them as quasi-intangible even as they affect both the reception and production of performance. In reception, atmospheres seem to appear as if from nowhere and can cause irrational or surprising moods, whereas the production of an atmosphere can be objectively discussed by designers who might use non-mimetic means of production—what Böhme refers to (after Plato) as 'phantastike techne' (Ibid., 4) or design (Ibid., 6). The atmosphere may result from an 'imaginative idea the observer receives through the object' that 'causes the action on the stage to appear in a particular light and … creates an acoustic space which *tunes* the whole performance' (Ibid., 4). By drawing together these two ideas—the tuning or 'tone' of a performance and the way an atmosphere emanates as a felt presence in space Böhme arrives at the conclusion that an atmosphere is 'the felt presence of something or someone in space' (Ibid.).

---

[1] This refers too to Jean-Luc Nancy's theorising in *Listening* (2007).

The importance of this work is that it demonstrates the pervasiveness and the slipperiness of the idea of atmospheres, producing subjective moods and affects in individuals, even as such results are objectively discussed and created. Whether or not a sound is consciously heard and no matter how much attention is paid to the sound world—and much theatre music, like film music, is specifically designed to be 'unheard'—the sound atmosphere affects perceptions of what is seen. Individual audience members may choose to focus on particular sounds or may not notice them at all, but they will, nonetheless, subconsciously respond to the atmosphere. The music called for by Portia in *The Merchant of Venice* that is to play while her suitor makes his choice among the boxes is atmospheric even as it is also diegetic. She calls for the music to underscore the scene so it becomes diegetic; nonetheless it remains incidental to the action and atmospheric in summoning a mood to accompany the scene. This mood has an effect on how she, the suitor and the situation are perceived by audiences—what do the director and composer want to say about this situation and how are audiences affected in their attachment to these characters?

But there is another step that pertains to the live theatre. Music becomes associated with the visual imagery to the extent that the delivery of actors is likely to be affected as well as the perception of audiences. This is clearly unique to the live interaction of theatre and music, and is one of the arguments for the importance of live music in theatre—that both musicians and actors can adjust their pace and delivery as an atmosphere is animated between them and the audience at each performance. Daniel Levitin describes a laboratory experiment by Ian Cross at Cambridge University that demonstrates how humans co-adapt and accommodate with each other's performance. In the experiment individuals are asked to tap their fingers on a desk and synchronise with each other. It emerges that they synchronise more closely with each other even though the beat may vary than with the precise time-keeping of the metronome, an effect of co-adaptation where the humans interact and co-ordinate with one another through a combination of sight and sound. Such co-ordination of sound/movement may have an evolutionary root since the facility to walk together, communicate through voice and gesture and develop collective activities (such as rowing, hauling and other heavy manual tasks) facilitates social and productive interactions (Levitin 2009, 51). A similar process occurs between musicians and actors in performance as they align their performances synchronising their efforts, and as described in "Musical Collaborations at the RSC", feel good as a result.

The effect of atmosphere on pace and energy is particularly notable in theatre for this reason. Music is not simply descriptive of Puck's flight but works alongside the actor's performance to create the perception of flight and ethereality through the combination of visible and audible images. It also causes changes in the physical biology of participants and listeners and in the neurochemicals of their brains that, while not yet fully understood, alter perceptions of mood. Meditative music has been shown to decrease levels of cortisol and noradrenaline, though the relationship between physical response and neurochemicals is still not entirely clear. Levitin describes how serotonin levels increase in listeners as a result of listening to pleasant music, while different genres of music cause different neurochemical activity such that mood can be altered in audiences not just by the connotation of lightness and flight but also by the mood-enhancing properties of some types of music (Levitin 2009, 99). Music works not simply by connoting feelings of calmness but by producing them: it has performative effects on actors and audiences.

When actors are speaking over music the rhythm of their speech can be affected by atmospheric music in a way that contributes not just to the acoustic environment of the production (Böhme's tone and emanation), but to the dynamic shape of speeches. This is fundamentally different from the process of making a film to which the music is added after the performance has been enacted, recorded and edited. In the theatre, since musicians and performers are working at the same time, the effects described above come into play so that a feedback loop is created as vocal and musical sound, emotion and atmosphere interact in a dynamic process. As Adrian Curtin notes, 'If the sound designer is substantially involved in the rehearsal process, he or she is able to fashion a sound design/musical score that adds another layer to the sonorous rhythms of Shakespeare's verse, in this way creating a specially crafted acoustic environment for the production' (Curtin 2016, 158), an effect that is sometimes referred to as 'heightening' the emotional pitch of a scene or speech. This is not just a general effect, though, and it is one that is even more dynamic when music is performed live.

Since music exists in time, the atmosphere and the mood it creates and its alteration even within the course of a speech can cause a dynamic shift in the speech and the character, but equally the musician can respond to the actor's performance. The performance of musicians is affected by the rhythm and dynamic structures that they accompany just as the actors are affected by the musicians' playing. In the canon of plays discussed here this applies particularly to scenes of magic, religious significance or nobility, but also in speeches that portend doom and disaster. Music can remove the scene or character from the quotidian and amplify particular characteristics that are atmospherically supported in the music. Not only is the language the actor is speaking poetic, metaphorical, stirring or inspiring, and not only is it removed from the quotidian by rhythm and possibly rhyme, but there is an additional effect that removes the vocal performance even further from the everyday. This effect of heightening is fundamental to music's power in theatre and is an effect that relies on the collaborative work of musicians and performers, something the RSC has evolved more consistently than other theatres for reasons illustrated in the chapters above.

Atmospheric music also includes what Woolfenden and David Collison had termed 'undertow' in relation to the *Henry V* tape as well as many other types of cue. Such cues generally act as empathetic music; they fade in imperceptibly under a speech, creating tension as they increase in pitch and intensity. If they stop suddenly they will draw attention to themselves, whereas if they fade gradually the emotional tension recedes imperceptibly. Starting or stopping suddenly, changing rhythm, pace or style tends to draw the attention of the audience and so is avoided in underscoring and in much atmospheric writing. By contrast, the playing of the pianola at the end of *Troilus and Cressida* that Ilona Sekacz described above, and the accompaniment of battle scenes with domestic piano music, are examples of anempathetic music that creates an effect because it does not reflect the mood of the events. In this case the domestic piano music demonstrates the continuance of social interactions and family life and its absence for the soldiers engaged in the war. It reveals a gap, and it is through the revelation of the gap, between the connotations of the audio and visual images that tenuous and individual interpretations might be generated and audiences encouraged to think for themselves. This type of atmosphere also affects both performers and audiences. In film the notorious rape scene in *A Clockwork Orange* (Kubrick 1971), in which the attacker, Alex, sings 'Singin' in the Rain,' uses this strategy both for the anempathetic effect created in the gap between the violent act and happy song, and for a later plot twist. Equally the cellos in the 2011 production of *Macbeth* playing during the murder of Banquo have an anempathetic relationship to the action but affect the vocal delivery of the actors because of the conflicting atmosphere they create, which they fight. In a very real way the music makes their actions harder to accomplish because the actors must transcend its atmospheric effect.

The importance here is atmospheric music's function as one of the tools the creative team uses to enact a particular mood that contributes to a reading of, and immersion in, the text. This might be perceived as the effect of stretching out and attending fully to the audio-visual performance whether empathetic or anempathetic. Atmospheric music is designed to be 'unheard' because of its importance in creating an empathetic relationship with the audience, drawing them into involvement with the story and/or characters, but it does not always work in that way. There are occasions when anempathetic music creates an entirely different atmosphere though it is unlikely that it would have the effect of distancing audiences since it remains an imperceptible manipulation of mood. At the same time, since it can also manipulate the actors and musicians, atmospheric music assists in altering the tone and emotional level of the performance and co-ordination between participants in a spiral of interaction.

Atmospheric Music: Some Examples

Roberto Gerhard's 1954 score for *A Midsummer Night's Dream* at Stratford (Devine) contains indications that it was played on panatropes. While it is certain that this or another recording device had been used for previous productions, this is believed to be the first that took advantage of the technology to create atmospheric effects 'to accompany certain actions, such as the casting of magic spells' (Llano 2013, 117). Samuel Llano notes that most of the score is devoted to providing musical renditions of magic by drawing on examples and techniques from throughout Western culture. There were sonorous effects for casting spells including the use of harp for magic and mystery, and a percussive use of spoken voice in the Witches' Song. However, the critics complained of the modernism of the work, that it was 'spiky' and that it completed 'the purge on prettiness' of Devine's production (Wardle 1978 quoted in Llano 2013, 118). Mostly the complaints concerned the decision to drop Mendelssohn's romantic score with its pleasant and unobtrusive atmosphere. It is obvious that the desire for fantasy and a romantic atmosphere in a musical score was embedded, at least among reviewers, and that this different atmosphere was too intrusive. It might well have created an atmosphere that amplified the director's vision but it was an unexpected one that disrupted identification with the romantic vision audiences anticipated. In a sense, simply by being noticed it had a distancing rather than an immersive effect on audiences.

Of his production of *Henry V* in 1966 Guy Woolfenden noted that atmospheric music can underscore speech, which at that time was still relatively rare in theatre, though it was becoming conventional because of its use in film. The list of French nobles summoned by the French King is accompanied by 'great braying calls from the French hunting horns, which makes the king seem gigantic and terrifying, and helps to build the speech to a huge climax' (Beauman 1976, 50). The effect here is of an undertow whether or not the sound was continuous—the energy and volume both contributed to the lifting of the speech in an interaction between musicians and actors. Thus the heightening of the speech, the nobility of the king and the call to arms are all linked to this heroic and climactic atmosphere. There are other quieter moments when the audience might not be aware of music, but that contribute to the overall interpretation of mood. 'There are signal trumpets off stage, for instance, which call each other all through the night in the English scenes before the battle. They help to re-inforce the feeling of doom in the scene, and they are like clocks—they mark the passing hours of this endlessly long night' (Ibid.). Such realistic sounds as trumpets signalling to troops are noticed only subconsciously since they blend with the realism of the scene, but they contribute to the atmosphere of waiting and create a tense undertow as the hours pass.

By 1994 the same effects were being produced through partially electronic means: synthesisers afforded composers the opportunity to create complex polyphonic sounds that functioned as atmospheric music and underscore. The electronically generated sounds obscured the identity of the sounds as music and so contributed to the abstraction of the atmospheric writing, while the volume was vastly more controllable by musicians as well as by sound operators and so encouraged ever more widespread use of underscoring and the effect of undertow. Ilona Sekacz remarked that such underscoring was much more common in film played by orchestral strings, so that when these sounds became available on synthesisers and samplers she used what she described as 'a fat string sound' to create a 'bed of sound' that an actor can speak over (Sekacz 2016). Whereas a melody is distinctive, this type of atmosphere is 'adding a frisson or an emotion to what might not be there, which is what you do in film' (Ibid.). This is particularly interesting in relation to the idea of undertow, which is an imperceptible sound element that causes an atmospheric effect. It is notable that it developed first in recorded sound and became more commonplace live only when the volume of sounds was controllable by electronic means so that there was no disruption to the immersion of audiences in the dramatic moment, only a heightening of the emotional stakes.

Sekacz's own scores use such undertow in, for example, *A Midsummer Night's Dream* and *Hamlet* (2016), the latter of which she describes as having 'some really lovely textures [...] underneath which unsettles or calms you'. What atmospheric music can do is to create a paradoxical reading where the music unsettles what the actor is portraying. This is a development of the idea that music is empathetic or anempathetic, but the atmosphere might relate to an individual character, an individual action or the scene as a whole. It is also likely that the reception of such moments, especially as they cause a subconscious response, contributes to a more complex atmosphere and potential range of interpretations. Rather than a single identifiable feeling among audience members, the subjective responses may vary even though the composer has an objective in mind in creating the musical cue.

As noted above, atmospheric music is not only used to create pleasant effects but can also heighten the emotional level of a speech or disturb its interpretation. For her score for *Edward II*, for example, Sekacz was asked to provide 'something really ear-ripping' as the play was to be conceived as cruel and bitter and difficult to listen to. On this occasion she modelled the score on George Crumb's *Black Angels* so that the effect was of 'the interior of the violin and the interior of the cello; pain, anguish and high notes and scraping nails down a finger board' (Ibid.). Such atmospheric writing has continued and become ever more pervasive in later scores at the RSC assisted by the ability of players to co-ordinate their playing with speech and the increased control of volume and timbres provided by computerised sound systems.

A further example of atmospheric writing occurs in *Comedy of Errors* (Dir. Supple, Composer Lee, 1996).[2] The underscore that plays as Egeon tells the history of the wreck in which his wife, one twin son and a servant were lost begins with the movement of the sea and the undertow supports the vocal delivery during his evocation of the storm. The atmosphere, still with the tension of the undertow, becomes sorrowful as he talks of 'the loss of whom I lov'd'. These are examples of a filmic use of underscore that adds colour, atmosphere, structure and complexity to a speech and heightens the delivery and energy of the performance building tension to a climax before fading out again. Such music is like film music in its ability to manipulate atmosphere and mood, often without being directly noticed as the manipulating factor by audiences, while the subjective interpretation it gives rise to might be varied. It is this ability of music to appear to

---

[2] I based this discussion on analysis of the AV recording and the score.

accompany the scene while in fact shaping and structuring the emotional engagement of audiences and actors with the text and action that is the key feature of atmospheric music.

SIGNIFYING CONTEXT

A historical or geographical context for a production can be signified using the structures of semiotics. A musical sign carries information based on genre, style, pitch, instrumentation, tone, rhythm and so on, to an audience that interprets the signs according to similar cultural codes. Philip Tagg (1979) demonstrated how detailed and complex a task this could be in his extensive analysis of the audio-visual combinations during the opening credits for the American detective series *Kojak* (CBS 1973–8). The key feature of how contextual music contributes to the audio-visual production is that it generates local meanings that are interpreted immediately on hearing them. Atmospheric music also relies on the same cultural codes to signify sadness or happiness but it functions principally in creating feeling and mood. Here I want to focus particularly on the signification of a historical and geographical context and stylistic frame for the production at the local level. This idea relates to what Chion describes as Semantic listening—listening to a cue that, by using a particular code or language, can communicate information. Gorbman refers similarly to the denotative and connotative powers of music in relation to the visual elements of film. In this case the meanings to be explored are the historical or geographical settings of the plot and the production, which might not be the same. For example *Two Gentlemen of Verona* might be set in a contemporary Italy, an early modern England or, indeed, any other two contrasting locations, thus creating a dialogue between the textual references to location and the aural and visual settings. Together the audio-visual combination of signs can communicate sometimes quite complex or intertextually dense meanings.

Equally, music can suggest whether or not something is ironic or comic through the use of widely understood signifiers thus framing the performance either in relation to a moment, a character or the production as a whole. An example of this is Bottom's song in *A Midsummer Night's Dream* which is generally performed using coarse vocal and orchestral sounds and a popular or folk inspired musical style. At this level the character is being framed by the type and style of music being sung. Meanwhile, it is unlikely that the production as a whole will be framed similarly since clearly the lovers and the fairies belong to different strata of society or have different functions in the play, so Bottom needs to be read as a comic buffoon within a different world. All this information can be semiotically encoded in the music.

The location of the action may change in the course of a production, from Verona to Milan in the case of the *Two Gentlemen of Verona*, between Venice and Belmont in *The Merchant of Venice*, and that transferral can be signalled and contrasted through music. Equally the character's home country can be suggested by locating music, such as the contrast between the Ephesian and Syracusian pairs of twins in *The Comedy of Errors*, or there might be a difference of status to be signalled perhaps between rural Bohemia and urban Sicilia in *The Winter's Tale*. Music that suggests a time and place to a contemporary British audience locates a production or even just a moment of a production—the important feature being that the composer has an objective meaning to communicate and a defined cultural framework within which the audience is likely to understand the terms of reference.

The use of pastiche or ironic contextual music, operatic or folk music might signify not only time and place but also the style of that scene and the class of the characters. This is particularly important given the relatively limited canon of Shakespeare plays and the number of RSC productions of them. *Romeo and Juliet* may have been located in Verona as a distant and exotic place in the sixteenth century, whereas a contemporary production could be located elsewhere if that gave relevance to the director's vision of what he wanted to communicate through this text and production. Finally, the music and production could be anachronistic by referencing many signifiers rather than a single time and place, or it could attempt to create a sense of universality through a combination of music and design that attempts to avoid stereotypical or recognisable signs. The ability of creative teams to discover new meanings by locating the plays in different historical and geographical contexts has contributed to the vibrancy and continued relevance of this extraordinary canon of plays, and the many innovative productions of them.

Contextual music can thus contribute to the director's vision of the text by providing a framework—a historical and geographical location for a scene and a performance style—which all frame that moment of performance so that interpretation by audiences is constructed or guided. The signification of theatre music is similar to the signification of film music. However, since film is generally used to create the impression of 'realism' there is much less diversity in the historical and geographical locations within which the work might be set, and consequently a narrower band within which to locate the contextual music. The number of remakes of films of Shakespeare plays is much smaller than the number of new productions of the canon at the RSC, and each creative team attempts to read the text anew. The opportunities for composers and designers to re-think the sound worlds in relation to the text are consequently much greater and the sound worlds themselves immeasurably more varied in live theatre performance.

Another local aspect of musical contextualisation is the effect it has on time perception, pace and energy—what Chion calls *Temporalisation*. He describes three aspects of temporalisation: that sound can render the perception of time in a scene as exact and detailed or vague and fluctuating; it can create a sense of temporal succession when a continuous music or sound cue plays through what might otherwise appear to be unrelated images; it creates a sense of forward momentum that the scene is progressing somewhere (Chion 1990, 13–14). The first of these was discussed above in relation to Ariel's lightness and ethereality. Montage is another word for the second of Chion's aspects of temporalisation, in which unrelated images are drawn into a perception of narrative continuity by music's auditory progress. It is less common for montages of unrelated images to be presented in theatre, but continuous music can create the perception of linkage between scenes in a montage—such as the battle sequence in *Macbeth*—so that one battle is perceived from a series of short scenes and images. It is potentially in the area of pace and energy, of forward momentum, that contextual music can impact the live performance most fundamentally, and for many of the same reasons as it impacts the actors through the creation of atmosphere. The opportunity to tell a story in montage, though not widely used, can be facilitated by contextual music that frames the audience's reading of the visual imagery, and it can create forward momentum. The sense of a plot driving to a climax, though, especially in the history plays, often relies on musical momentum and volume.

Contextual Music: Some Examples

A comparison of two productions of *Comedy of Errors*, from 1996 (Dir. Tim Supple) and 2000 (Dir. Lynne Parker), demonstrates how music can contribute to the understanding of the historical and geographical locations and the performance style, but this area very easily overlaps with the ways in which music can help to articulate the themes of the play to which I will return below.[3] The key feature here is that the signification is immediate and local. This play, for the plot of which Shakespeare turned to Roman comedy, is one that does seem to be relocated quite frequently. In 1976 Trevor Nunn set the story in a Greek taverna, and notably there is a musical derived from this play, *The Boys from Syracuse* (Rodgers, Hart and Abbott, 1938), that, although being notionally set in ancient Syracuse and Ephesus, uses 1930s swing and jazz to create a farcical and anachronistic context.

By using the 'ud, a type of fretted lute and the primary instrument of the Arab world to signify Ephesus in Turkey, and the Zarb, which is the essential percussive instrument in Persian art music for Syracuse, Adrian Lee locates the 1996 production in a distant 'other' place (Dir. Supple). Although an expert might well appreciate the authenticity and distinctive source locations of the two instruments, a general audience is likely only to perceive the difference between the two sound worlds and to understand the exotic location of the play in broad terms. However, although a reading of location might be somewhat generalised, violin and accordion as well as voice are all used within the melodic and rhythmic patterns of Asia Minor and Turkish traditions, so that the overall impression is that there is a sense of authenticity in this Middle Eastern setting. A fairly specific location in an historic 'every-time' is represented, rather than the time and place of the play's modern performance or of the early modern period. Equally, this music through its exoticism creates a strong sense of alienation; an alienation that is somewhat uncanny.

The strangeness of the misunderstandings is the focus of this production that unsettles through the perceived authenticity of its representation of the distant location. Interestingly there are frequent uses of a bowed saw to underscore speeches creating an atmospheric tension that is equally non-specific. For example, Adriana's speech begging Antipholus of Syracuse 'do not tear thyself away from me' (Act 2, Sc. ii) is accompanied by chords on the 'ud that become more dissonant and lower, reinforcing the mood of the speech and the pitch and volume of her voice (Cue 13) such that the music might be signifying her anger and upset. The local signification relates to her mood as atmospheric music, but also locates the performance as a whole and her cultural heritage. The consequence of the

---

[3] This discussion is based on my analysis of the AV recording, score and prompt book of the production.

combination of alien sounds, Middle Eastern rhythmic and melodic patterns and timbres, is to create quite a serious production that explores the uncanny misunderstandings and the emotional depth of the characters even as the usual comic business takes place.

By contrast the 2000 production composed by Bell Helicoptor juxtaposes a cool jazz beat and a walking bass for the Ephesian twins with a swung rhythm using a vaguely 'oriental' sounding melody for the Syracusian pair. The sound world is one that is more familiar, or rather stereotypical, for Western audiences and the comedy of the plot is enhanced by contrasting a non-authentic reference to Arabic music alongside the 'cool' symbolism and dance rhythms of different types of jazz. The two sets of twins are identified with similar but subtly different music, while the comedy of this production is exemplified in the stereotypical 'Eastern' music. For example, the Courtesan performs a snake charming trick accompanied by music reminiscent of 1940s and 1950s Western variety acts depicting comic/magical performers of the exotic East. There is also a sand-dance performed in drag by the Merchant, again reminiscent of the Music Hall and early comic film traditions. Here the themes articulate two worlds: a stereotypical representation of the exotic orient framed as nostalgic and comic within Western popular culture contrasts with jazz to accompany the sexual farce in the present. These two themes provide a context for the production that is located in a highly sexualised and farcical but nostalgic popular vernacular in its acting style, design and music. The distance between the locations provides a comic caricature rather than a disturbance.

In relation to temporalisation, the pace of the comedy is different in these two productions. The latter focuses on a fast comic production with stereotypical chase music for fights and runarounds and has the audience laughing heartily at the physical antics heightened by comic stings and punctuation. The former, whose focus centres on the uncanny developments in the plot, is paced differently so that although the comic stings and chases are present they are much more subtle, and are not perceived within the comic tradition of farce. Consequently the audience response is more muted though no less appreciative. The performances too demonstrate a difference in pace in response to the music. Even the physical style of the actors' bodies is affected by musical genre and the construction of 'farce' and 'authenticity' in the musical language.

The comparison above demonstrates how music creates meanings, though interpretation is often much more varied and subjective when musical sounds and styles are not widely known within the cultural context (as in the first of these productions). Such musical signs as have been discussed generate local meanings about the time and setting of the production. The use of music hall traditions and comic stings in the second production in contrast with the authentic sounds of the first create a very different understanding of how audiences might respond to the comedy. Such signifiers are read immediately and locally but have the potential to contribute to the wider dramaturgical understanding of the power structures in the play or the performance of characters. In the case of the RSC it is the diversity of potential readings of the canon that demonstrates the ability of music performatively to interact with actors suggesting physical language as well as genre, framing and location.

Supporting the Director's Concept

Conceptual music has a function in expanding how the director imagines the overarching structural composition of a play and a production, a function Claudia Gorbman terms 'metadiegetic' (1987, 22–3). The concept includes the overarching structural oppositions or dynamic polarities in the production that inform the design, the sound design, music, and all aspects of the production. As such the concept relates to the themes or political ideas the director might choose to highlight in her interpretation of the work, and the ways in which a composer can focus attention on or amplify such readings.

Musical motifs that are first heard in conjunction with a character or action can take on an association such that later in the performance the sound can stimulate a memory of that character or action. This is the basic premise of leitmotif—that musical motifs become associated with ideas or characters and draw them into conjunction with the current plot moment. In theatre, music motifs can act as a momentary flashback or premonition moving away from the present action through musical reminders of earlier events, or it can add complexity by juxtaposing images and actions that take place at different times in the production. Equally, as we have discovered in the discussion of context above, the identification of a place with a musical style is locally significant, but can set up binary polarities in the work as a whole. This part of the discussion focuses on these larger scale dramaturgical structures of a production.

At the start of the period of this study motivic writing provided unity in scores and the reprise of musical ideas at intervals through a production is a feature that continues in theatre music (and film music). John Eacott's score for *Taming of the Shrew* (Bailey 2010) is developed in a series of interactions of four themes that are introduced in a prologue before the Induction scene. The themes are adapted and developed with other music throughout the score so that there is a sense of unity, but also so that the music supports a series of dramatic relationships. There is a lively alto saxophone scale-like melody over a swing accompaniment that in Act 2 is called 'Hortensio throws in the towel' and later transforms into 'Lucentio's theme'. Another theme is a tango whose melody is reprised in Waltz time creating a relationship between moments with a similar musical character. A fast 6/4 theme for 'Baiting the shrew' is associated with Katherine and later becomes a waltz and a tarantella for the wedding sequence demonstrating her journey. A 'sweet and sexy' swing tune with the sound of New Orleans jazz is associated with Petruchio. These themes say something about the characters, and their associations (signifying in the ways discussed above) but their development and transformations can reveal larger scale themes in the work.

As Bruce O'Neil remarked, 'the most successful scores … are kind of a group of themes and variations' through which composers allow their thematic material to evolve in relation to the characters and situations in the play (O'Neil 2016). Although audiences might not notice key structures or thematic links consciously, O'Neil is sure that the transformations of music that reflect the transformations of characters provide an approach and structure that are appreciated at a subconscious level. As an example he described the 'statue waking' moment from the 1992 production of *The Winter's Tale* with music by Shaun Davey as follows:

> The music starts with this minor key, low octave, slightly slow moving repetitive figure that moves a bit and then pauses and moves a bit again. It is obviously reflecting what was going on in the production about Hermione's statue gradually coming to life… It is slightly halting and then it chromatically moves up a little bit further. Then eventually that subsides and what you get is this very lyrical beautiful major key tune (O'Neil 2016).

At this moment the music is working contextually describing and accompanying the action. However, O'Neil speculates that Davey reverse engineered the score, dropping in little elements of this final theme, associated with Hermione throughout the play, that finally come together at this moment to utilise the emotional impact that a thematically constructed music score can have.

Ilona Sekacz describes such thematic construction as 'being authentic'; the attempt to be 'true to the feeling of the production, which comes from the director' (Sekacz 2016). For a production of *Henry VIII*, Sekacz discussed the music with director Howard Davies who described the bureaucracy and laws of the period when the law was being used to change and mould the church. This was something that also featured in the set design with scrolls and paperwork to represent the legal frameworks of politics and religion, and black and white pictures of buildings in London that created a kind of formality. As a result of thinking about this approach to the production she developed the idea that the bureaucracy might sound like an old Underwood typewriter (with a microphone to amplify it) that could be played live as a percussion instrument. As she said 'it would often lead into the cues and then lead out […] subliminally saying office and bureaucracy.' She concluded that 'the idea of bureaucracy was good and that spoke to me about what to do with the music. It was neither a place nor a time, it is a thread really. It is a thread that if you get hold of and you can look at it, examine it and make something of it, then it will find its way in' (Sekacz 2016). It is this sort of approach that most clearly exemplifies the idea of the conceptual use of music. Sekacz gave one further example of what she meant by 'conceptual' drawn from her very first production for the RSC, a production of *King Lear* (Dir. Noble, 1982). When Lear is sane the music should be 'very square, very loud and ceremonial. The brass was very useful there with fanfares—absolutely traditional RSC type fanfares. Then once the storm ends and his brain goes I had this idea that the brass starts to melt, the drum skins started to rip and everything burst into flames, crumpled or got wrecked' (Sekacz 2016). In this description it is clear that the large-scale structures of the music reflects the director's approach to the play that she has translated into a musical concept.

As noted above some of the plays are constructed around broad binary oppositions between places, such as Bohemia and Sicilia (*The Winter's Tale*), Belmont and Venice (*The Merchant of Venice*), Padua and Verona (*Romeo and Juliet*); a score that represents these oppositions musically can also reinforce the poles that pull on the characters. These poles may be geographical and are locally signified, such as those mentioned above. As Yershon describes it; 'in the case of *The Merchant of Venice* … basically you're doing a score for Belmont and you're doing something for Venice' (Yershon 2016). However, other plays are trickier, as for example with *The Comedy of Errors* that is located in one place, or *Macbeth* that uses a number of locations. In these cases there might be an opposition between characters, or the metaphysical and the physical, the magical and the mundane, the good and the corrupt characters, or the military and the familial, between aristocracy and peasantry, male and female, or between warring parties focusing on legitimacy and illegitimacy.

In *The Tempest* the breakdown is even more complicated with three groups of people; Prospero and Miranda, the shipwrecked visitors and the magical contingent, or the creative team might separate the groups into the comic and noble characters and Ariel (Yershon 2016). O'Neil discusses how a series of Shakespearean opposites are useful parallels for music to mirror, since music has major and minor, fast and slow, loud and soft, high and low, consonant and dissonant as well as a vast range of musical styles and genres. To a greater or lesser degree these types of binaries in the music 'reflect on what is going on psychologically in these characters' journeys' (O'Neil 2016). These qualities are dressed in subtle ways, tapping into particular timbres and the accent of music within a particular period and location, but underlying it the music adds these very broad but important structural qualities within a production to reinforce the director's particular vision or message.

On the other hand Yershon perceives some of the plays as a gigantic arc in structural terms, such as *Twelfth Night* and *Love's Labour's Lost* and even *The Comedy of Errors*. This only reinforces the importance of understanding the director's vision for the piece so that the structural facility music offers can support that reading. Comparing scores and identifying the local or contextual meanings in them and then looking for the broader structures reveals how music contributes to the articulation of a particular dramaturgy for each new production. This is accomplished partly through the signification of atmosphere and context as described above, but also through the structural relationship of themes, the juxtaposition of genres and the exploration of different types of 'authenticity'. How such confrontations are worked out varies from composer to composer, production to production, as each writer creates a sound world that fits the directorial and design concepts. It is here that the employment of composers who work regularly with the RSC, are employed over a significant preparatory period, and who attend rehearsals becomes significant. It is through the collaboration of the team that concepts develop that amplify or transform the director's initial ideas into an effective and conceptually sophisticated audio-visual world. This is a process that is significantly different from film music which, though it may be equally sophisticated, is often added only after the film is completed and edited. This process of collaboration between director and composer/sound designer, which began at the RSC and continues mostly in the subsidised sector, has produced models of practice that, interestingly, feature in the devising practices of contemporary companies such as Filter Theatre and Kneehigh and in the development of actor musician productions as well as in the processes of sound design more widely across the country.

Conceptual Music: Some Examples

Many scores at the RSC contain a relatively small amount of musical material that is developed and adapted as thematic or motivic content to represent aspects of the play: the 34 cues of Sekacz's score for *A Winter's Tale* for example, contain a much smaller number of thematic elements that are developed and adapted to signify within the production. The story of *A Winter's Tale* contains oppositions between Sicilia and Bohemia and between aristocracy and peasants. There is also potentially an opposition between a world of speech and a world of song fixed around the presence of the singing character Autolycus. Certainly the rural world is presented as the more free, joyful and loving and contains the songs. Thus there is the potential for a dramaturgy between these larger institutional and moral frameworks that can be played out in musical worlds. It is possible that one production might focus on the Bohemia/Sicilia opposition, another on the aristocracy/peasantry opposition and yet another on the speech/song opposition. The reality is rather more nuanced as the musical dramaturgies of the productions considered here contain elements of all these debates.

There is very little music in Act 1 in either the 1998 production (Sekacz, Dir. Doran) or the 2002 production (Yershon, Dir. Warchus), though that little comprises 17 cues in Act 1 in Sekacz and 15 in Yershon—and both have a total of 34 music cues.[4] That means that while there are half the music cues in the first act they are predominantly short atmospheric and contextual music cues that occur at scene changes, whereas in the second act there is extensive singing and dancing and the music becomes much more apparent and pervasive. As Yershon explains, 'the whole thing made quite a lot of sense in terms of depression America'. The issue he explored is that the music for Bohemia, because it is song and dance, has to be

---

[4] The discussions in this section are based on analyses of AV recordings, scores, and prompt books of these productions.

much more historically and geographically specific, so 'it's to your advantage to be vague with Sicilia'. Despite this comment the 2002 production of *The Winter's Tale* (Dir. Warchus) locates Sicilia in a 1930s American underworld whose costume design has elements drawn from gangster movies, the jazz age and film noir—a world consciously steeped in contemporary film references—perhaps drawing on the cinematic link between Sicilian and American mafia representations. In very broad terms, Yershon writes bluegrass music for the peasants' masque played live onstage by fiddle, mandolin, banjo, guitar, percussion and voices that sets the scene in the countryside around Polixenes' castle. This contrasts with the ceremonial formality and timbres in Leontes' state, which is rather less specific of time and place.

There was no attempt to unite the two worlds in that production, or indeed any of the productions Yershon has composed, so the two distinct sound worlds are maintained. When the Bohemians return to Sicilia they bring their comedy and endearing nature but not their music since by the time they arrive there is no time to celebrate. It was only in the bows of that production that the bluegrass music returned. As Yershon noted: 'the shape of the play bizarrely is that you start with Leontes and you finish with Leontes, so in a way his is the framed story ... and you have this puddle of activity in the middle ... that takes you right away from Sicilia to another world' (Yershon 2016). He noted that one of the key moments of the story is the transition scene with the bear, but that the important feature of the two main locations is their dissimilarity. Thus he proposes an arc with the bluegrass festivities at the central point.

In the 1998 production, Sekacz contrasts the military ceremonial of brass and drums at the formal court with folk music played on woodwind, harp, tabla, accordion and bodhrum for the rural idyll, again played live onstage. A new binary separation appears here—music is widely used and celebratory in some scenes, in contrast with the absence of celebration and of diegetic music in others, and can be linked to the presence and absence of loving or joyful emotions and relationships. This idea is further developed in Hermione's trial scene which requires speech through a static microphone; Hermione sometimes conforms to the requirements of the court and speaks through the microphone and at others moves from the microphone and speaks directly to her husband, thus creating a tension between the distancing effect of technology for formality and the 'authenticity' of liveness for the personal. It could be argued that this distinction between live and not live projects a greater level of 'authenticity' onto the

Bohemian community with their live songs and dances. The binary relationships between aristocracy and peasantry, Sicilia and Bohemia, are broken down by the depictions of happy and successful relationships aurally portrayed as a community with live music, communal singing and dancing, and a joyous, lively involvement in the performance of music in both locations at the start and end of the performance.

Broadly what might be deduced in both productions is a binary separation between the aristocratic world of Sicily and the peasant setting in Bohemia, and a corresponding 'authenticity' in the Bohemian peasant idyll, though those worlds are located differently according to the parameters of the production. As Yershon reminds us, Polixenes talks about grafting two plants together so that a stronger plant will spring out as a third—which leads him to suggest that 'the more diverse the two parts of the score are, the more I'm serving the play' (Yershon 2016) and in fact both composers use this strategy.

A key event in the story is the reading of the oracle: 'Hermione is chaste; Polixenes blameless; Camillo a true subject; Leontes a jealous tyrant; his innocent babe truly begotten: and the king shall live without an heir, if that which is lost be not found' (Act 3, Sc. ii). This moment might be linked with the final scene of the play in which Leontes acknowledges his daughter, Hermione returns to life and all is forgiven. The oracle (a magic device to foretell the end of the story) is read at the darkest moment of Leontes' jealousy, and the final scene is a magic device to resolve the dilemma foretold by the oracle. For the reading of the Oracle, Sekacz offers a formal stately entrance to the court with consonant chords over a steady beat, portentous and harmonious. This is the introduction to a sung hymn built of open fifths with brass and bells. There is something of an orthodox modal influence in the music reflecting the Delphic origin of the oracle. Thunder and thunderous rolls on the timpani attack and then underscore Leontes' denial of the oracle and prefigure the storm that will afflict the sailors. The music that awakes Hermione in Sekacz's score contains similar open fifths on the harp under the scene before a guitar adds a melody and then the harp accompaniment becomes more rhythmic—and derives from the earlier Oracle music, linking the two magic moments. This is not a strategy Yershon follows, perceiving these as different moments entirely, demonstrating the consequence of the different dramaturgical structures.

In both cases the Curtain Call music contains elements of the music from both worlds: Yershon's score brings together the ceremonial music of tremolo strings and regular slow drum beats that transforms into the bluegrass dancing music, while Sekacz draws on the 5/8 dance music and the music for the oracle and awakening. Thus a dramaturgy of contrasts underpins both productions, separating the two worlds (aristocratic Sicilia and rural Bohemia) in a number of ways, and articulating a number of different discourses within the productions. Contrasting musical genres or creating identifiable sound worlds, incorporating motivic development, and the opposition or entwining of themes can all be used to articulate overarching and large-scale dramatic structures or dynamic changes, while providing conceptual unity and continuity to a production.

As noted above this relies on significant involvement in the production beginning with directorial meetings when ideas are being conceived. Conversations and composition continue throughout the pre-production and rehearsal periods. There is significant involvement in adapting lengths, dynamics and volume at the technical rehearsals and there may be further changes during previews or for a subsequent touring version. The details of this process are outlined in "Collaborative Composition at the RSC" above, but the importance here is that for the composer to contribute effectively to the total concept, and to shape the dramaturgical structures of the production, they need to be involved from the outset, which relies on the institution's commitment to music. This (and the resource required) was clearly in place at the RSC in ways that were unparalleled at the time though this practice has been followed, first at the National Theatre and more recently elsewhere including at Shakespeare's Globe.

Contributing to the Diegesis

Whereas the first three aspects of music discussed in this chapter have focused on the relationship between the narrative and the story-telling aspects of the playtext and how they might be amplified by music, this next category refers to music that is actually inside the narrative. Diegetic music is the live music played onstage that is heard by the characters (rather than the performers)—what Woolfenden referred to as the music of the play, and as we will discover in the next chapter, what Auden described as the 'called-for song'. It includes music as well as song that are mentioned in the text, and as such it contributes to the sense that the dramatic world is a coherent and complete object that audiences perceive from beyond the fourth wall. In many recent productions the musicians' playing space is within sight of the audience, but this does not come under the heading of diegetic music if it cannot be heard by the characters—though directors may choose to explore the potential of negotiating this gap.

Clearly diegetic music features in the categories above by being either contextual or atmospheric as well as diegetic, but it also directly responds to and features in the onstage events. So, for example, the arrival of hunters might be presaged by the onstage performance of a hunting call, a song or dance might feature musicians as part of the scene, or musicians might be commanded to play by characters in the action. When Feste sings 'Come Away, Death' Orsino is listening; when Lorenzo and Jessica open Act 5 of *The Merchant of Venice* with 'How sweet the moonlight sits upon this bank', the 'touches of sweet harmony' can generally be heard by them and audiences together. Music is playing at the start of *Twelfth Night* too, and could be quite pervasive in *The Tempest* as the articulation of the noises of the isle.[5]

The reason onstage music is featured here is that the onstage presence of musicians as performers adds a dimension to the performance that is becoming increasingly common even in small-scale shows using actor musicians, but in the early years of the RSC was innovative. The presence of musicians onstage within the action is connected to the early modern experience of theatre and draws attention to the presence of music played live by musicians elsewhere in the theatre at other points in the performance. Thus the live performance of musicians onstage, while being immersive in the sense that audiences are drawn into observance of a dramatically coherent world, actually draws attention to their absence when music is performed at other times and sometimes to their awkwardness as performers in the environment. So diegetic music can contribute equally to the awareness of theatricality and immersive involvement in the plot. Figure 1 shows players as part of a scene from the production of *Taming of the Shrew* (2010) that was discussed above, but here is important because it demonstrates the musicians as simultaneously within and without the dramatic action. They are clearly seen and heard within the action but are not characters as such.

As seen in Fig. 1 musicians appear as something of an anomaly; they are not named characters in the plot, yet they are onstage performers. They

---

[5] The last three plays, *The Winter's Tale*, *Cymbeline*, and *The Tempest* are clearly different in the amount of music that might be anticipated because they were indoor plays for which a professional band might have been available.

appear onstage and are also members of the creative and backstage teams. They bring this double image with them onto the stage, even as they contribute to the production's design and reception. They contribute to the situation, and sometimes provide aural or physical comic gestures, while becoming non-speaking characters locating themselves in relation to actors and audience. As a result musicians might take part in Bert O. States' categorisation of 'presence' in any of the three modes he describes in his study, *Great Reckonings in Small Rooms* (1987). As in Fig. 1, in *The Taming of the Shrew* (Bailey 2012) the musicians are playing in the street attempting to avoid the debris as Katharine expresses her anger, remaining within the illusion of the plot and accompanying the action in the representational mode. At other times they might comment on the action through physical or musical gesture in the self-expressive mode, or, perhaps (though not in this image) through the choice of musical gesture, placement in the auditorium or physical action they can enter the collaborative mode. Thus the choice to have musicians in sight or onstage at any particular moment is part of the design and directorial concept and feeds

Fig. 1 *Taming of the Shrew*, 2012. Katherina Rages. (Photo by Sheila Burnett. ©RSC)

into the overall theatre experience by negotiating a path that might contribute to the illusion of realism in the plot or the disruption of immersion in the dramatic world depending on the content of the diegetic material they perform.

The negotiation of diegetic music in film is rather different, though as noted at the start of this chapter, some directors explore the effect of moving between awareness of diegesis by, for example, appearing to begin a scene accompanied by incidental music only to pan the camera and reveal a player or radio from which the music is emerging. This fluidity is not possible onstage in the same way, though it would be possible for actors or lighting designers to direct attention in ways similar to the act of panning on film. However, the presence of musicians and what they are to accomplish can be complex to negotiate and is unique to the live theatre since the musicians must negotiate the framing of the performance and the fourth wall. It is also a particular feature of productions at the RSC, where the practice of using musicians as onstage performers was instituted in the 1960s and continues to this day. It relies on the presence on the staff of a music team and the availability of employed and freelance musicians who learn the music and feature onstage.

Diegetic Music: Some Examples

At the beginning of *Twelfth Night* a band is already playing when the speech 'If music be the food of love' begins. It is likely that the music will stop and start again as a result of scripted instructions, and that draws attention to what they are playing. Music in that play is integral to a relationship with feelings and is spoken of in the script, so even if the players are not actually onstage the music and players have a diegetic presence.

The players often have a much more obvious physical presence, however. For a production of *The Plantagenets* (Dir. Noble, 1988) Ian Reynolds describes a music cue that required six drummers to flank Queen Margaret (played by Penny Downie). Only four of the players were expert drummers, the others were doubling to augment the effect of both sound and spectacle. Every four beats the whole group took a step down stage, then every two beats and then every beat so that the effect was produced of a great noisy Lancastrian army accelerating into battle before the formal mass of bodies dissolved and the band fled into the wings as the battle was joined. This is the self-expressive mode where the band remains within the illusion of the drama. As far as the performance was concerned the noise of the drums and the physical advancement down stage will have created not only a call to arms and to battle but the aural exhilaration to build towards the climactic battle sequence.

As an example of the collaborative mode (where performers step outside the action) one might refer to *The Taming of the Shrew* directed by Michael Bogdanov in 1978. The wind band, dressed in costumes that were 'sort of like front-of-house staff … jackets and peaked caps', were to march round the stage and at one point perform a move they called 'the Shrew crossover' in which one line crossed through the other as they were playing. The band finished with some comic business and always ended with 'the Bugs Bunny music' then stopped dead before the last note 'at which point the first trumpet would look at his watch and jerk his thumb to get us off-stage. This was the Winter of Discontent, everybody was on strike, so this was quite topical' (Reynolds 2016a). A comic effect and a topical political reference momentarily exceeded the frame of the narrative and confused the separation of illusory and external worlds. Figure 2 is surprisingly similar from the 1995 (Warbeck, Dir. Edwards) production. Note, in particular, the attitude of the side drum player and the shoes of

Fig. 2 *Taming of the Shrew* (1996), The Band in Formation. (Photo by Reg Wilson. ©RSC)

the bass drum player, both of which set a particular visual tone and contribute to the representation of the players as characters.

Other productions directed by Bogdanov and occasionally Nunn appeared in Reynolds' memory as ones in which the band was required to engage in physical activity, interaction with audiences or even acting—negotiating the categories of presence. For a production of *Venetian Twins* (Dir. Bogdanov, 1993) the band was to be a shambolic Italian marching band, making the music as horrendous as possible while shambling around the stage. At the end of the music they marched to the downstage edge of the stage where Reynolds was to take off his big floppy hat and put it down as though requesting tips. 'There was one performance where some idiot threw a pound coin from one of the galleries and it plonked me on the side of the head—so we abandoned that idea' (Reynolds 2015). The intention, though, was to use the moment to maintain the illusion of the drama (and the busking musicians) while drawing the audience into interaction with the stage. It is possible this would have exemplified the representational mode.

By contrast, for *Elgar's Rondo* (Dir. Trevis, 1993, with additional music by Dominic Muldowney), the group had to impersonate a military band—and for the first rehearsal they were drilled by a sergeant from the Royal Engineers 'and didn't play a note' in an effort to choreograph the correct visual image. The playing of 'Land of Hope and Glory' by what appeared to be a ghostly band was timed so that the band would begin playing in the car park outside the Swan theatre, march in, peel off in fours, march across the stage in three groups, then turn down stage ending up with the very last pace coming to a halt right on the downstage edge of the stage followed by a complete blackout within which they swiftly exited (Reynolds 2015). This was another coup de theatre accomplished by the combination of sound and spectacle from the onstage diegetic players, though this time there was no interaction or breaking of the frame, but in the self-expressive mode they remained within the narrative world.

Of course such precise action while playing requires more rehearsal and more performers than are available in many theatre companies and so could only have been instigated in the particular circumstances at the RSC. Nonetheless such scenes demonstrate the ways in which sound and spectacle with the presence of the non-acting players can create a combined energy that moves beyond the narrative confines of the scene even though the music itself is diegetic.

Creating a Sense of Theatricality in Music

Theatricality in music is a way of describing music that contributes to the avoidance of immersion in the plot. The terms 'dramatic' and 'theatrical' have been debated since the Greek philosophers, but in broad terms the dramatic is concerned with the story and its mimetic representation onstage, whereas the theatrical relates to the production as a whole rather than just the actions in the plot. As Albert Weiner explains it, 'that which is dramatic is … concerned solely with the art of telling a story. That which is theatrical is concrete, is in the visible realm, and is concerned with illustration' (Weiner 1980, 207). In recent times theatricality in narrative theatre has been related to some aspects of Brecht's epic theatre whose 'essential point … is perhaps that it appeals less to the feelings than to the spectator's reason' (Willett 1974, 23). For Brecht the dramatic theatre involves the spectator in the plot to the extent that the spectator 'shares the experience', whereas his epic theatre turns the spectator into an observer and so arouses the capacity for action in the world (Ibid., 37). I use the term 'theatricality' here since some examples may have a Brechtian political intent while others may be intended as entertainment, but both rely on particular aspects and combinations of music (often including pastiche or parody) and of the players' presence.

Theatrical music is intended to draw attention away from immersion in the plot and focus instead on the production and in some ways theatricality in music might be perceived in direct opposition to atmospheric music. However, even music that distracts from immersion also creates atmosphere and context. One example is from the 1991 production of Henry IV Part 1 (Dir. Noble) that culminates in a battle scene with Hotspur and Hal. This scene included a tableau of performers that arose from under the stage looking like a World War 1 memorial. On this occasion the entire band was placed in the tableau along the back of the stage with 'every conceivable percussion instrument … we were just welting everything in sight' (Reynolds 2016a). Here the separation of action and the performance of music were indeed theatrical and spectacular, but the effect of the sound also contributed to the aggression and chaotic mess of the battle scene, thus contributing to the diegesis.

Theatrical and diegetic music may overlap at times as in some of the examples above of the onstage band appealing to the audience or otherwise breaking the fourth wall, or indeed, actors playing instruments on which many are skilled, but these functions also have differences. Although theatrical music might carry out any or all of the other functions above it deliberately locates the audience in a blended combination of the present moment and the world of the drama rather than immersing them entirely in the drama. This type of theatricality constantly stages the performance in a state of becoming, a process of creation in flux rather than a completed and final illusion, and such interactivity, in some cases, may require the co-presence of actors and musicians in rehearsal. This is a feature that emerged very early in the development of the RSC though it has now spread to other companies, especially companies like Filter Theatre and Kneehigh that prize the opportunities afforded by the theatrical use of music and the involvement of musicians as performers. It is possible that the work of the RSC may have been one of the inspirations behind the development of actor-musicianship in devised and later mainstream theatre in the UK—but that is fairly speculative. However, the opportunity to explore the theatricality and musicality of performance has been facilitated in those companies that use actor musicians following a practice at the RSC where extended exploration of how music might contribute to performance was enabled by the working practices. At the RSC this included a music department to support actors, musicians and actor musicians, and the luxury of extended rehearsals and long-term collaborations. In small companies actor musicians and the presence of musicians in significant long-term roles has facilitated the exploration of similar territory. It may be that the funding model allowed such developments to emerge at the RSC that have subsequently transformed the British theatre landscape.

Theatricality in Music: Some Examples

Peter Brook's production of *A Midsummer Night's Dream* (1970) is one of the most influential works in reimagining the performance of Shakespeare for contemporary audiences and it incorporated music into its theatricality.[6] Its design rejected all the styles that had preceded it including the bowdlerised nineteenth century productions and even the more poetic, uncut interpretation by Harley Granville-Barker in 1914. While Granville-Barker's production replaced Victorian scenic illusion and musical romanticism in favour of a stylised design and English folk tunes, Brook moved even further away from romanticism and presented the play in a

---

[6] The score is available in the Shakespeare Birthplace Trust archive as is an AV recording and the prompt book. All of these informed this discussion.

white box in which performers are understood to re-enact characters and create the sound world. It introduced male fairies performing circus tricks to represent the magic of the forest and altogether explored the darker adult themes of the play using a Brechtian inspired theatricality. As Brook himself noted in an interview published in *Plays and Players*, 'A *Midsummer Night's Dream* is, amongst other things, a celebration of the arts of the theatre. On one level the actors have to display a physical virtuosity—an expression of joy. Hence our production at Stratford involves acrobatics, circus skills, trapeze acts' (Ansorge 1970). Both David Savran and Helen Cole King remark on the magical, festive, circus-like quality that turned the performance into 'a ritual, an initiation, a purging, a purification. Effected by laughter and awe. A true—and utterly simple—theatrical sublime' (Savran 2017).

The 1970 score by Richard Peaslee[7] that was developed with Peter Brook and the actors was not remotely illusionistic. The score calls for Percussion 1 to be stage left and Percussion 2 to be stage right while the guitarist enters and exits as required and performs onstage. However, although this is detailed in the score and performed in touring productions (seen in Fig. 3), in the initial production the percussion instruments were predominantly played from the top of the white box, while the guitarist played onstage. All the musicians played live onstage only in the Mechanicals' scenes. The musicians were not the only sound makers in this production though, since the actors also played instruments and noises in other scenes to contribute to the sonic effect.

The musicians who developed the production with Peaslee, Brook and the company were Tony McVey and Robin Weatherall on percussion and Edward Flower on Guitar (Martin Best played guitar in the touring version). The two percussionists also doubled on trumpet and trombone. Figure 3 shows the musicians sitting with the actors (or actor musicians), during the Mechanicals' performance of Pyramus and Thisbe. The percussionists played a barrage of instruments including a bullroarer[8] and lion roar, and the guitarist also had a zither and autoharp. Various different tubes, metal tops and musical saws allowed different pitches and vibrations of sound to evoke the magic flower and its spell, while every one of Hermia's dreaming movements produced a metallic buzz of a serpent.

---

[7] Peaslee had previously worked at the RSC with Brook on *The Marat-Sade* in 1964.
[8] This is described in the score as a bevelled piece of wood or ruler on the end of a stout cord, swung around rapidly creating a roaring sound (Peaslee, p. 2).

Fig. 3 *A Midsummer Night's Dream* (1972) Touring version showing the onstage band. (Photo by Reg Wilson. ©RSC)

Increasing use of sound effects contributed to the 'confusion and inarticulate states of the characters trapped inside' (King 2008, 419) as sounds jarred against gestures. These are features of theatricality—that sounds are unexpected and jarring, that they draw attention to themselves and their construction, and that they interfere with or disrupt immersion in the dramatic world. This theatricality is the precursor of a type of collaborative and reflexive theatre music at the RSC that was exemplified in the previous chapter in the 1999 production of *Macbeth*.

There are 66 cues in Peaslee's score, some of which have multiple sections, but many of which are stings and effects, or short comic and disruptive *a capella* songs rather than orchestrated compositions. The majority of cues in the score are for the musicians, and include a brisk up tempo jazz march for the entrance of the performers. Cues 4, 5 and 6 are all for guitar only and require *ad libbed* improvisation based on composed thematic material played under the actors' dialogue, with the further proviso that while cues 4, 5 and 6 should be serious and classical, cue 7, using similar thematic material, should be gayer and lighter. These are effectively atmospheric writing in this most theatrical of productions.

There are many short songs in the production including a 5/4 rhythm of gong and Indian bell for the entrance of Helena and Demetrius who chant a song. 'Fair Love' is a song for Lysander accompanied by guitar that is echoed by Hermia. 'And so it came to pass' is a jazz waltz on guitar and trombone accompanying antiphonal singing by Puck and Oberon. Demetrius sings of sorrow's heaviness, 'why should you think that I should woo in scorn,' in a mock melodramatic song marked as 'Grandioso (operatic accompanied by guitar)'. The paradox of this instruction is itself evidence of the pastiche and theatricality of the score. Trumpet and trombone with tambourine on the off beats accompany Bottom singing the pastiche pop of 'The Beard Song' with the chorus of mechanicals providing backing vocals. This intertextual profusion of styles contributes to the theatricality as attention is constantly drawn to the comic performance of songs and music from throughout popular culture.

At other times the percussionists highlight jokes or tricks as though in a variety show. Figure 4 contains a page of the score that demonstrates the way short stings and buttons punctuated speeches.

There are 'tapped side-drums, finger-bells and Eastern arpeggios' for Titania's entrance and Oberon's 'Ill met by moonlight' (Selbourne 1982, 213). When Titania says that she has foresworn Oberon's bed and company there is an antiphonal effect as a snare shot from one percussionist is followed by the choke cymbal by the other—the traditional 'boom chick' response to a joke. The subsequent lines have similar sting effects, which turns the scene into a game of repartee, a competition to deliver the best line that completely undermines the atmospheric reverie with which the fairy world had often been represented. As Brook remarks, 'the actor should say to the audience, "I am a man as other men are". That is the necessary beginning for a play about the spirit world ... It's from the hidden inner life of the performer that the magic, the unfolding possibilities of the play, must emerge' (Ansorge 1970). This is true too of the way the music is put together in this production, so that it is visibly generated as well as audible, and contributes to the distancing effect of the performance (Ibid.).

There is some instrumental music for entrances and dancing too: a minuet for clarinet and bassoon accompanies the entrance of the lovers after they leave the forest, and Mendelssohn's Wedding March (written for between Acts 4 and 5 and often used during the marriage scene) is here used to parody such serious institutions when played as Bottom

THEATRE MUSIC AT THE RSC 169

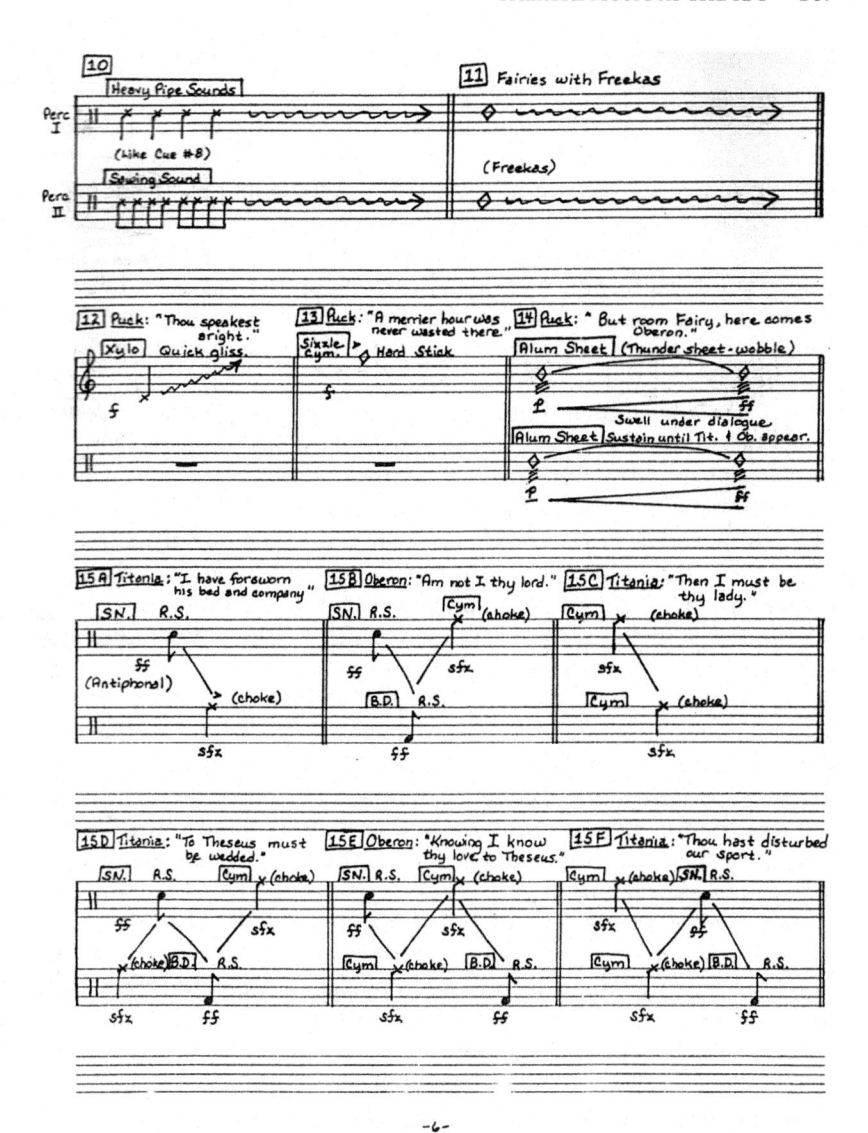

Fig. 4 *A Midsummer Night's Dream* (1970). (Score by Richard Peaslee. By permission of the RSC)

enters Titania's bower.[9] As Selbourne remarks Mendelssohn's *Wedding March* is sent up 'in a sardonic gesture [as] Titania strokes this "as if" standing phallus amid a lascivious clutch of fairies, who seem to hang upon every sexual impulse and erotic gesture. Mendelssohn's sentimental ghost is about to be laid' (Selbourne 1982, 237). Altogether the musical score incorporates diverse popular and high cultural references, and is used in ways that highlight the comic or ironic potential of the play. Its non-conformity to existing practices in theatre composition and its use of musical stings and commentary derived from popular performance both complement the effect of alienation that the staging and design have established.

As Peter Brook notes, 'With an explosion of percussion from the composer Richard Peaslee, the whole cast literally burst onto the stage, climbed up the ladders and swarmed across the top level of the set with such joy and energy that they swept the audience along with them' (Brook 2013, 80). Savran recalls how 'Everything seemed to come out of the actors, or to the actors, especially Oberon and Puck who cast the spells. In that sense, the whole production felt so hand-made, with tricks always perceptible as tricks, as theatrical feats. Which is also why I thought of it at the time as a 60s hippie-like de-industrialization, de-mystification, de-sanctification of a "classic"' (Savran 2017).[10] This type of theatricality that, according to King was at this point already a fully integrated part of Brook's stage scenography (Ibid., 418), draws attention to the constructed nature of performance; it rejects illusionism and integration in favour of the revelation of the theatrical production. It took theatre 'back to the basics, the basics of theatre and of human relationships: an empty space and people' (Savran 2017).

Savran remembers the music and sound effects as a kind of composite created from such 'fanciful props as noisemakers, those funny plastic pipes the actors would whip around in the air [freekas], the percussive use of other props, especially associated with magic and transformations … cymbal rolls and swells and the way that the entire space became

---

[9] Mendelssohn's nineteenth century incidental music was very widely used or excerpts performed during productions of this play until at least the 1930s, so its significance was likely to have been recognised. (See Manifold 1956, 156, and Lindley 2004, 111.)

[10] Some short clips are available on YouTube that include the sound of the Freekas (https://www.youtube.com/watch?v=Kg-FiWX4uWI [Accessed 08.10.2015]), but very little of the performance was recorded at the time.

percussive, a white box that could be slapped and smacked against' (Savran 2017). The score requires Lysander to imitate bird calls using a clarinet mouth piece, an effect that could have been recorded—but that was the point; that these sounds were not realistic added to the effect of theatricality. The Bergomask is a dance improvised by the actors accompanied by rhythmic sounds using found objects such as beating on a box, using spoons, slapping thighs, sounding police whistles on the offbeat and so on. The score at this point notes that although the dance is improvised the musical performance should be carefully organised so that the effect is 'not sloppy' (Peaslee 1974). Helen Cole King, meanwhile, remarks on the 'sing-song voices and operatic speech […] echoed by percussion instruments played by the musicians on the catwalk around the top of the set' (2008, 419). This gives an overall sense of the appearance of a noisy, chaotic sound world generated as a result of the collaborative rehearsal period involving actors as musicians and musicians in a thoroughly conceptual production.

From a purely musical perspective it is obvious that this influential production marked a turning point—however slowly its effects filtered through to other compositions in the RSC canon. The genres of music it incorporated were not historically related to Shakespearean productions following the 'authentic' movement, or to any nineteenth-century classical or tonal framework, or indeed to the atonal and electronic developments noted in other parts of this book, but to twentieth-century popular culture. This type of musical interaction with the text is unimaginably different from anything that preceded it in the literary theatre, but not in popular comic performance. This production can be seen as one of the transformational moments in the development of music at the RSC because it utilised sound, music and actor musicians to avoid the immersion of audiences and to increase theatricality. 'Combining the strange and the familiar, the "alienating" and the plausible, the sound effects of these productions invite us to stretch our imagination beyond its usual limits' (King 2008, 424) and to become aware of the nature of the theatrical illusion. Such detailed interactive responses to the text—the stings and mickey-mousing noted in this production—did continue if somewhat infrequently, and especially in the comedies.

This type of theatricality is also apparent in the 2000 production of *Comedy of Errors* with music created by Bell Helicoptor (Parker) that was discussed above, and which is a very physical and comic production of the play. One of the plot devices in *A Comedy of Errors* involves the purchase of a gold chain by one twin and its delivery to the other twin who is not expecting it, leading to confusion about whether it has been delivered, paid for, or stolen. In this production the chain is delivered in a box and every time the box is opened angelic voices sing until it is closed again, articulating the femininity and desirability of the chain (that was destined for the courtesan), but also creating a momentary theatricality reminiscent of pantomime. Other such comic sound effects that derive from popular comedy in theatre and film are the ringing of the bell tree at the appearance of or reference to the courtesan and bird song when Adriana appears. There are percussion effects for bumps and beatings, and running semiquaver scale patterns for chase and fight sequences. The effect of such close articulation is to draw attention to the impact of a particular physical contact, but also to render it comic, just as it is in film cartoons, commedia and pantomime performances. Where a naturalistic slap might be considered unpleasant, a slap accompanied by a cymbal sizzle or a wobble board has the pain removed by the comic framing of the sound.

Filter Theatre, who first adapted its postmodern, non-illusory staging methods in a production of *Twelfth Night* created in association with the RSC, use music and sound to create a level of 'knowingness'. According to Curtin 'they create illusions, but they also show how the illusions are made' (Curtin 2016, 163). It is this feature of sound and music performance that allows audiences either to 'suspend their disbelief' or to 'revel in pretence and artificiality, in theatrical make-believe' (Ibid.). It is a feature that Filter has explored much more extensively in recent years than the RSC itself, but such theatrical knowingness remains a feature of some productions. Drawing awareness to similitude, or as Brecht explained it 'show[ing] that [they] are showing' (Brecht 1979, 341 in Curtin 2016, n. 26) destabilises the narrative and encourages audiences to reconsider the texts. It requires musicians to be part of the company, to be involved in rehearsals and for the same musicians to be available throughout the run since depping this type of show is difficult. That such practices arose at the RSC is somewhat unexpected, though given its focus on reconsidering a relatively small number of canonical plays, this exploration drawing on developments in European expressionist theatre is not so surprising. The result is that the opportunity provided by long rehearsals and a collaborative environment led to significant innovations in the way music was conceived that have had effects throughout the theatre landscape.

Conclusion

As noted above, all these functions have the potential for overlap, but through the examples of each I have attempted to highlight the ways in which they contribute to the total experience of live performance. The nature of theatre music is deeply complex since it contributes not only to the plot but also to the framing of the plot and the theatricality or immersive nature of the event. In particular I have been concerned to demonstrate that theatre music's functions cannot simply be conflated with the ways in which music contributes to film; the liveness of the event, the collaboration and responsiveness between performers, and the involvement of the audience in the energy of the event all feed back into the creation of a shared theatrical experience. Fundamentally, though, in a book about theatre music at the RSC what becomes apparent is the way the institutional structures, the collaborations among long-serving staff that led to musicians being involved in devising and performing music onstage and off in direct interactions with the stage led to innovations. Such innovations have transformed the ways in which theatre music can be conceived. Practices that were innovative at the RSC are used by actor musicians in devising companies or by sound designers in ways that are interactive and immersive, theatrical or distancing, that guide the audience's attention and involvement in productions.

From *Macbeth* to *Matilda* at the RSC

> *The man that hath no music in himself,*
> *Nor is not moved with concord of sweet sounds,*
> *Is fit for treasons, stratagems, and spoils;*
> *The motions of his spirit are dull as night,*
> *And his affections dark as Erebus.*
> *Let no such man be trusted.*
> *Mark the music.*
> *The Merchant of Venice* Act 5, Sc. i

This chapter will explore the musicality of RSC productions and consider the relationship between those productions that are viewed fundamentally as plays with music, and those that openly embrace the identity of a musical. It will question whether the difference between plays and musicals is a matter of the scale of musical intervention or whether there are aesthetic differences in practice. It will consider whether they can be analysed like for like, or whether the cultural assumptions we hold about the distinctions between plays and musicals mean that any sense of a coherent musical approach in the RSC's work is challenged. In the end, I will ask whether it is theoretically possible to link all the RSC productions—from *Macbeth* to *Matilda*—along a continuum of musical practice. This idea arises from Shakespeare's expression of an idea prevalent in the early modern period, that well-being was profoundly affected by music and the sounding of the world, such that an absence of musicality might suggest a dark and untrustworthy nature. While I will not engage with the philosophical background to the speech quoted above it opens up a question about the ubiquity of sound and music in the plays and the musicality of performers and performance more generally.

The discussion will begin by considering the importance of voice and verse speaking since verse speaking was a fundamental driver of acting practice in the UK in the early/mid part of the century and a significant value underpinning the formation of the RSC. The rhythms its rhyme schemes and metres establish slow down naturalistic time, while the combination of the lyric qualities of voice and music has the effect of poeticising language. Later discussions will consider the aesthetics of voice and song before turning to song and musical theatre as extensions of the RSC's practice.

Vocal Training and Musicality

Despite training for performers within an ensemble system having been considered by the company since 1875 it was only Peter Hall's company that began any sort of consistent practice as part of his actor development system (Darnley 2013, 42ff). Hall utilised voice, verse and movement teachers, including Michel Saint-Denis who ran a studio training programme in Stratford from 1962 to 1966. John Barton left Cambridge to teach verse speaking at Stratford along with Geraldine Alford, Iris Warren and Denne Gilkes who were all involved as voice, singing or verse speaking coaches. As a result a style of vocal practice emerged led first by Iris Warren and Bertie Scott and from the late 1960s by Cicely Berry, but it was Barton's way of teaching verse speaking that was first perceived as an RSC style in the 1960s (Darnley 2013, 54–5). Berry's work went further than Barton's as it encompassed the production of voice as well as the delivery of verse, and her practice incorporated the 'release'[1] of the performer's voice, training the muscles for increased efficiency, so that the inner life of a character could be most effectively expressed (Berry 1973, 3 and 7).

---

[1] I note the issues raised in respect of this terminology by Richard Knowles, but use it here in referencing Berry's and Rodenburg's work with actors. The ideologies Knowles critiques are not really relevant to the discussion here that explores the relationship between spoken and sung texts rather than the practices of actor training. In any case, Lyn Darnley has mounted a strong defence of Berry's terminology in her PhD thesis *Artist Development and Training in the Royal Shakespeare Company* (RHUL 2013).

Berry began working at the RSC in 1969 when she joined the company led by Trevor Nunn and became the first voice expert to work in-house for a theatre company, heading the new Voice Department and being fully integrated into the rehearsal process (Darnley 2013, 75). Notably it was Berry who led the development of voice practice for Peter Brook's production of *A Midsummer Night's Dream* in that first year. Her method, that has been honed over many years with many directors, many of whom espoused different approaches to language, involves 'challenging the status quo by disrupting "smooth speech" through exploring the soundscape, physicalizing language and releasing the in-built rhythms of the text' (Darnley 2013, 75). Her work 'enables actors to feel comfortable with the text and empowers them to "own" the language' (Darnley 2013, 95). As Berry concludes in *Voice and the Actor*, 'you have to prepare the voice as well as possible and make it as skilled as you can. You have to stretch it so that it can compass and respond to whatever text you have and so that it can be surprising' (1973, 136). Rather than requiring a particular type of voice, she encouraged actors to discover the most effective way of relating to others using their own voices in order to bring out the poetry and musicality of Shakespeare's language. In an article in *The Guardian* she remarks that 'Peter Brook always says there's a million ways of saying one line. It may be a bit exaggerated, but not much. The actor has to make that line work for themselves, yet feel the rhythm behind it. That's what's exciting: it's like singing the blues' (Barnett 2011). Here again there is reference to the musicality inherent in Shakespeare's writing epitomised at the top of this chapter in the example from *The Merchant of Venice*.

As Lyn Darnley notes, writing in 2013, 'the ensemble ideal and desire for continuing development for artists that was originally instigated by Hall has remained at the heart of the RSC' through the work of Peter Brook, Trevor Nunn, Buzz Goodbody, Adrian Noble, and into the artist development programme established by Michael Boyd (2013, 62). The actual training arrangements varied considerably and some were more effective in practice than others; sometimes overt training was offered separate from rehearsals and at other times training was subsumed into the support mechanisms within rehearsals, but throughout the period voice and verse training for performers was part of the experience of being a member of the company. Beyond the basic rehearsal process Trevor Nunn established a company culture in which actors should focus on self-improvement by taking classes in singing, movement and speech among other things (Beauman 1982, 298), and later Buzz Goodbody's work at The Other Place focused on the development of educational work, experimentation and contact with audiences. The most recent stage of this process was the development of a training programme by Michael Boyd which included the evolution of the public understudy run as an opportunity for young actors to gain experience in larger roles. The training programme and its historical precedents have been documented by Darnley who was one of the staff employed on the project (Darnley 2013). Whatever the pros and cons of the various practices Darnley discusses, the commitment to a training programme is interesting for its promotion of the ensemble, the creation of a company ethos and sense of community as well as the development of musicality in verse speaking. However, the focus here remains on the voice as a constituent of the sound world.

As Peter Hall remarked in an interview with Richard Eyre in which he promoted the primacy of Shakespeare's verse and the importance of verse speaking, 'playing Shakespeare is like playing jazz – play the line, listen to the beat, it's how you nearly break the rhythm that enables you to express the emotion and allows you to express what the character feels' (Eyre 2010). Thus we find that the vocal delivery, that is, the performance of text—whether spoken or sung—has a relationship to music. The rhythmic regularity of poetic stress equates to the pulse of music, while the articulation of consonants and the punctuation of grammar provide the detailed rhythms. Melody arises from the intonation of voice and the pitch of vowels while the timbre and tone of the voice, its breathiness and its grain, contributes to the distinctive performance of character. Berry and Brook both focus on 'the sound dynamics of words as well as their literal meaning' and discuss the sensations produced by consonants, vowels and the resonance of the voice in the body (Darnley 2013, 78). This is similar to the experience of singing in which the sound of the voice produces an effect in the singer and in audiences that is excessive of the rhetorical meaning of words and music.

In a related initiative 2010 saw the development of the Hip Hop Shakespeare Company which began working with spoken word and Hip Hop artists to explore the links between the poetry of Shakespeare's Elizabethan England and the contemporary lyrical styles of UK poetry and lyrics. This eight-week project was developed with secondary school children at a season in London in autumn 2010 and the results presented at the Roundhouse with a live band. The aim was to engage young people with a love of words, confidence in rhetorical speaking, as well as a connection with Shakespeare ('Hip Hop and Shakespeare' *RSC Members News*

June 2010). Of course, it also made a direct connection with popular music, musicality and improvisation, and accompanying instruments added to the physical and emotional interpretation of the words.

Brook and Berry as well as Hall and later Nunn speak about the musicality of Shakespearian verse and the viscerality of vocal sound, encouraging actors to connect the sound of their delivery of language to the material content of the words. As Helen Cole King notes, Brook sought 'the life within a sound', using the actor's voice and amateur musical skills as his starting point (Ibid., 413). He wanted to draw on vocal and acting skills in ways that would restore the musical dimension of speech to adequately reflect 'the poetry of dramatic texts' (Ibid., 413).[2] During his experiments in the 1960s and 1970s he worked with actors whose musicianship allowed them to create a 'more subtle relationship between the music of verse and of voice, between actors and audience' (Ibid., 413). Patsy Rodenburg devotes a whole chapter of her book *Speaking Shakespeare* to describing how to speak the rhythms of iambic pentameter since, as she describes it, the rhythm is 'a wave, sometimes small and almost still, sometimes mighty'. She continues '[t]he genius of Shakespeare is such that as long as you follow his rhythm, you will be on and in the meaning of the text' (2005, 98). Throughout the discussion of rhythm she uses musical terminology: the regular and irregular beats that create the rhythm and that relate emphasis to thought, while the tone through which the beat is varied, and through which meaning and interpretation emerge are, she argues, more important than obedience to rhythm. She explains this as follows: 'Locate the iambic to release its power; then allow it freedom to harmonise with the meaning and intention of the text' (Ibid., 104). This is similar to the process of learning a song in which the notes, the words, the melody, the rhythms and the rhymes provide the shape and structure that underpin meaning, upon which the 'imaginative actor' extemporises with feeling and sense, allowing the alterations of pace, rhythm and pulse to feed into interpretation. As she notes—in terms similar to those used by Brook and Hall—'Great jazz musicians extemporize with feeling and sense, but they know structure and rhythm intimately: only then are they free to improvise' (Ibid., 106).

---

[2] It must be noted that all these references to the idea of a 'total communication' or the 'echo' of the play and the 'life within a sound' point to a certain ideological essentialism that I don't have space to address here. The vocal practices created through the methods of these creative practitioners are the objects of my consideration rather than the ideologies of the language used to produce them.

It is this type of musicality in verse speaking that combines the revelation of the body through voice with the awareness of melody and rhythm, tempo and beat. Together these aspects of vocal performance demonstrate the continuum between verse speaking and singing. This is an argument developed by Trevor Nunn, who proposes a link between the function of verse in the classical plays and songs in musical theatre, relating both sound structures to two qualities: heightening emotion and the extension of time (Yershon 2016). The lyrical function of verse speaking and the rhythms its rhyme schemes and metres set up slow down naturalistic time. The same is true of song. When Emile de Becque sings 'Some Enchanted Evening' in *South Pacific* the show expands into what Scott McMillin refers to as 'lyric time' for the character to sing that moment in what is effectively a bubble of time (2006). The same thing occurs when Hamlet delivers the soliloquy 'to be or not to be'. Both of these events move outside a 'realistic' sense of time, but because they retain a coherent meaning and expand on the psychological state of the characters, audiences perceive both orders of time to be part of the fabric of the scene and story. It is the combination of the lyric quality of voice, the poetry of the language, and the effect on the structures of time that unites musical theatre and Shakespearean productions at the RSC through the sounding of the voices, rhythm and resonance, and accompanying music.

The Aesthetics of Voice and Song

Within the performance of voice, though, there are different vocal qualities that contribute to the representation of character. There is a 'rough' aesthetic used by singers of working class, rural or bawdy characters as befits the character stereotype. This is used to deliver prosaic spoken language and, even in the songs, the rhythms and rhymes are direct and obvious rather than containing metaphorical or poetic imagery. In contemporary settings the melodies are often at or near speech pitch and close to speech rhythms with straightforward harmonic structures based on the patterns and structures of generic popular forms. The timbre of the voice is thicker, articulation of notes or consonants might be slurred and the voice is likely to contain gravelly textures and a certain rhythmic gusto that arises from an over emphasis on the beat. This can be readily perceived in the songs of Autolycus, Caliban and friends, and more especially Bottom, since the musical language of song-settings is likely to allow for, or even encourage, this type of performance of voice.

David Lindley's comprehensive survey of music and song in the play texts confirms that many songs are sung by characters of lower social status; but he notes that often the music needs to be 'shared between characters of different social status, and with the audience' (2006, 144). Thus, he argues, these characters are likely to have used a common language set to the tunes of well-known songs, or indeed the songs themselves might have been incorporated in what we now refer to as 'jukebox' fashion. Cultural patterns and fashions change, however, and what was current in the sixteenth century fails to signify in the contemporary period—the popular songs of the period would no longer be recognised or their inferences understood. Therefore, the RSC practice has been for songs to be set to music freshly composed for each production using musical genres or styles that are familiar to the audience so they signify through style and genre rather than through recognition of a particular song. There are few examples of the use of existing songs, jukebox style,[3] in the work of the RSC, but the employment of a composer like Laura Marling, for example, makes a particular connection to contemporary popular culture, and the availability of her songs to download or listen to online perhaps equates to the familiarity that might have been present as a result of some song choices in the early modern period. It is not necessary for the song itself to be familiar in order for it to signify, however, since using generic similarity or parody also chimes with the idea of contextual music discussed in "Theatre Music at the RSC". The musical style aids characterisation in terms of signalling history, geography and status, but it also communicates to the audience in the musical language of contemporary culture. Songs thus overlap with the other music of the play to create a context for voicing characters and action that is popular and fresh, but it also implicates the singing character more completely than underscore in its intertextual, generic and aesthetic signification.

In the Shakespeare texts, as has been noted above, it is not always certain whether a particular ballad or verse might have been sung or spoken, or how the intertextual juxtaposition might have been interpreted, a situation that opens up the parallel opportunity to explore diverse processes for incorporating songs into the play texts. This situation perhaps accounts for the diversity of practice at The Globe, at the RSC and, for example, at Filter Theatre. Adrian Curtin documents the ways in which Filter Theatre

---

[3] One of the exceptions is Woolfenden's adaptation of the songs of Cole Porter in *Two Gentlemen of Verona* directed by David Thacker in 1991.

relies on audiences understanding the conventions and associations of particular songs to evoke a shared cultural knowledge in the same way that it is assumed Shakespeare used popular songs of his time. The use of pastiche in Filter's work is similar to that at the RSC, though perhaps more pronounced and shocking. In respect of Ophelia's mad scene in *Hamlet* Bruce Johnson suggests that 'by playing with an established popular repertoire, disordering and fragmenting it, presenting it in inappropriate settings and juxtapositions, the sense of a known world turned inside out, of poignant ironies, is far more disturbingly achieved than would overtly "mad" music' (Curtin 2016, 163).

Work songs, of course, were sung by men such as the Gravedigger in Hamlet, thus using music in a utilitarian way that overlaps with the idea of diegetic song in musical theatre. Songs are also more common in the tavern than the court (Lindley 2006, 148), and music often signifies the difference between these worlds or the level of drunkenness of the singer. Falstaff sings, as does Iago when encouraging Cassio to drink in the song 'And let me the cannikin clink'. But it is not only lower class or drunken characters who sing. Theatrical convention requires that women sing when they lose their wits, as Ophelia does, whereas Desdemona's song is associated not so much with madness as with her lovesickness. In the later seventeenth century 'mad songs' became a defined sub-genre (Lindley 2006, 155 and note 32, 262), while in the early nineteenth century a trope of extraordinary and excessive arias sung by mad heroines emerged in French and Italian opera, including Ophelia, Norma and Lucia di Lammermoor (Taylor and Symonds 2014, 144). These are just examples of a wider conception within literature and the arts of a coalition between madness, women and song. But to return to the specific example, in the Shakespeare plays madness is the only factor that causes noble women to sing. It is possible that Hamlet might sing, or at least he might chant, since to do so would be to accentuate his madness through the indecorum of such a practice. He taunts Polonius with 'quotations from a popular ballad of King Jeptha'. The fact that, in reality, it is unlikely that Hamlet sang in the early modern period and is equally unlikely to sing today may be perceived to support the argument that singing remains a gendered activity (Lindley 2006, 158–9) and a class-defining one. However, it is likely Benedick might sing a popular ballad 'in the throes of his love for Beatrice' in Act 5 of *Much Ado* (Smith 1999, 169), thus linking madness and love as lovesickness which causes even upright men to lose their wits sufficiently to sing.

Since the mad scenes may be characterised by song in which the vocal timbre needs to be perceived as appropriate to character, the question of vocal timbre becomes relevant again. How does a noble mad woman or a lovesick man sound? It is an open question whether identification with the 'real' emotions of such characters as Ophelia requires that the performance of song also be 'real' where 'real' is interpreted as 'sounding untrained'. This is an interesting debate since it is likely that the amount of singing undertaken in the home and at court in the early modern period would lead to a relatively high level of proficiency, though voice pedagogies had not then been developed. At the RSC for many years there was an aesthetic that no special technique should be used when singing, since an 'amateur' or 'untrained' vocal timbre and delivery was most appropriate for the performance of madness, and, indeed, for most singing where 'realism' was required. Although there has been a constant development of voice training this has always focused on the development of voice for speech with song taking a poor second place. Denne Gilkes, the singing teacher for the Studio in 1965 felt that the standard of voice practice was poor, while Geraldine Alford who taught voice reported that 'Generally, I have been struck by the lack of any sound basic training or understanding of the use of the voice … ignorance and misconceptions about such basic things as breathing, tone, articulation, etc.' (Darnley 2013, 59). What they are pointing to is a lack of consistent or coherent training in the use of voice for speech, let alone for song, in the early years of the company. This was remedied in relation to speech by the Voice Department from the 1970s onwards and improvements were made, but song was largely left to the oversight of music directors who were dealing with teaching songs rather than training voices, so that the quality of sung voice did not advance. This seems like a deliberate separation of speech and song, musical and play at the very core of RSC practice, and perhaps points to the elitism that was signalled at the start of this chapter. I will return to this debate below, but in respect of singing, Richard Brown remembered that he and the other music staff 'used to get quite cross occasionally that directors lumbered us with actors that had to sing and we had to work truly hard to get them to deliver the goods' (Brown R. 2014).

Occasionally songs are transferred between performers because of the particular skill of a cast member. It is likely this was also an issue in Shakespeare's day as some of the debates about whether one character or another sang a particular song revolve around voices of actors breaking or the employment of a new performer with musical skill. Lindley records a suggestion that the reallocation of 'Come away death' in *Twelfth Night* from Viola to Feste was because the boy actor's voice broke. However he also presents a counter to that hypothesis based on the accepted dates of composition, the unreliable nature of documentation of the texts which led to the removal of Desdemona's 'Willow Song' in the Quarto text, and the unproveable hypothesis about who were the performers (Lindley 2006, 149). This is also an issue faced by the creative teams at the RSC. As Richard Brown explained, some RSC directors thought carefully about the requirements for singing when casting productions, whereas others were less concerned with musical expertise than with the performers' acting abilities (Brown R. 2014).

Ian Judge was mentioned as an example of a director who, like Nunn, was very interested in the musical aspects of plays, and the singing capacity of the cast, perhaps because he too was a director of opera and musical theatre. Judge cast Derek Griffiths in *Twelfth Night* because in addition to his acting ability he has a wonderful tenor voice 'and of course it meant that Nigel [Hess] was able to write these delicious songs which were really made for the voice' (Brown R. 2014). Later when the show was revived and Griffiths was not available Clive Rowe, another highly capable and inventive musical theatre performer, took over the role. On other occasions the casting was adapted, as, for example, in *As You Like It* (Thacker 1992) which had a 'magical score' by Gary Yershon (Brown R. 2014). As Brown records, 'Jenna Russell was in the company and David Birt [both of whom are experienced and excellent singers and musical theatre performers], so in actual fact the [director] managed to engineer it that Jenna and David sang the song even though [the script] says it's "Touchstone and two page boys"' (Ibid.). This is not a new practice, however, since, as Lindley reminds us, it is not always certain whether a particular portion of text was or was not sung in the early modern period, or by whom. As such, contemporary composers, directors and actors might jointly make decisions about whether some material should be sung and how it should sound. The Fool in *King Lear* might sing his rhyming ballads, and is asked by Lear about his singing (Act 1, Sc. iv: 162), but there is no certainty of a precedent for this (Lindley 2006, 161). In Ilona Sekacz's score for *King Lear* (Noble) in 1982, the Fool, played by Antony Sher, sang snippets of song accompanying himself on the violin. After Lear has killed him a soldier playing the violin in the final scene brings a memory of the Fool and his singing, thus extending the association between Lear and the Fool into the final scenes.

Despite the separation of training for speech and song that seems to have occurred at the RSC, and the relative importance clearly given to them, song was widely used in the plays, though the amount of song varied from production to production. The musical version of *The Comedy of Errors* (Nunn 1976) with lyrics by Trevor Nunn, set to music by Guy Woolfenden, is an early attempt to musicalise one of the plays rather than creating an adaptation (such as *West Side Story* or *The Boys from Syracuse*).[4] Starring Judi Dench, Michael Williams, Roger Rees and Francesa Annis it illustrates many of the issues of casting around voice discussed above and raises further issues about adaptation. Judi Dench had starred as Sally Bowles in *Cabaret* in 1968. Sheridan Morley noted that, at first, Dench thought the producers were joking when asking her to audition for this part, since she had never done a musical and she has an 'unusual croaky voice'. He continues: 'So frightened was she of singing in public that she auditioned from the wings, leaving the pianist alone on stage'. When the show opened, Frank Marcus, reviewing for *Plays and Players*, commented that: 'She sings well. The title song in particular is projected with great feeling' (Morley 1986). Almost 30 years later Dench also created an award-winning interpretation of Desiree Armfeldt in Sondheim's *A Little Night Music* for the 1995 revival, in which she performed the song 'Send in the Clowns' to great critical acclaim, but these songs have a very limited vocal range and she is a great actor. For many performers, as the vocal range of a song is extended and the performance becomes more dependent on vocal technique, the performance of character and plot is affected to the extent that audiences feel uncomfortable. This is certainly apparent in *The Comedy of Errors* where all the lead characters (including Dench) struggled with retaining resonance and breath to phrase the songs appropriately during sustained musical lines. For example, during Act 2, Sc. ii, the lines 'Why call you me love? Call my sister so' are used as the catalyst for a sung duet between Luciana and Antipholus (from Syracuse). The song completes their scene effectively and Nunn has extended and repeated the lines of the following speeches to create a lyric. However, the practice in musical theatre and film is for the prospective happy couple to sing lyrically together as a prediction that they will end up happily married. Since neither actor is able to sustain an extended musical phrase the song is set as a light-hearted number using fast running words at the pitch and pace of speech leading into a short (also basic) dance routine. This is in contrast with the beautiful

---

[4] A DVD is available produced by Granada Ventures in 2012.

lines and voices (or skilled dance routines) of most heroes and heroines of musical theatre. Here is a compromise created by a skilled musical theatre director, Trevor Nunn, that demonstrates the plot point, but fails to energise the end of the scene or raise the emotional stakes between the characters.

The comic characters fare much better with both Dromios (Michael Williams and Nickolas Grace) performing comic song and dance numbers using the articulation of patter type songs and physical theatre/clown skills very successfully, Williams in the opening number of Act 2 and Grace in Act 4, Sc. iv. The Merchant, played by Keith Taylor, who is clearly a comfortable and experienced singer, leads the opening chorus thus expanding his role, while the same happens with Robin Ellis as Pinch whose role now includes a production number as a quack doctor/magician charged with the task of restoring the Ephesian Antipholus and Dromio to sanity in a Jewish Klezmer style with full chorus and dance routine. This example has therefore served to illustrate the difficulties of casting without real attention to the musical requirements, but also the potential solution that allocates songs to other characters, thus increasing their roles in an adaptation. However, it also draws attention to the vocal requirements of musicals and the challenges that were faced when the RSC began to engage in their production.

The issue of creating a song lyric that works in a contemporary pop style is also contentious. Richard Brown remarked that 'You can repeat lines [...] the old trick if [...] you wanted to get what we know as a "hook chorus" in contemporary pop terms – quite often you just have to repeat a line.' Brown described Shaun Davey's score for *The Winter's Tale* (Noble 1992) as follows: '[the actor] Richard McCabe ended up singing a complete chorus that Davey had created out of "with hey, with hey, the doxy over the dale, over the dale, over the dale, with hey"' (Brown R. 2014). Nunn had been rather more liberated in translating Shakespeare's words into songs for the musical version of *The Comedy of Errors* (1976) discussed above, using the Shakespearian scenes as a catalyst from which lyrics were newly created. Syracusean Antipholus' soliloquy at the start of Act 4, Sc. iii is turned into/replaced by a chorus number within which all his many female friends call on him—a song that turns into a dream sequence, then a nightmare before returning to reality. The substance of the song derives from his material in the scene, especially his soliloquy, turned into song and action. Remaining much closer to the original text, the final couplet of the play, 'We came into the world like brother and brother; And now let's go hand in hand, not one before another', is set to a repetitive trope that turns into an effective (if lyrically dull) refrain for the bows.

Even when setting the obviously diegetic songs in the plays it is now accepted that it may be helpful to change the function of songs and perhaps move them around. Michael Bruce gives the example of the diegetic song 'Sigh No More' from *Much Ado About Nothing*, which he wrote for a performance not at the RSC, that was transformed into a summer dance anthem of the 1980s to be performed at the end of the play. It was replaced in Act 2, Sc. iii by a softer ballad with acoustic guitar and voice. Here the tempo, rhythm and instrumentation were changed as well as the structure being adapted so that it suited the context of the performance (Bruce 2016, 123).

It might not only be a question of changing the musical style and repeating lyrics, but sometimes of quite wholesale adaptation and alteration of the lyrics more in keeping with Nunn and Woolfenden's translations for *The Comedy of Errors* (1976). In "Theatre Music at the RSC" it was noted that two different versions of Autolycus' songs in *The Winter's Tale* had different titles, verse structures and choruses. In the early period of this study, and right up until the 1980s 'the Bard was regarded as sacred, and we were the company that shouldn't be mucking around with it, but doing it as well as we can in whatever style' (Brown R. 2014). Although there was enormous freedom for directors to envisage modern day productions, productions set in different times and places, or cutting and moving scenes, the adherence to the words was regarded as almost sacrosanct. However, it is certainly clear that the interaction between the fixed elements, the words, and their order appears to be looser in the songs and in musical versions of the plays than elsewhere even in the earlier period, and more recently it has become increasingly possible for new songs to be added. All this leaves the field open for composers to create songs in musical genres that signify to a contemporary audience and to adapt verse structures as required.

In the production of *Two Gentlemen of Verona* (Godwin 2014) Michael Bruce was asked to add a new song and dance sequence at the start of Act 2, Sc. iv for a contemporary-styled production set in modern day Italy. The idea was to create a contrast between the sleepy rural Verona and the spectacle of Milan, and since a song didn't exist at this point in the play, new lyrics were needed. Bruce found an Italian translation of a Shakespearean sonnet so that the language and poetry was in keeping with the play, but to increase the sense of alienation on arrival in Milan, he used the sonnet in Italian. This was set with an 'energised Eurobeat musical influence' and gave a modern vigour to that moment (Bruce 2016, 131). As mentioned above, another example of new music and lyrics being written is the incorporation of songs by Laura Marling into the production of *As You Like It* (Aberg 2013).[5] Bruce O'Neil who was music director for the production gives the example of 'He comes to steal my heart', which is a song that doesn't exist in the play, but is a moment where there is a suggestion of music that Marling developed into a new song to expand on the character's emotional world. In the other songs for this production she also adapted the Shakespearean lyrics as most writers now do, but in her case she created fresh songs and lyrics by taking 'the essence of the song' rather than the exact words (O'Neil 2016).

In the non-Shakespeare canon of plays at the RSC there are many more examples of singing and song that incorporate original music and lyrics. *House of Desires* (Meckler 2004) is a bawdy comedy written by a sixteenth-century Spanish nun. It was directed at the RSC by Nancy Meckler with music and songs inserted between the scenes by Ilona Sekacz. Sekacz did a lot of historical research exploring potential music and lyrics that might be effective as songs that would contribute to the contextualisation of the plot. She discovered some Spanish poems by the author (Juana Ines de la Cruz) that she set to a kind of reconstructed period music and sung in the original language. The music was derived from Sekacz's research into Mexican music of the late 1600s and early 1700s, particularly its rhythmic complexity and the emotional quality of the singing voice in Spanish and Mexican traditional music. Sekacz explained that 'whereas to the audience the [performers] could have been singing 'I Do Like to Be Beside the Seaside' in Spanish, the fact is that it was authentic; it was this woman's words'. There were three women singing, one of whom managed to get 'that big sob in the voice,' the second had 'a warm motherly tone' and the third 'a pure soprano tone' (Sekacz 25 April 2016). Importantly here, these vocal qualities were made possible by the employment of professional singers who sang between the scenes. This separation of acting and singing is one strategy that seems to be employed from time to time to counter the problem of non-singing actors. This practice was followed in the recent production of *The Tempest* (2017) when the masque was performed by two classically trained singers appearing on stage, whose voices were used from the band box throughout the rest of the score.

---

[5] My notes relate to the live performance of this production.

What is revealed is an enormously diverse practice that allows great flexibility for repetition and reinvention of lyrics, composition of new songs, altering the placement and function of songs and even who sings. The voice is sometimes treated as a musical instrument requiring specific expertise and separation from the actors and at other times actors are required to sing—thus calling on a different set of strategies. All this results in a very open field within which songs can be interpreted and their dramaturgical functions re-envisaged.

The Functions of Song

In musical theatre there are many different types of song that have been categorised by surveying the golden age musicals of the 1940s–1960s—they include 'I want songs', 'soliloquies', 'the 11 o'clock number' and so on—but all these song types could be subsumed into a much broader binary framework of functionality for the audience—one that W.H. Auden used when describing 'Music in Shakespeare'. He categorised songs into two types as the 'called-for song' and the 'impromptu'. The 'called-for songs' are songs that are sung by a character at the request of another character, and Auden refines this by explaining that the character 'ceases to be himself and becomes a performer; the audience is not interested in him but in the quality of his singing' (Auden 1962, 511).[6] The 'impromptu' 'reveals, as the called-for song cannot, something about the singer' and is sung by a character (and audience perception remains with the character rather than the performer) who is expressing feelings and thoughts for themselves whether or not other characters are listening (Ibid., 522). For the audience, the latter allows them in to the inner thoughts of the character, to understand or empathise, to have private knowledge about the character and her motivations within the narrative—whether or not they are truthfully expressed, and in this way they mirror the function of soliloquies. It is these songs that might be regarded as requiring a less developed vocal technique.

In musical theatre the 'called-for song' is often termed 'diegetic'—song that is perceived as sung performance within the world of the play or musical. But there is a grey area where the character sings within the world of the play or musical only for themselves. Examples of this might include 'The Hills are Alive' from *The Sound of Music* or 'Oh What a Beautiful Mornin'' from *Oklahoma!* Clearly these are impromptu songs but they are

---

[6] *The Dyer's Hand* (London, 1962, 511, 522).

also diegetic since they exist within the world of the play or musical. To a large extent it is the presence of non-diegetic impromptu songs—songs that allow characters to reveal their inner thoughts, feelings, emotions or motivations to the audience—that is one of the defining features of musical theatre, while it is perhaps the predominance of 'called-for song' that sits most comfortably in the play with music. So while Auden's typology is helpful in identifying the place of audience perception in plays with songs it cannot account for the diversity of songs' functions in the dramaturgy of musical theatre. Where it is particularly useful, however, is in clarifying which songs he believes would require an effective singing technique. Perhaps this is helpful in understanding the separation of these vocal practices at the RSC.

The fact that certain character types are unlikely to sing separates these plays to some extent from musical theatre in which most characters sing.[7] However, even those diegetic songs that appear to be inserted simply as entertainment in reality serve multiple functions at the same time. Time passes in the narrative, tension is created or released and the atmosphere is altered in, for example, Autolycus' songs in Act 4 of *The Winter's Tale* (Lindley 2006, 164–5). 'It was a lover and his lass' is clearly an interruption of the action (*As You Like It* Act 5, Sc. iii) and an entertainment inserted by two fortuitously passing page boys who are asked for a song as Touchstone and Audrey wait for their wedding on the following day, but it is also a song about the joys of love, a cheerful song to set the mood for later celebrations and a light-hearted 'foolish song'. It is an entertainment for the two listeners and the audience, but it also sits between the more serious scenes in which the principal characters' noble sentiments are worked out, and as such provides a contrast and a prediction before the denouement when all the lovers will be reunited with their lasses. Another example is 'The Willow Song' that appears simply as an interruption before Desdemona's death, and which, as Lindley notes, has the quality of impromptu (and possibly unaccompanied) song. Its dramatic purpose, though, is to provide a hiatus during which the dramatic irony of what is about to occur increases tension for audiences. Desdemona sings of her sadness and loneliness, revealing her vulnerability and the change in her mood from the liveliness and independence she displayed in the early part

---

[7] There are notable exceptions such as Mayor Shinn in *The Music Man* or Zach in *A Chorus Line*, and Rex Harrison famously performed a kind of speech/song as Professor Higgins in the film of *My Fair Lady*.

of the play. At the same time audiences are aware of Othello's jealous rage and the extreme contrast it presents with Desdemona's resignation. The extreme emotional range of these passions, and the delay in their fulfilment, intensifies the emotional experience of the tragic outcome for audiences, and the vocal performance is clearly not a prime consideration.

Examples of diegetic songs from *Twelfth Night*, one of which can be seen being performed in Fig. 1, are 'Come away death' and 'O Mistress Mine', which are beautiful reflections on getting old that, although they interrupt the action, are also commentaries that contribute to the understanding of character. Feste is called upon to sing 'Come Away, Death' (*Twelfth Night* Act 2, Sc. iv), while Orsino is listening to it within the world of the play. Lindley expounds on this moment at some length discussing the choice of Feste to sing the songs (Lindley 2006, 199–202) and how that feeds into the dramaturgy, but here it is more important to

Fig. 1 *Twelfth Night*, 1969. Actor musicians performing on stage. (Joe Cocks Studio Collection. ©Shakespeare Birthplace Trust)

understand how the background music and then the lyrics and musical atmosphere interact with the conversation between the Duke and Viola and feed the despair he feels and the frustration of her position. In musical theatre that song might have been sung by Orsino himself to express his sentiments and emotions, but since an aristocratic character in the Shakespeare plays would not sing he calls instead for a singer to perform. Requiring someone else to perform the song during the conversation between Orsino and Viola results in a layering of speech, lyrics and melody that all interact producing a complex picture. It also potentially allows the song to be performed by a more skilled singer.

Despite the multiple purposes some songs serve, the lyrics themselves are often straightforward since a lyric needs to be heard and understood in the time frame of the music. Sekacz commented on the complexity of Shakespearean soliloquies in comparison with the relative simplicity of his song lyrics, which were written that way because audiences must listen to lyrics in real time in association with music. But it is not quite so simple, since as noted above the songs create a brief hiatus in the action that has its own purpose within the rhythm of the play—and this rhythmic function is important in the creation, development or release of tension. More importantly, alongside the constriction of time a song always incorporates a second element that must be heard simultaneously—the music—and the music signifies in addition to the lyrics. So while it could be argued that the lyrics are less complex, the combination of music and lyrics might result in a more complex aural presentation.

Sekacz suggests that depending on the musical accompaniment songs can either reinforce the mood or suggest alternative interpretations of the lyric. As she explains, 'whatever music you play you can say, "Gosh he is being very kind to her, but underneath he is seething." Or, "He is being very openly funny, but underneath he is dying"' (Sekacz 2016). What she is articulating is the power of music to suggest meanings other than those being communicated in the lyrics, so that, despite commenting that songs are often static in narrative terms, the composition of a musical score and a vocal performance all contribute layers of meaning and so add nuance. Lindley explores a similar idea when he suggests that the tavern songs in *Henry IV* Part 2 are not a sign of riot and drunkenness, but act 'as a melancholy reinforcement of the darkening world of this play' (Lindley 2006, 146), and if the musical composition of the song has a gentle melancholic character it can serve 'rather to underline Falstaff's wistful observations "I am old, I am old" than to suggest the incitement of lust' (Ibid.,

147). He concludes that the music is associated with old age and declining performance in a way that is picked up in the final Gloucestershire scenes. These examples demonstrate how songs in performance have the capacity to contribute in ways that are not immediately obvious and rely less on a developed vocal technique.

Performing Verse and Song

There is additionally an interesting counterpoint produced as a result of the actor's material presence in the corporeal world at the same time that music or rhyme, rhythm and metaphor are raising the image beyond the quotidian. Music operates uniquely in the live theatre in this respect, since the corporeality of bodies in a shared space with the audience creates a different counterpoint to that experienced in film and television where there is no shared corporeality. Since the early twentieth century the direction of travel in the development of acting technique has been predominantly a move towards 'realistic', or mimetic acting on television and film, reproduced in theatre. Within this style of performance 'the play on stage is understood as diegesis of a separated and "framed" reality governed by its own laws and by an internal coherence of its elements and which is marked off against its environment as a separate "made up" reality' (Lehmann 2006, 100). This has possibly reached an apotheosis in postdramatic theatre in which audiences are encouraged to engage with the 'real' moment of performance and the 'real' presence of the performer rather than the 'intentional object of the staging' (ibid.), but nevertheless there is a material reality in performance: 'Theatre is *at the same time* material process – walking, standing, sitting, speaking, coughing, stumbling, singing – and "sign for" walking, standing, sitting etc.' (Ibid., 102). The result of this is that there is a material reality and a represented reality that are contained within a performance even while the verse structures, musical phrasing, underscore or accompaniment alter/heighten the emotional range of that reality.

In musical theatre there has been a significant move towards the appearance of 'integration' and the 'realistic' delivery of speech and song,[8] so that audiences will identify with or believe in coherently presented characters. Raising the poetic level of speech beyond a quotidian delivery—a

[8] Although these are contested terms I use them here as shorthand in order to pursue the argument.

delivery that is almost unheard of in the popular mediums of mainstream film and television—provides an extraordinary sense of intensity especially when characters are speaking modern dialogue.[9] That is similar to the moment of song that requires the performer to negotiate the material requirements of technique and presence in the representation of coherent characters. Audiences too perceive these two realities that are brought into relief at such heightened moments. The moment language becomes poetic, moving towards the condition of music, not only is the intensity of the experience enhanced, but the time frame is transformed such that there is more space and time for music to create atmosphere and emotion. Consequently the performance contains both the material presence and a significantly heightened/intensified 'reality'. As Gary Yershon explains, '[music] is helping to poeticise the prosaic fact of the physicality of the actor in front of you' (Yershon 2016).

It is here too that the development of sound design has fed into the sense of a continuous concept for performance. Sound effects are separate, but since the concept of soundscape was articulated in the 1970s (encompassing the types of theatre music that have been discussed above) there has been an increased experimentation with texture as a legitimate expressive tool, and, as has also been seen in some of the examples above, a move to replace melody and harmony with colour and texture. What sound designers and composers do when creating soundscapes for performance results in a poeticisation of space similar to that achieved by performers speaking verse. There is an increased intensity resulting from greater artificiality to more fully represent a coherent poetic space, and the two combine to accomplish this to the greatest effect.

The increased emotional intensity that can be aroused as a result of song is somewhat controversial. Michel Poizat in *The Angel's Cry* describes the emotions of opera-goers at moments of extreme vocal excess, an argument that draws on a Lacanian idea that the sound object is perceived by audiences as separate from the articulating body at such climactic moments. This idea of vocal excess, whose basis in neuroscience is explored by Carlo Zuccarini in 'The (Un)Pleasure of Song', suggests that some responses to the performance of voice, especially excessive vocal power and technical virtuosity, inspire a neurophysiological response among audiences (2014, 31). While this is a more extreme case than might be discovered in the

---

[9] Steven Berkoff explored this type of alienation and intensity to great effect in such plays as *East, Decadence,* and *The Greeks.*

Shakespearean canon, in which vocal delivery is firmly rooted in the material articulation of the body, poetic language, along with rhyme and rhythm, have the potential to heighten speech, giving a level of intensity different from everyday speech especially in performances by luminaries such as Gielgud, in a style showcased by the RSC and the Old Vic. It may be that one of the reasons for the extraordinary longevity of the Shakespeare plays is exactly this poeticisation of language which translates the action from the mundane or prosaic world to another, more excessive and other place. Song has a similar power to intensify emotion generated through the musical structures of rhythm, melody and vocal mirroring as well as metaphorical and lyrical poesy, but it also has a musical accompaniment that adds another level of signification and affect.

Moving into Musicals

It was Trevor Nunn who took the RSC in the direction of formal musical theatre, though clearly an interest in the use of music had already been demonstrated by Hall and Brook among others, and in fact there was a 1962 production of *Comedy of Errors* directed by Clifford Williams with music by Peter Wishart that could almost be called a musical. Building on the musicality and ensemble nature of production that had been his vision for his artistic directorship, Nunn first introduced the much longer and broader epics and musicals directed with John Caird. These include a production of *The Merry Wives of Windsor* (1979), then the nine-hour version of Dickens's *Nicholas Nickleby* (adapted by David Edgar, 1980), as well as *Peter Pan* (1982), before the same team—that included John Napier as designer—reunited to develop the musical version of *Les Misérables* (Schonberg et al. 1985). In between these and many other productions at the RSC Nunn worked in the commercial sector, where he directed the 'immersive musical spectacular' (Dickson 2011) *Cats* (Lloyd Webber et al. 1981). This variety demonstrates a catholic approach to theatre and musical theatre that Nunn explained as follows: 'I've never seen any dividing line, and I don't think Shakespeare saw one' (Dickson 2011). Nunn saw theatre as one continuum of practices, requiring particular skills of directors and performers that utilised the heightening effect of music and the poeticisation of language and space. Clearly there is an economic imperative that to some extent accounts for the infrequent attempts by the RSC to produce full scale musicals, but there are aesthetic and dramaturgical arguments both for and against such an extension to the remit of the company, and indeed, the company's attempts at full scale musicals is not universally successful.[10]

However, the presence of a music department, the increasing amount of incidental music being composed for Shakespeare productions (and indeed for other works as the company grew), the introduction of Christmas shows that were often musicals in all but name and the increasingly hazy separation between plays with songs and musicals as described above suggests an investment in music and song beyond that of a literary theatre. This is especially apparent in works such as *The Beggar's Opera* (1963), *Toad of Toad Hall* (1973), *Comedy of Errors* (1976), *Privates on Parade* (1977), *Piaf* (1978), *Hansel and Gretel* (1980), *Poppy* (1982), *Peter Pan* (1982), *Les Misérables* (1985), *The Wizard of Oz* (1987), *Kiss Me Kate* (1987), *Carrie* (1988), *Show Boat* (1990), *The Blue Angel* (1991), *The Beggar's Opera* (1992), *The Lion, the Witch and the Wardrobe* (1998), *Alice in Wonderland* (2001), *Beauty and the Beast* (2003), *The Canterbury Tales* (2005), *Merry Wives: the Musical* (2006), and *Matilda the Musical* (2010) as well as *Caucasian Chalk Circle* (1979), and *Mother Courage* (1984), and such other Christmas oddities as *The Shakespeare Revue* (1994). Alongside these productions that perhaps sit more easily in the field of musical theatre, there are debates about the masque-like nature of the later plays—*Cymbeline*, *The Winter's Tale* and especially *The Tempest* that Lindley discusses. Taken together, the presence of these works in the RSC's canon and the debates about form they inspire suggest that it is at least theoretically possible to link all these works along a continuum of musical practice—one that counters the elitism of a historical separation of plays with songs from musicals in the UK despite the RSC's own training practices.

Some people regard the difference between musicals and plays with songs as one of scale as well as narrative responsibility. Bruce O'Neil commented that 'if there is enough music so it feels like the dialogue scenes, as it were, are islands within sequences, where music is really moving things on and that leads into songs, then I suppose you can describe that as a musical rather than a play-with-songs' (O'Neil 2016). This issue is, in the end, immaterial and is only discussed here to highlight the fact that

---

[10] *Carrie* is the musical most often referred to as a flop, though it received only mixed reviews and in this was not substantially different from *Les Misérables*, though ultimately they have fared very differently. My own opinion of *Les Misérables* and *Carrie* is that the former is a far more musically coherent, developed, and satisfying musical than *Carrie*.

British culture seems to have a greater concern about the act of breaking into song than, for example, the Americans. There is a continuum of practice, and performers work in very similar ways in both types of performance, though as discussed above there are technical demands of vocal training and issues of vocal aesthetics that separate performers. There are also some technical differences for the sound and music departments to consider that are also issues of scale and resource rather than differences of practice. In "Electronics, Sound and Fury at the RSC" the issue of the placement of the sound board and the miking of actors was discussed, and in all the interviews and discussions with creative teams there was a sense that a different level of investment in sound and music was required for musicals. Richard Brown noted that for the production of *The Lion, The Witch and The Wardrobe* (1998) it was 'budgeted as a musical' meaning that there were 'more than a dozen' musicians, and for *The Wizard of Oz* (1989) there were 23 musicians. This was an exceptional production, directed by Ian Judge, the first re-creation of the old MGM film score performed live with an American orchestrator, a big score and many performers, and that 'emphatically was a musical' (Brown R. 2014).

Brown recalls Woolfenden's score for *The Comedy of Errors* as 'almost a musical' and Sally Beauman writes of it as a 'musical version', whereas Woolfenden referred to it as a musical, and one that won an award for Best Musical of the Year at the Society of West End Theatres (SWET) awards in 1976 (Beauman 1982, 343). The smaller number of songs and the smaller amount of underscore driving the narrative led Brown to question the designation of 'musical', but felt that it was a very grey area. For *The Beggar's Opera* (Caird 1992) Sekacz describes 'modernising what was already there' rather than writing original material as the work was turned into a parody rock opera. This was appropriate since *The Beggar's Opera* which was written in 1728, was, itself, a parody of early eighteenth century opera. Because each song is so short she needed to have a single idea for each song, compose an introduction that revealed the pastiche through the orchestration, and create the setting for the voice, but the melodies and harmonies remained from John Gay's original text. As the score was updated for rock instruments with electric bass guitar and kit the voices had to be miked, thus creating the modern sound that was contrasted with a harpsichord for the underscore. Despite the work having 'opera' in its title, and the large number of very short songs, whether or not it is an opera, a musical or a play with songs remains debatable because of the lack of musical direction, thematic unity or underscore.

Of the Christmas shows *The Lion, The Witch and the Wardrobe* that was adapted with lyrics by Adrian Mitchell and music by Shaun Davey was one of the most successful and perhaps most clearly a musical version. It was directed by Adrian Noble and had a large amount of underscore, but it didn't have a life beyond the Christmas seasons at the RSC. Not all the Christmas shows had songs, though they had a lot of music and were generally regarded as musical versions of literary classics, and it is this idea of the importance of the literary that perhaps provides one of the ways of thinking about what was acceptable to the RSC when commissioning new works of musical theatre such as *Piaf* written by Pam Gems, or *Privates on Parade* and *Poppy* by Peter Nicholls. These works incorporated only, or predominantly, diegetic songs, were written by contemporary British writers, had West End runs and have been frequently revived in commercial productions.

One of the more recent musicals that appeared for a Christmas season was *Merry Wives: The Musical* (2006), adapted by Gregory Doran with music by Paul Englishby and lyrics by Ranjit Bolt.[11] *Merry Wives of Windsor* is one of the plays that has inspired many operatic adaptations including by Salieri (1798), Balfe (1838) and Verdi/Boito (1893), though all of these were called *Falstaff*. Ralph Vaughan Williams adapted the play as *Sir John in Love* in 1935 using English folk song themes including 'Greensleeves'. There have been productions of the play with new music by luminaries such as Arthur Sullivan and Oscar Asche, and Stratford Memorial Theatre hosted a Viennese operetta type production directed by Theodore Komisarjevsky in 1932. All of this demonstrates the potential for musicalisation of this play; it contains a gallery of colourful, well-drawn characters and sound plotting despite unlikely situations, romance and an energetic ensemble. As Gregory Doran notes, it is the only one of the Shakespeare plays that is a domestic middle-class comedy (Programme Notes, 2006).

The creative team spent two years developing the first 'full-scale musical version' of the play by the RSC, created by 'extract[ing] the juice from this great Shakespearean orange without letting the useless pips slip into the little glass' (Doran 2006—Liner notes). They transported the show to a Berkshire town but maintained the links with the Histories, *Henry IV* parts 1 and 2, and *Henry V*, that precede and succeed this play and contain some of the same characters. In fact the adaptation stresses the previous 'shady' relationships between Mistress Quickly, Falstaff and Pistol so that

---

[11] This discussion relies on the AV recording, the score, and the prompt book.

she has a stronger reason to reject Falstaff and leave with Pistol in this musical as preparation for being married to him in *Henry V* (Doran 2006). Anne and Fenton have very little material in the play, but the adaptation gives them a stronger emotional journey as a counterpoint to the story of Falstaff and the Merry Wives. Englishby's score for *Merry Wives* is an eclectic mix including 'Tangos, Vaudeville and Big Band Jazz, all sewn together with Elizabethan twine' (Englishby, 2006). My own observation is that the structure of the narrative and the way it was presented has more in common with twentieth century pantomime and farce than contemporary musical theatre, but perhaps that merely demonstrates the derivation of so many aspects of British musical theatre from Shakespearean roots.

After the classic musical comedy overture a pantomime style set design of village houses outlined in a cartoon fashion is revealed within which, as the chorus sings the opening number, all the characters are introduced entering from the upstage entrances and walking down stage centre. Falstaff's entrance on a motorbike (shown in Fig. 2 with some of his companions from the ensemble) mirrors that of the Dame in many contempo-

Fig. 2 *Merry Wives: The Musical*, 2006. (Photo by Stewart Hemley. ©RSC)

rary pantomimes, though (s)he doesn't then perform an opening comedy routine. This style of presentation is intensely theatrical, acting as a reminder of the history of British musical theatre performance and directly referencing moments within it. The appearance in Act 2 of a pastoral masque in the woodland that appears to reference *A Midsummer Night's Dream* and the ballets of 1930s and 1940s musical theatre only adds to the sense of intertextual familiarity. Anne and Fenton are staged one on the balcony and the other below for their first duet—a reminder of *Romeo and Juliet* and its adaptation, *West Side Story*. That they sing together is symbolic of their true love as in the classic Hollywood and Broadway musicals, and that they sing lyrically in soprano and heroic tenor ranges also symbolises their position as thwarted lovers whose love will win through. By contrast the comic characters sing at the pitch and pace of speech in, for example, Falstaff's comic vaudeville routine with his servants in 'Falstaff's Plot' and Mistress Quickly's rhythmically interesting round robin routine 'I know her mind'. Mistress Quickly has an opportunity to express her response to Falstaff's lies and cheating in the lyrical 'Honeysuckle Villain' which adds complexity to her character. The songs for Ford are rather less successful, with a quite difficult and rather dull soliloquy for Ford that, despite some wonderful lyrics and an appropriate position in the first act reprised in the second, seems to be undecided as to its function.

Notwithstanding all these elements derived from pantomime and musical theatre, it is the opportunity for ensemble song and dance that really turns this piece into a musical comedy. Pistol's contribution to 'Canaries' turns into a big jazz style dance number, while the sequence of hiding Falstaff in the Buckbasket becomes a musical ensemble during which the farce is enacted, all the characters' themes are combined in an ensemble, and the whole concludes with a company song and dance. After a short entr'acte Act 2 begins with a song and dance routine set in the pub that begins colla voce, becomes 'Medium jazz-Loungey' and includes soft-shoe routines, stop time and even some acrobatic dancing before an applause-inducing finish. The farce of Act 2 is entirely musicalised in another ensemble tour-de-force, 'The Windsor Forest Quintet'. 'Merry Wives' is a hoedown that includes courtly dancing accompanied by the harpsichord as a nod towards the Elizabethan before turning into a riotous dance that includes a percussion section played on pots and pans. This song recurs as the Finale.

There is no question, as a result, that this is a musical or that it is fun, lively and entertaining, but as was noted by the *British Theatre Guide* reviewer, some of the singing and dancing is not of the highest standard, and some of the music is a little unmemorable (Orme 2006). While praising some of the performances, Charles Spencer of *The Telegraph* wrote that 'In one of the most eclectic scores I can recall we get soaring agonized love ballads a là Andrew Lloyd Webber, Elizabethan madrigals, echoes of Brecht-Weill, music hall turns and even a country and western hoedown with the company beating hell out of dustbins and saucepans' (Spencer 2006) and he did not intend those comments as a compliment. Michael Billington was even less enthusiastic about the eclecticism of the adaptation's music and design commenting that 'we are in a musical fantasy-land rather than in Shakespeare's world of simmering middle-class resentment' (Billington 2006).

One of the problems may be that despite the best intentions and the investment of time and money in the production the end result, while eclectic, energetic and entertaining, was rather dated in musical theatre terms, having more in common with pantomime than with what was happening in contemporary musical theatre. However, there is no suggestion that this musical was ever intended as any more than a Christmas amusement for the Stratford audience—a pantomime in all but name and audience interaction. More important to this discussion is the focus on ensemble practice. Although this production was not one of the musical theatre successes of the RSC, demonstrating some of the weaknesses in singing and dancing technique discussed above, the commitment to the ensemble within it is a feature that will be discussed further below.

Les Misérables (1985)[12]

Clearly there was something of a financial imperative that led to the RSC mounting the production of *Les Misérables*, but as noted above, Trevor Nunn's tastes in theatre were wide ranging and he saw no problem in mounting a musical at the RSC. Importantly, too, Victor Hugo's novel was a literary classic which fitted with the pattern of Christmas shows and musicals that had been developed in Stratford and London. Now at the

---

[12] For this section I referred to the prompt book and score for the RSC production. There were many changes made for the West End opening.

Barbican theatre there was the opportunity to rework the musical version of Victor Hugo's novel that had already been developed as a concept album in French (by Schönberg and Boublil with poet Jean-Marc Natel). A staging of the concept album took place in 1980 at the Palais des Sports in Paris where half a million people saw it during its 100 performances (Vermette 2007). Cameron Mackintosh was offered the show by a young Hungarian director, Peter Farago, but once he had listened to the album Mackintosh decided it would be perfect for Nunn, whom he had already worked with on *Cats*. Nunn, who was then artistic director of the RSC had worked with John Caird on the adaptation and direction of *Nicholas Nickelby* at the RSC—a similar epic story adapted from a nineteenth century novel—and brought him on board (Tims 2013). Nunn agreed to direct the production with Caird as co-director since they had developed a technique for adapting material during earlier collaborations (Behr 1989, 66). He also stipulated that the show must initially be presented at the Barbican as an RSC production. Mackintosh raised £300k to match the 'in kind' support of the RSC, with another £300k required for the transfer to the Palace Theatre (Nightingale and Palmer 2013, 20). This meant that the RSC would benefit from a possible West End transfer financially—in fact as a result of the success of the show a royalty would continue to be paid to the RSC for some years and was recorded as £19m in 2012 when the company was still receiving £400k annually (Nightingale and Palmer 2013, 20). Thus one of the significant consequences of this musical was that it improved the RSC's finances and continued to subsidise the company's less commercial ventures for many years.

From Mackintosh's point of view if a transfer to the West End transpired the show would have preview time as well as the kudos of the RSC opening and the word of mouth for advance sales. However, he was not convinced the RSC had a sufficiently experienced creative team for a full scale commercial musical, so he brought in sound designer Andrew Bruce, music supervisor, orchestrator and synthesiser programmer John Cameron and Martin Koch as MD. Designs were created by the team from the RSC's *Nicholas Nickelby*, lighting designer David Hersey, set designer John Napier and costume designer Adriane Neofitou. Napier was required to create a set that would fit the stage of the Palace Theatre where the show might move after the Barbican opening. The music staff at the RSC were part of the team too, one example being that the copyist was Peter Washtell, a regular timpanist and assistant MD at the London home of the RSC. He also played piano/synthesiser for the Barbican season and on the original cast recording, and in fact half the band of 20 were RSC regulars supplemented by a further 10 freelance players.[13] The additional cost of the sound fit up and sound operator for the 12 weeks at the Barbican amounts to what now seems a meagre £3050, though clearly that was a not inconsiderable extra cost at the time. Guy Woolfenden, in memos to the production manager, was concerned at this stage with all the nitty gritty of band calls, making space for the players, ensuring they had the correct equipment in the right places and the use of vans for transport. Many of the cast were also new to the RSC and were experienced commercial musical theatre singers, including Michael Ball as Marius, and Francis Ruffelle as Eponine, while RSC actors Alun Armstrong playing Thenardier, Roger Allam as Javert and Sue Jane Tanner as Madame Thenardier were the only three from the company whose singing was perceived to be strong enough for principal roles. The Irish tenor Colm Wilkinson was recruited to play Jean Valjean and the American Patti LuPone was brought in to play Fantine and all were required to sign 12 month contracts (Behr 1989, 71).

This co-production, using a combination of commercial know-how paired with the creativity and ensemble practices of the RSC, seemed to bring out the best in all participants, though there is evidence of some friction between the commercial company and the RSC company despite the planning committee being unanimously in favour of the project (Behr 1989, 67). As Behr comments: 'for all the RSC's classical theatre expertise and reputation, in-house musical theatre might be regarded by some of its members as a kind of light-hearted intermezzo, an end-of-term lark' (Behr 1989, 67).

The book and lyrics continued to be developed throughout the rehearsal period with lyrics by Herbert Kretzmer building on the poetic starting points provided by James Fenton. Nunn and Caird brought their experience of adaptation to bear so that the moral/religious battle between vengefulness and redemption was comprehensible through action as much as through the lyrics. As Mackintosh recalls, 'we went into rehearsal with what we thought was the finished script, but stuff kept being added or edited out. 'On My Own' was originally called 'L'Air de la Misère' and sung by Fantine; but the words didn't translate, and we didn't want

---

[13] There are notes in the Production Records at the RSC archive about concerns relating to the number of chairs and lit music stands as this was the biggest musical production the company had mounted.

Fantine singing two ballads back-to-back before expiring—so we rewrote it and gave it to Eponine' (Ibid.). Several songs were suggested by the cast to help develop their characters: 'Stars' was written because Roger Allam pointed out that his character, Javert, needed to express why he was so driven, and Beverley Klein[14] also recalls 'Stars' being written and 'hearing Claude-Michel sing it at the piano in the rehearsal room' (Klein 2017). Similarly Alun Armstrong felt Thenardier needed a song in the second half where 'Dog Eats Dog' subsequently appeared.

Rehearsals were conducted in the same fashion in which Nunn and Caird had undertaken the work on *Nicholas Nickelby*. Klein recalled the luxury of rehearsing for 12 weeks before opening night and even having a revolving stage in the rehearsal space to work on (Klein 2017): after six weeks, on 9 September, the cast of 27 moved into the old Astoria Theatre (hired for £1000 per week) to rehearse on the revolving stage in preparation for working on Napier's set. Both the length of rehearsal and the availability of parts of the set were unique to the subsidised sector and opera companies at the time (Klein 2017). The co-directors required their performers 'to immerse themselves in French history and ideas […] ensuring that the performers fully inhabited their characters' so that thoughts and feelings emerged into song (Nightingale and Palmer 2013, 25). A talk about Hugo, France and the novel began the rehearsals that Klein recalls as follows: 'I remember sitting around the table before we even began any form of improvisation, where we did research into aspects of the society of the time in France'. This followed the pattern Nunn and Caird had instituted with *Nicholas Nickelby* where the huge sprawling novels had to be unpicked 'cherry-picking how to tell the story very directly and dramatically … eliminat[ing] characters … eliminat[ing] whole passages of subplots and focus[ing] on what's going to carry your story forward' (Klein 2017).

The next stage of the process was that 'we did a lot of improvisation', starting off with basic exercises and games before improvising around the subject matter (Klein 2017). Exercises and improvisations were designed to allow performers to understand their characters, and the ensemble created entire background stories that meant that new material kept appearing. As Nunn recalls 'We extracted something like twenty paragraphs from the book which were descriptions of minor characters and we built up a series of individual improvisations, with people switching from one character to another, partly to get people to understand the nimbleness that

---

[14] Klein was an original cast member.

would be required of them as actors, to populate the scenes' (Behr 1989, 98). Later improvisations included developing the prologue sequence and, as those scenes and others were being created music was added based on the various themes. Klein recalled that 'Claude-Michel was writing music and they certainly were writing lyrics as we went along because Herbert Kretzmer was translating the lyrics that existed but also writing completely new sections' (2017). There were also constant changes to the material as it developed such that she remembers different versions of 'Do you hear the people sing'. The result of this rehearsal process is that a musical and physical language was developed by and with the ensemble that allowed for the rapid transformation between times and places, compressing the novel into a manageable length and many years and plot events into continuously moving company sequences. Jessica Sternfeld commented on this feature noting that the chorus 'as a group and in ever-changing subgroups, these several dozen players become one of the most important unifying features or "characters" of the show' (Sternfeld 2006, 205).

Some of these developments are apparent in the vocal score at the RSC's Stratford archive that is annotated throughout. On page 13, for example, there is an insert scrawled on paper and stuck into the score that contains melody and chord symbols to replace section K for Fantine. At the end of the number there are new lyrics written in, bars scribbled out or replaced and then a short play off to segue into the next song ('I Dreamed a Dream'), which is now the well-known introduction to the song, written in pencil. Other songs such as 'Lovely Ladies' are fairly complete since they existed in the previous production, but in many other places the accompaniment is signified by chord symbols once specific motifs and musical styles have been established, with shorthand symbols suggesting repetitions or instrumental doublings. Sternfeld analyses the song 'One Day More' and its reprises, references, motifs and new material at some length; an analysis that demonstrates the extraordinarily complex weave of vocal lines and materials that resulted from this working process and produced the momentum of the show and the number (Sternfeld 2006, 190–206). Frank Rich of the *New York Times* commented that 'this particular number summarized the show's accomplishments' as the various themes of the characters are all brought into 'an accelerating burst of counterpoint' (in Sternfeld 2006, 214). The show was further revised for its West End season, but the point is that these materials demonstrate the fluidity of the script and score and the contribution of all participants to the creative process. Such a process was much more unusual in the commercial musical theatre world where the shorter rehearsal time would have rendered this type of adaptation and devising impossible.

However, this resulted in one of the features of the show and the score that Sternfeld comments on—that 'the seams are often covered by Schönberg's virtually continuous orchestra that picks up a turn or motif and develops it, preparing the mood of the next scene' (Sternfeld 2006, 193). The result of this fluid use and reuse of motifs and thematic materials is that there is a sense of continuous evolution and organicism that arose at least in part from the extended period of improvisation and development and recalls the style of *Nicholas Nickelby*. Sheridan Morley, one of the reviewers who immediately praised the show, noted its organic nature 'which, rather than being structured in a way that set up and delivered hit songs, worked more like pieces of a puzzle' (Sternfeld 2006, 187). The combination of this musical language with the 'sweeping' construction of the plot and the almost cinematic ability of the production to race through time and space using the revolving stage to continue the momentum of music and action meant that the whole production had a seamless quality that was unique in musical theatre of the time. The impact of the RSC working practices altered the structure of this musical and had a profound effect on subsequent musical theatre.

By the time the show opened at the Barbican, previews had been greeted with standing and shouting, cheering, whistling, tears, and audiences jumping to their feet, but the reviews for the show that opened on 8 October 1985 were famously largely negative apart from Michael Coveney's review in the *Financial Times*, Benedict Nightingale's commentary in the *New Statesman* and a rave review from Sheridan Morley in *Punch*. Nightingale and Palmer speculate that a combination of cultural snobbery and the effrontery of the subsidised RSC and its artistic director for daring to tackle a commercial musical may have accounted for the critical opinion, but it was audience word of mouth and the queues at the box office that kept the show open through the Barbican run and again when the show transferred to the Palace Theatre on 4 December. By 2015 the show had been 'seen by more than 70 million people in 44 countries and in 22 languages around the globe, it is still breaking box-office records everywhere. The original London production celebrated its 30th anniversary on 8 October 2015'. (http://www.lesmis.com/uk/, Accessed 26 July 2016). Its success brought many people unfamiliar with the RSC into the theatre. The performance itself with its strength of acting, ensemble style performance and filmic design concept represented a transformational moment in musical theatre history, but it also set a pattern for a new form of creative process arising from the combination of commercial and RSC practices that arose because of Nunn's ability to 'bestride both musical form and theatre form like the colossus' (Klein June 2017).

The production model is one in which the entire production 'complete with full cast, orchestra, and revolving-barricade set' was required in new locations. This resulted from the team's desire for creative control, but also from their commitment to delivering 'the Broadway treatment, not a scaled-down version'. And as Sternfeld notes, 'Caird defended this practice on the basis that each new company had the chance to improvise and become familiar with the story, just as Nunn and Caird did with the original RSC cast' (Sternfeld 2006, 219). The devising process made possible by Arts Council subsidy and the collaborative rehearsal practices at the RSC, along with Cameron Mackintosh's business acumen, ultimately changed many aspects of musical theatre, including the production and marketing models. To stick to the theme of this book, though, it was the organic development process with musicians and singers that stimulated a new style of production that was seamless, sweeping and company based. Rather than inserting songs into a play the musical emerged as an organic whole whose story is told through the combination of art forms and the efforts of all the creative team and all the performers. Collaboration and community re-emerged as aesthetic qualities that arose from the company's previous collaborations with composers, musicians and sound designers, into the London working practice and then fed out in an extraordinary way into global musical theatre.

Matilda (2010)[15]

The second huge hit musical for the company was *Matilda the Musical*, which opened in 2010 at the temporary Courtyard Theatre. There had been a practice at the RSC for many years of producing literary adaptations as Christmas productions aimed at a family audience. The interesting thing about *Matilda*, though, is that it is not only a classic of children's literature, but also that the content of the plot revolves around

---

[15] For this discussion I refer to the AV recording and photographs from the Shakespeare Birthplace Trust archive, the live performance at Stratford, and the publicly available materials such as YouTube clips, vocal album, and CD.

storytelling, writing and genius, all of which are subjects that seem quite appropriate for the RSC (O'Neil 2016).

Whether these Christmas shows were plays with songs or musicals is something of a moot point since as has been noted above, that might rely on the amount of music, the narrative function of music, the aesthetic of the piece as a whole, the way dialogue and music are interwoven, the genre or contemporaneity of the music, or even the amount of underscore between songs. Aside from the question of what a musical is, Bruce O'Neil wondered whether the RSC is perhaps more self-conscious about singing and the term 'musical' than other companies. Noting that the most recent examples, *Matilda* and *Merry Wives* both have the tag *The Musical*, he speculates that it may be a concern of marketing departments that audiences should understand the nature of what they are coming to see (O'Neil 2016). More interestingly, this particular musical, like *Merry Wives* contains a number of features that reference the British pantomime tradition. In this case the evil Miss Trunchbull is played in drag as a Dame/villain, the Wormwood parents have the function of evil sidekicks in providing a catalyst for events, while Miss Honey is to all intents and purposes a good fairy and the story has a happy ending after the villain gets her comeuppance. Where the adaptation differs from pantomime is in the strength of the characters and particularly in the agency of Matilda, who, as heroine,[16] saves not only herself but the other children and even Miss Honey.[17]

A further feature, though, is the investment in the piece at its inception. Most RSC Christmas shows have a shorter gestation period from the commissioning of rights to a workshop before coming into rehearsal, but some productions may have been under discussion for two or three years before they arrive on stage (RSC 2009). In this case there was a sense that the show might have a further life and so the piece was given this long gestation period, even though in an interview Tim Minchin suggests that the show was only initially commissioned for a three-month run at Stratford (Minchin 2013). He believes that was important because of the intimacy it brought to the show: it was designed for a small theatre space in which the children in the audience were very close to those on the stage, and the important thing was to tell the story rather than to please a

---

[16] Robert Gordon refers to her as a kind of Fairy Godmother in Gordon, Jubin and Taylor *British Musical Theatre Since 1950* (London: Bloomsbury Methuen, 2016), 78.

[17] Whereas it has been argued that *Les Misérables* is an anti-feminist musical it could be argued that *Matilda* is rather more feminist with its leading (young female) character saving everyone.

diverse audience in a grand theatre. As he put it just before the opening of the show at Stratford, he was trying to write something entertaining and emotional, fun and funny, that takes people on a rollercoaster ride (Minchin 2011). For similar reasons of proximity to the audience he felt the need to maintain a sense of truth in the behaviour of the characters, in what and how they sing.

The reality of whether the show was intended only for the Stratford Christmas season or for a longer run elsewhere may be the difference between having a theatre booked and deposit paid (as with *Les Misérables*) or investing in a show with the hope of a further life but with no firm commitments. Whatever the understanding was for different members of the production team the RSC nurtured the project and invested in it over several years but it was written for a small theatre. This is an unusual combination of conditions that allowed the creative team to flourish without pressure.

It was Jeanie O'Hare, the dramaturg at the time, who brought the creative team together. She decided to approach Tim Minchin, though it was actually Matthew Warchus, the director, who had the first meeting with Minchin. It turned out that Minchin had considered writing a musical version of *Matilda* some 10 years earlier when writing children's shows in Australia (Minchin 2011). His abilities as a lyricist, composer and comedian gave added zest to the lyrics, and he was looking for the opportunity to do something theatrical. He was paired with writer Dennis Kelly and director Matthew Warchus who brought in his regular team of designer Rob Howell, lighting designer Hugh Vanstone and choreographer Peter Darling. Just like with Nunn and Mackintosh all those years before, the creative team had an established working relationship that facilitated the process.

Bruce O'Neil, who was MD for the production and who joined the project after the first workshop, remarked that the success of the piece was largely the result of Matthew Warchus' ability to structure a piece and to know how to make it work. 'No matter how good the material is you need someone who understands that' (O'Neil 2016). But the most important thing the RSC did was to give the production time. During this time there were several workshops that included showings to children (Kelly and Minchin 2011). The final workshop in July 2010 was a two-week workshop with a four piece band (piano, keyboards, kit and guitar) in which 'a cast of young people perform[ed] the latest draft of the script' (RSC 2010). The final workshop, which can be seen in Fig. 3, was still not a fully staged event, but what such workshops offer is the space and resources to

Fig. 3 *Matilda the Musical*, 2010. Workshop with band. (Photo by Manuel Harlan. ©RSC)

try out ideas. The limitation is that there can be no visual spectacle since the actors read or perform with scripts after a limited rehearsal period, but this makes it imperative to maintain the focus on story, and performing for young people ensures that the dramaturgy is effective for the intended audience. In many ways this process mirrors that of *Les Misérables*; it was developed by a creative team used to working together, and resulting from a long gestation and development process that included restructuring the material through a collaborative process of continuous evolution. It is different, however, in the series of workshops through which it was developed into a complete script and score, and that there was no commercial transfer booked. So the show was created for the intimacy of the Courtyard Theatre and only later scaled up for the Cambridge Theatre after an interruption from 30 January 2011—when the Stratford performances ended—until October 2011 when the West End version began. This process gave more flexibility and time for ideas to be nurtured as each workshop process was followed by thinking and revising time that also allowed the team to continue with other work. The lack of a fixed deadline in the early stages allowed the material to grow through an organic process and to be fitted into the performance schedule when everyone agreed the production was ready, and only when the show had a secure dramaturgical structure was it scaled up for the West End production.

During early discussions the idea of Matilda being a puppet was discussed, and in fact Kelly and Minchin joke about Matilda being either a puppet or even a robot in one of the online interviews (Kelly and Minchin 2011). Although this idea was apparently discussed in the early stages it was dismissed in favour of there being just one child in the show, who would play Matilda. It was not until the penultimate workshop that the idea was trialled of having Matilda's contemporaries also being child actors. Bruce O'Neil recalls that

> there were a few days in Clapham rehearsal rooms where we rehearsed one or two sequences including the opening sequence which is 'Miracle' with a bunch of kids. There was a meeting after the showing of that workshop and all the creative team... Denise Wood who is now a producer on the tour ... [went around] the room just canvassing opinion about how they felt about the idea of the children being in the cast. Without fail everyone was going, "Yes, we are onto something here this is really good. This actually works really well." You get that difference in scale. What Roald Dahl does brilliantly is see the world through the lens of a child, so that difference in scale where you have got teachers, big Trunchbull and then these tiny little kids standing next to them – it is just superb.

Although everyone agreed that it worked really well, the realisation began to dawn that using children would make the production much harder. It is one thing to put on a musical with a professional cast, but to have 10 children in the cast, which means you actually need 30 children working in cycles, was a very different logistical undertaking. But then there was a final workshop before rehearsals began (in Fig. 3), and 'it was clear that the material was fantastic, and, interestingly, the songs had not changed very much from Tim Minchin's early demos' (O'Neil 2016). This demonstrates the fluidity of the process and the organic nature of decision making that built the work around the core material.

Minchin's approach to writing is that each musical number needs to have a complete imaginary world in which the songs give the character something extra that they do not have on the page, and perhaps it is here that *Merry Wives* was less successful; since the characters, apart from Anne and Fenton, were already fleshed out there was little that the songs could add. The process for *Matilda* was that Dennis Kelly wrote a script that followed the atmosphere of Dahl's book then Minchin wrote songs to suit the mood of the script. He found it hard to write for Matilda herself because she is somewhat undemonstrative and unemotional as a character, so for the first two workshops she didn't have a song at all. Then he wrote the song 'Naughty' which 'brought her alive and made her a character who held her own destiny in her hands' (Minchin 2013); he wanted to communicate a sense of agency, that each person is responsible for changing their own story. As noted above, in a musical songs offer the opportunity for characters to reveal what drives them. Without a song Matilda's motivations and impulses would have been much less clear leaving her less clearly defined and appealing. The emotion Minchin wanted to inspire in audiences, and especially children, was a feeling of invigoration and defiance; that they could instigate change and act independently. He wanted to create a modern sensibility but within a musical theatre aesthetic rather than by using contemporary pop music with an anti-establishment style and message, especially in 'Revolting Children' (Minchin 2013).

It is in 'Revolting Children' too that the examination of the difference between sung and written words, the literary examination of the text, demonstrates Minchin's witty poeticism. The words 'We can S-P-L how we like' are anarchic, further confused by the overlaying of 'Why' and the letter 'Y', 'You' and 'U' before the final coup de grace, 'It is 2-L-8-4-U E-R-E-volting', all of which speak of a contemporary lyrical intelligence that seems appropriate to the work of this company.

Although Minchin said he focused on Kelly's script he had known the book very well since childhood and took influence both from the grotesque characters of Dahl and from the angularity and spikiness of Quentin Blake's drawings which inspired him to use broken and unexpected rhythms and intervals (Minchin 2013). In this sense there is a parallel with the inherently musical shape and texture of Shakespearean language. Dahl's language and Blake's drawings offer a stylistic theatricality that Minchin followed so as to maintain a certain cartoon or 'unreal' quality. Miss Trunchbull's song, for example, starts in 5/4 as a response to the drawings, but since she had been an Olympic hammer thrower hemmed in by the turning circle and the rules of competition she wanted to impose rules on everyone else—to the extent that it becomes equivalent to a religion for her (Ibid.). The refrain of her first song 'The hammer' sounds anthemic in a lyrical and regular 4/4 time with lyrical inserts in mock Latin. Elsewhere, unexpected time signatures and angular melodies make the songs just a little bit unexpected leaving the characters with distinctive representations that are immediately recognisable even when they are melded together to drive the plot.

Rather than having the character sing about her own evil and vengeful nature Miss Trunchbull sings about what inspires her (Minchin 2013), though she does refer to the children as 'little squits' even in her most lyrical moment. By contrast in 'The Smell of Rebellion' there is something of the poetic quality of language in the lyrics as Miss Trunchbull sings 'The smell of rebellion, the stench of revolt, the reek of insubordination, A whiff of resistance, the pong of dissent, the funk of mutiny in action' (Minchin 2011, 109–110). This demonstrates the metaphoric quality and witty use of language that drives character even while it connects the work to a poetic tradition.

It is not just the song lyrics that demonstrate continuity with the RSC's ongoing practice. The underscore contains repeated reference to thematic materials that are reprised as necessary to underpin the story organically. This material was developed at the rehearsal stage when Laurie Perkins, Christopher Nightingale and Bruce O'Neil worked collaboratively sitting around a piano during rehearsals. They played with the themes to develop underscore and links from Minchin's material. For example, the scenes are heavily underscored when Matilda is at the library talking to Mrs. Phelps and telling her a tale about an acrobat, his wife and a child (called the Acrobat stories). The thematic material links the four library scenes and then comes to a climax when Miss Trunchbull is finally confronted by the children. Miss Trunchbull is revealed not only as an evil headmistress but as the villain of the piece who has defrauded Miss Honey of her inheritance. Thematic and motivic repetitions help to drive the narrative and link together these characters' journeys giving them momentum (O'Neil 2016). At the same time the presence of music in these scenes means there is less of a jolt when characters break into song in other parts of the story. The overall style, while not in one musical genre, maintains a sense of coherence and thematic unity. Just as with *Les Misérables* the end result is a score that is not so much a series of songs as an essential and inseparable element in the dramaturgy. These features demonstrate the idea of a continuum; a certain desire for unity similar to that developed in *Les Misérables* and brought in by the orchestrator, arranger and MD.

This doesn't suggest a direct connection between the two musicals since they have completely different teams and processes, but that the desire for thematically driven music has become much more pervasive in composed musicals since *Les Misérables* and is similar to the kinds of strategies being used in other forms of theatre music and sound design at the RSC. This idea of a thematic and conceptual focus for a work is similar to that in *Macbeth* 1999 and 2011 discussed in "Collaborative Composition at the RSC", whose sound worlds construct a coherent musical dramaturgy for the productions. It could even be argued to demonstrate a continuum of musical practice with, for example, the scores of Gerhard in the late 1950s and 1960s, discussed in "Electronics, Sound and Fury at the RSC", that were unified either by thematic interactions or a sonic continuity.

O'Neil commented that it was not an accident that the show was a success—in his opinion 'the right people were approached to work on the right subject matter and they were given time to develop it properly' (O'Neil 2016). I would add that the collaborative nature of working at the RSC also may have contributed to the success of this production. As O'Neill remarked, 'someone pointed out to me recently that the RSC's hit rate of really quite successful musicals is remarkably high … but it wasn't by chance, it was completely deliberate and it worked because everything was achieved in the right way' (Ibid.). When the RSC chooses to make this investment and gives time to the right project it can be hugely successful, and obviously the global success of *Matilda* helps the RSC; the '*Matilda* bonus' is used to fund one-off projects or capital projects rather than ongoing costs since ultimately the show will close and the funds will disappear. Interestingly the RSC has just hosted Sarah Llewellyn under the auspices of the Cameron Mackintosh resident composer scheme managed by Mercury Musical Developments and Musical Theatre Network. Under this scheme an emerging composer has been based at the RSC for one year, where she had the opportunity to create music and songs for *Three Tales From Ovid* as well as writing music for several other projects. This is an exciting development that offered a creative opportunity for a new composer/sound designer to continue the evolution of theatre music and musical theatre.[18]

---

[18] Sarah Llewellyn's website contains information and a blog detailing some of the work she did during this attachment. It illustrates many of the practices outlined in the chapters above: http://www.tonal.org.uk/production/composer-residency-with-the-royal-shakespeare-company/ [Accessed 16.04.18].

Conclusion

Clearly what the RSC has achieved in *Matilda* is a brilliant entertainment whose utopian story appeals to children of all ages around the world, but how does this most recent global commercial success fit into the narrative of this book about music at the RSC? *Matilda* and *Les Misérables* are, of course, just two in a whole series of musicals produced by the company, most of which occupy a slightly different middle ground. Many of the others are not as innovative in terms of the musical theatre dramaturgy or the way the musical themes drive the narrative, but they nevertheless benefit from the ensemble practice at the RSC. The presence of these works in the RSC's canon, and the debates they inspire about the musicality of performance, the function of song and music and the development of ensemble practice in musical theatre suggest that it is at least theoretically possible to link all these works along a continuum of musical practice.

There are a series of different areas where the idea of a continuum can be identified: the production practices and focus on the ensemble has produced a performance style that leads to an integration of music, song and speech; the resources of the company mean that development periods can be extended to allow creators and performers to work together to produce a dramaturgically unified concept; musical scores become thematically or conceptually unified as a result of the investment in composition, workshop and rehearsal time and the involvement of regular teams; finally, to return to the discussion of lyricism and the poeticisation of space at the start of this chapter, there is a continuum of vocal practice from verse speaking to the rhythms and rhymes of song. It may be that the place where there is a gap in practice is in the vocal development and training for song and speech since musical theatre practitioners are brought in for big musicals and singers for featured songs in the plays as well as the musicals. Other areas that have been mentioned elsewhere in this book that retain a somewhat different practice between plays and musicals include the different levels of amplification and miking, placement of the sound desk, the numbers of musicians, and the concerns of the marketing department.

Clearly there are many individual factors that have led to the RSC producing two globally successful musicals, a number of nationally renowned musicals and hundreds of successful plays with music and songs, and the investment of time and resources has to be part of the picture. Crucially, though, as discussed in "Musical collaborations at the RSC", there is a sense of flow to which all parts of the organisation contribute and as a result of which no single moment or idea can be regarded as the originating or catalytic stimulus for the project. One of the most important things the RSC provides is the luxury of time and support to develop material whether through the workshop process of *Matilda* or the rehearsals of *Les Misérables*, and it is possible that only the subsidised theatres can support this type of development. It is notable that other substantial innovations in musical theatre writing in recent years, *London Road* and *Jerry Springer the Opera*, were produced at the other major subsidised venue The National Theatre after a similarly supported development process. The other factors that may have played into the success of these shows is the collaborative and ensemble nature of the working process in the rehearsal room that creates the possibility of fluid and driving narratives using music and song as integral parts of the process. This is no different from the process undertaken in creating *Nicholas Nickelby* or indeed Peter Brooks' production of *A Midsummer Night's Dream*; it has simply been applied to sung works. Music drives both types of work, using the fluid transformation of themes to drive narrative whether in song or as underscore, for theatrical distancing or immersion. All this relies on a fundamentally strong system of collaboration at the heart of the organisation that is stimulated by the presence of freelance professionals alongside a core team, and a structure within which creativity can thrive.

Epilogue

> But this rough magic
> I here abjure; and, when I have requir'd
> Some heavenly music—which even now I do,—
> To work mine end upon their senses that
> This airy charm is for, I'll break my staff,
> Bury it certain fathoms in the earth,
> And, deeper than did ever plummet sound, I'll drown my book.
> *The Tempest* Act 5, Sc. i

Last night I attended *The Tempest* again, this time at the Barbican where Gregory Doran's production (2016, music by Paul Englishby, sound by Jeremy Dunn and Andrew Franks) had transferred after its Stratford season.[1] In many ways it represents a summation of the themes addressed in this book: the music and sound worlds were almost inseparable as entities and both were embedded in the physical, live and computer generated world of the island. Ariel wore a suit that transmitted an avatar augmenting his physicality while his voice was amplified and processed through microphones with added reverberation, accompanied by music and sound from instruments and voices. The magical Ariel was a combination of live and digitally created visual imagery and sounds. It was clearly not possible

---

[1] Alongside the live performance I had access to the CD of this production and the publicly available YouTube promotional materials.

© The Author(s) 2018
M. Taylor, *Theatre Music and Sound at the RSC*, Palgrave Studies in British Musical Theatre,
https://doi.org/10.1007/978-3-319-95222-2_7

to speak about music separate from sound, or indeed separate from the visual and physical aspects of this immersive production.

There are some practical or material considerations that can be outlined on a factual level. In this production there are three songs sung by Ariel, 'Come unto these yellow sands', 'Full fathom five thy father lies' and 'Where the bee sucks', an unaccompanied chant for Caliban and a round for the unholy drunken trio of Stephano, Trinculo and Caliban, and a wedding masque that provides the opportunity for formal music.[2] These sung moments, the vocal qualities with which they are sung and the music that accompanies them, demonstrate the relative status of the characters through a combination of musical style, sound quality and the effects used in producing them.

Ariel's voice is enhanced by digital echo effects to make it sound 'other worldly' and possibly to correct pitch, and his melody accompanied by a low flute (useful if an actor is not a trained singer in thickening the sound and making it more melodious, holding the performer in tune and maintaining the sense of a 'natural' voice). Thus there is a combination of the issues of sung performance discussed in "From *Macbeth* to *Matilda* at the RSC" above with the use of digital sound manipulation and sound design discussed in "Collaborative Composition at the RSC" that together result in a performance that is other worldly and magical and whose processed sound complements the visual projection seen in Fig. 1. Ariel is a computer generated avatar as well as a live performer and his voice similarly explores the continuum of the live and the processed.[3]

The first song, 'Come unto these yellow sands', begins with the tinkling sounds that presage the fairy world and there are bell sounds in the keyboard/percussion accompaniment to maintain this sense of a magical world. The melody itself is quite simple but accompanied by a rich texture of keyboards, bells, flutes and whistles that give the song something of a folk feel. However, the song is in no way like folk music because of the combination of keyboard, bell, flute, whistle and voice sounds and the electronic processing and echo effects that transform them all. Then the spirits onstage sing and dance with Ariel, an effect further enhanced by

---

[2] Some of the music including Ariel's three songs and part of the masque are available on the recording *The Tempest: Music & Speeches* (RSC Enterprise Limited, 2016). RSCE 016.

[3] The performer wears a special body suit that transmits gestures via a computer to the computer generated avatar projected above him that mirrors his physical movements at a larger scale.

EPILOGUE 219

Fig. 1 *The Tempest*, 2017. Ariel and his avatar. (Photo by Topher McGrillis. ©RSC)

the two sopranos whose amplified voices are heard from the band box. Each voice enters separately in imitation of the melodic motif creating the effect of a canon of very high echoing voices that combine with the rest of the music as the song takes off into a magical, high pitched, constantly shifting texture. The signifiers include the polyphonic vocal music of Elizabethan England; the folk-like timbres of whistles, voices and flutes; the magic of fairy bells; and the echoing enhancement of the digital present. The overall effect is to create a context for the performance that contains signifiers of magic, otherness and the historical context in a contemporary computerised present that draws the audience into an immersive experience of the magical world of the island.

The second song, 'Full Fathom Five' follows, in which Ariel's voice is placed much lower in his vocal range, perhaps to signify the depths of the oceans within which Ferdinand's father is lost or to echo a dirge or funeral march. The song begins with the strumming of a guitar pitched low as a kind of tolling over which the modal melody meanders. Melismatic phrases stretch individual syllables of the melody over several notes as a reminder of the ornamented cadenzas of the early baroque period. A slow steady pulse is created by the tolling guitar, to which is added the voices of the spirits singing the 'ding dongs' of the death knell. Then a three part round begins that restates the first lines of the song over which the sopranos sustain a rhythmically augmented phrase. The composer has arranged it so that there is a gradual increase in the number of sounds, their different colours, their rhythmic individuality and their spatial diversity to build the song to a climax. Like Ariel's other songs and the moments of magic in the show, this song has a dramatic structure and development produced through increasing complexity rather than through tonal harmony. Instead the music appears to hang, directionless, in the air; the 'sweet airs' of the isle. Rather than the structures of tonal harmony being used to create the musical climax it is the accretion of sounds and themes that accomplishes this task—a feature that relates to the ways in which sound design and sound timbre as well as atonality and minimalism have affected music composition in the last 50 or 60 years.

The third of Ariel's songs, 'Where the bee sucks', occurs as a celebration in Act V, and while livelier and happier contains similar signifying material. Elements of these magical sounds then feed out into the world whenever magic occurs, and in this production it occurs frequently since much of the design is created through projections and the avatar of Ariel. For all of these songs Ariel's voice is manipulated as a result of discussions between the music and sound departments about who would trigger the effects and what level of digital sound should be created (Dunn 2016). As a result of pitch correction technology voices can have chorus effects added expanding them into harmony, but simply using pitch correction adds a level of sonic digitisation that when overdone might 'sound like a dalek' or like 'Cher singing 'If You Believe''' (Ibid.). The sound department and the composer were exploring the possibilities of vocal manipulation at the time I spoke to them, as well as deciding whether many other elements of the show were to be created by sound effects or music. Dunn and his colleague Andrew Franks were at that time contemplating introducing a continuous underscore of 'drones' or to use Woolfenden's word, undertow, that would transform for different locations/characters but would unite the island's ambient world.

This is clearly apparent in the production when, for example, Caliban chants unaccompanied except by his own stamping 'No more dams I'll make for fish'. The song signifies his lower status through the raucous voice of the performer's delivery and demonstrates his lack of magic power to generate musical accompaniment. Nonetheless there is a sonic environment within which he performs. The catch—a three part round common in the Elizabethan period and after—to the words 'Flout 'em and Scout 'em' sung by the drunken Stephano, Trinculo and Caliban is interesting because it is a polyphonic style of singing that was popular in the Elizabethan period. Even as recently as the late nineteenth century Gilbert and Sullivan wrote a catch for the ordinary seamen of *HMS Pinafore* though it was used there to signal the incongruity of their courtesy and their labour. Here too, the vocal roughness and the lack of accompaniment signifies that these men are the lower orders—the workers and the drunkards—while they nonetheless are sufficiently educated or enchanted that they sing a round in their drunken pleasure. Thus the vocal and musical aesthetics signify something of the background of the characters, the history of the play, while the lack of musical accompaniment also suggests their status on the island.

The other substantial sung performance is the wedding masque that Prospero conjures for his daughter and Ferdinand, in which Ceres, Iris and Juno appear accompanied by the spirits. This scene revels in the excessive operatic voices of the two sopranos and intertextually references the Elizabethan and Jacobean development of the masque as a courtly allegory on a classical theme that was sung and danced as entertainment at the courts of Tudor and Stuart monarchs. In this song there is a bed of accompanying sound provided by the orchestral pads on the keyboards and the magic bells of the percussion, while the voice is echoed by flute and accompanied by harp before the two soloists begin a duet to bless the marriage. Clearly, the gods have the best voices, singing in high pitched perfection, referencing the aristocratic in the new (in the Jacobean period), high-flown styles of music and incorporating the atmospheric effects of the latest (in the contemporary period) digital processing technology.

The sound team were also exploring new types of reverb such as 'Convolution' to create 'texturised noises' such as the creaking of wood for the ship and shipwreck, and the sound of flames for when Ariel dismisses the feast since the magic in this play 'get[s] sound designers excited' (Dunn 2016). As Dunn described it, 'sound and lighting creates a context, it gives you a warning of what's about to happen, it tells you how to react'. As has been seen in the previous chapters such uses of musical and sonic signifiers that work in partnership with the visual action and design have developed exponentially throughout the period of this study, but the ways in which those signifiers have been produced is only one part of the story of theatre music and sound at the RSC.

In the course of the preceding chapters the practical working processes have been documented, noting the ways in which changes in musical practice and the development of sound technology have led to changes in the way theatre music and sound is made, and thus how the composite of music and sound interacts with the visual elements of performance. As a consequence theatre music and sound have developed strategies for becoming more immersive and less noticeable as they manipulate the relationship between audiences and performance. Meanwhile the liveness of music has effects not only on audiences but on performers, altering the dynamic shape of performances while offering opportunities to break the fourth wall and promote the theatricality of an event. Many of these aspects of music's performance have not changed except insofar as signification exists within culture and so develops alongside creators' and performers' experiences of a changing global context.

Much more fundamental have been the developments in technology and physical infrastructure that have reduced the isolation of the theatre in the Midlands. Musicians and creators can now easily commute to Stratford and retain freelance careers rendering the earlier continuity of staff less marked and the opportunities for collaboration potentially more expensive and unpalatable for musicians. Jeremy Dunn remarked on how many productions the RSC now produces, the amount of technology being used, and the numbers of musicians involved, commenting that consequently the level of collaboration in rehearsal has been significantly reduced since the time Woolfenden was music director, albeit for entirely practical reasons (2016). Meanwhile the increased reliance on technological support including click tracks and digital enhancement of sound has changed the aesthetic quality from fallible and acoustic liveness to the distance of perfect recorded quality even when played live.

What are the consequences of such changes on the ways in which music and sound work together with the visual elements of theatre to create a total experience? Working practices have changed for musicians, as well as the amplification and digitisation of the types of sounds they produce. Over the same period sound design has appeared and, as was noted in *The Tempest*, has become a pervasive element in the environmental ambience of a production, almost to the extent of immersion. As a result of the increasing digitisation of sound and music it is possible that the individuality of musical and vocal tone have been reduced, and that the relative impact of individual musicians as performers is no longer so great or so important—that is certainly true of *The Tempest* though perhaps less so of other productions where musicians continue to appear onstage and to interact with actors and audiences. On the other hand the amount of music and sound has increased exponentially since it became possible to control volume and blend texture within the overall aesthetic of a production. Thus an element of control in performance has shifted from the composer and MD to the sound designer and operator within what remains a creative collaboration, and the effects of liveness have been somewhat reduced.

In the midst of this there is the company itself that has professionalised and commercialised its output in order to generate the income required to produce consistently high quality innovative productions, to maintain its investment in the theatre infrastructure, and to become a global brand. Yet despite all these historical and practical changes in circumstances music has remained a feature of the experience of performance at the RSC. Throughout more than half a century of productions music and sound have remained absolutely integral, and it is the story of the contribution of music and sound to an audio-visual theatre that this study documents. Although the processes and practices continue to change, and have already evolved still further during the time of this writing, the presence in such an important theatre nationally and globally of a continuous focus on the development of the aural world demonstrates the extent to which theatre music and sound are fundamental to the way audiences attend and experience theatre. Many of the discussions in this book focus on the pragmatic questions of how music and sound operate in theatre; how they manipulate attention, structure time and space within socio-historical contexts and collaborative processes, but the arguments demonstrate the importance of theatre music. What this book shows is that performances at the RSC are now considered as interdisciplinary totalities with which audiences interact. That total experience relies on music and sound that communicates, affects, and transforms audiences, who are encouraged to stretch themselves and to attend to the nature of perception (Home Cook 2015, 172) as they listen in to the audio-visual performance of theatre.

To return to the questions I posed at the start of this study that began with the pragmatic and ventured towards the philosophical: what are the practical working processes within which live and recorded, onstage and offstage music performance have been produced since the inception of the RSC in 1961? What are the consequences of developments and alterations in these processes for creative teams, performers and audiences? How has the development of sound design and the collaboration of sound and music changed the way music and sound signify in performance? Have the functions of theatre music and sound altered as a consequence? Can the vocal sound of performers be excluded from a discussion of sound and music, and if not, where are the limits of the sound world? Later I questioned whether there might be a continuum of practice between theatre music and music theatre.

In the course of this book we have seen how changes to working practices affected process and the consequence of technology on aesthetics. This has not been seen at any stage as a value judgement but a document of evolution, one that probably has parallels across many art-forms and in offices and workplaces everywhere. The idea of collaboration, though, has been fundamental to the discussions in this book, and it seems that, although collaboration continues across the departments and disciplines and in the rehearsal rooms of the RSC, the opportunities for musicians to be part of a lively collaborative experimentation might have diminished. Nonetheless the functions of music and sound, in scores now created (and sometimes at least partially recorded) by composers and sound designers, have been retained. The aural world created by composers and realised in the performance of musicians and sound designers contributes to the clarity of dramaturgical concepts, to theatricality or immersion, to atmosphere and affect, to context and hierarchy, to perceptions of time and space. The voices of performers have changed through training within the RSC and (although not documented here) without, as has the freedom of composers to adapt or create lyrics, move songs between performers and develop vocal performances from beyond the characters in the narrative, mixing intertextual references and using popular genres.

Finally there is the question of whether the poetic space of Shakespearean production is really so far removed from the musical space of the musical theatre. I have argued, for all the reasons outlined in "From *Macbeth* to *Matilda* at the RSC", that the ensemble nature of production, the rhythms and rhymes of language and the dynamic structures of performance, are not so different across the spectrum of theatre forms, and that Shakespearean language in particular lends itself to this comparison. There are historical and cultural practices that separate these types of performances that include the concerns of marketing, the investment in amplification, the availability of singing actors, the requirement for more musicians and possibly a more integrated musical score, but the ensemble production, the collaborative process and the dramaturgical and atmospheric drive of music and sound are really not so different.

Some things that have been most surprising during this research are the consistent investment of the company in an audio-visual continuum to most effectively represent the dramaturgical perception of a work; the ideas about the musicality of language, structure and performance, and the poeticisation of space; the sense of collaborative flow in development and performance; and the possibility that the RSC, that has never advertised itself as an innovative institution for music production, may have provided a catalyst not only for innovations in theatre music and musical theatre but also for the development of actor-musicianship.

Now, as Prospero suggests, it is time to drown this book—or at least resolve that it is done and commit it to the uncertain waters of publication and interpretation, simply exhorting readers as Lorenzo does Jessica in *The Merchant of Venice*: to mark the music.

BIBLIOGRAPHY

Addenbrooke, David. *The Royal Shakespeare Company*. London: Kimber and Co, 1974.
Adkins, Monty and Russ, Michael (eds). *The Roberto Gerhard Companion*. Farnham: Ashgate, 2013.
Ansorge, Peter. 'Interview with Peter Brook', *Plays and Players*. October 1970.
Auden, W. H. *The Dyer's Hand*. London: Vintage, 1962.
Beauman, Sally. *The Royal Shakespeare Company's Centenary Production of Henry V*. Oxford: Pergamom Press, 1976.
Beauman, Sally. *The Royal Shakespeare Company: A History of Ten Decades*. Oxford: Oxford University Press, 1982.
Behr, Edward. *Les Misérables: History in the Making*. London: Jonathan Cape, 1989.
Berry, Cicely. *Voice and the Actor*. London: Harrap, 1973.
Bohme, Gernot. 'The art of the stage set as a paradigm for an aesthetics of atmospheres'. Ambiances [Online] 10 February 2013. URL: http://ambiances.revues.org/315
Brook, Peter. *The Quality of Mercy*. New York: Theatre Communications Group, 2014.
Brown, Ross. *Sound: A Reader in Theatre Practice*. Basingstoke: Palgrave Macmillan, 2010.
Bruce, Michael. *Writing Music for the Stage*. London: Nick Hern Books, 2016.
Carroll, William C. (ed). *The Two Gentlemen of Verona*. The Arden Shakespeare, Third Series. London: Thompson Learning, 2004.

Chambers, Colin. *Inside the Royal Shakespeare Company*. London: Routledge, 2004.
Chion, Michel. *Audio-Vision*. New York: Columbia University Press, 1990.
Collison, David. *Stage Sound*. London: Studio Vista, 1976.
Collison, David. *The Sound of Theatre: A History*. Eastbourne: PLASA Ltd, 2008.
Cross, Ian. 'Music and Communication in Music Psychology.' *Psychology of Music* 42(6), (2014), 809–19. Available at http://www-personal.mus.cam.ac.uk/~ic108/PDF/PoM%20Nordof-Robbins.pdf [Accessed 19.01.16].
Csepregi, Gabor. 'On Sound Atmospheres.' in Jim Drobnick (ed), *Aural Cultures*. Toronto: YYZ Books, 2004.
Curtin, Adrian. 'Designing Sound for Shakespeare: Connecting past and present' in John Brown and Stephen di Benedetto (eds), *Designer's Shakespeare*. London: Routledge 2016, 152–69.
Darnley, Lyn. 'Artist Development and Training in the Royal Shakespeare Company'. PhD Dissertation, Royal Holloway University of London, 2013.
Gorbman, Claudia. *Unheard Melodies*. Bloomington and Indianapolis: Indiana University Press, 1987.
Gordon, Robert, Jubin, Olaf and Taylor, Millie. *British Musical Theatre Since 1950*. London: Bloomsbury Methuen, 2016.
Home-Cook, George. *Theatre and Aural Attention: Stretching Ourselves*. London: Palgrave Macmillan, 2015.
Hosley, Richard. 'Was there a Music-Room in Shakespeare's Globe?' *Shakespeare Survey* 13, (1960), 113–23.
Irigaray, Luce. 'The Property Model' in Colin Counsell and Laurie Wolf (eds), *Performance Analysis*. London and New York: Routledge, 2001.
Kaye, Deena and Lebrecht, James. *Sound and Music for the Theatre* (3rd ed). Burlington MA: Elsevier, 2009.
Kendall, George R. 'Sir Barry Jackson and Stratford-upon-Avon, 1945–1948'. PhD Dissertation, University of Birmingham, 1981.
King, Helen Cole. 'The Echo from Within: The Role of Stage Music in Peter Brook's Performance of Shakespeare.' *Contemporary Theatre Review* 18(4), (2008), 412–424.
Knowles, Richard Paul. 'Shakespeare, Voice, and Ideology: Interrogating the Natural Voice' in James C. Bulman (ed.), *Shakespeare, Theory, and Performance*. London: Routledge 1996, 92–112.
Lehmann, Hans-Thies. *Postdramatic Theatre*. Trans. Karen Jürs-Munby. London and New York: Routledge, 2006.
Leonard, John A. *Theatre Sound*. London: A & C Black, 2001.
Levitin, Daniel. *The World in Six Songs*. New York: Plume, Penguin Group, 2009.
Lindley, David. *Shakespeare and Music*. London: Bloomsbury, 2006.
Llano, Samuel. 'Roberto Gerhard, Shakespeare and the Memorial Theatre' in Monty Adkins and Michael Russ (eds), *The Roberto Gerhard Companion*. Farnham: Ashgate, 2013, 107–130.

MacDonald, Laura. 'Sometimes you have to make a little bit of mischief.' *Studies in Musical Theatre* 6(3), (2012), 355–362.
Manifold, J.S. *The Music in English Drama from Shakespeare to Purcell.* London: Rockliff, 1956.
McMillin, Scott. *The Musical as Drama.* Princeton and Oxford: Princeton University Press, 2006.
Merleau-Ponty, Maurice. *Phenomenology of Perception.* London and New York: Routledge Classics, 2002.
Morley, Sheridan. *The Great Stage Stars: Distinguished theatrical careers of the past and present.* London: Angus & Robertson, 1986.
Nancy, Jean-Luc. *Listening.* New York: Fordham University Press, 2007.
Naylor, Edward. *Shakespeare and Music.* New York: Da Capo Press and Benjamin Blom, Inc. 1965 [1931].
Niebur, Louis. *Special Sound.* Oxford and New York: Oxford University Press, 2010.
Nightingale, Benedict and Palmer, Martyn. *Les Misérables: From Stage to Screen.* London: Carlton Books, 2013.
Peaslee, Richard. *A Midsummer Night's Dream.* Score. Magellan Music Ltd., 1974.
Poizat, Michel. *The Angel's Cry: Beyond the Pleasure Principle in Opera.* Trans Arthur Denner, Ithaca, NY: Cornell University Press, 1992.
Quayle, Anthony. *The Sphere* 8 March 1952, Reprinted as Director's Note in Festival Season Programme, 1952.
Rodenburg, Patsy. *Speaking Shakespeare.* London: Methuen, 2005.
Roesner, David. *Musicality in Theatre: Music as Model, Method and Metaphor.* London: Routledge, 2014.
Roesner, David P. and Curtin, Adrian (eds). 'Sounds Good': Special double issue. *Theatre and Performance Design*, Vol. 2. London: Routledge, 2016.
Roesner, David P. and Kendrick, Lynne (eds). *Theatre Noise. The Sound of Performance* Newcastle: Cambridge University Scholars, 2011.
Roesner, David P. and Rebstock, Matthias (eds). *Composed Theatre. Aesthetics, Practices, Processes* Bristol: Intellect, 2012.
Sawyer, R. Keith. *Group Creativity: Music, Theater, Collaboration.* New York and London: Routledge, 2003. e-book.
Schafer, R. Murray. *The Soundscape: Our sonic environment and the tuning of the world.* [*The Tuning of the World.* New York: Knopf, 1977]. New York: Destiny Books, 1994.
Sekacz, Ilona. 'Composing for the Theatre.' *Contemporary Music Review* 11(1 & 2), (1994), 261–66.
Selbourne, David. *The Making of A Midsummer Night's Dream.* London: Methuen, 1982.
Settle, Ronald. *Music in the Theatre.* London: Herbert Jenkins, 1957.
Smith, Bruce R. *The Acoustic World of Early Modern England: Attending to the O-Factor.* Chicago and London: The University of Chicago Press, 1999.

States, Bert O. *Great Reckonings in Little Rooms: On the phenomenology of theatre*. Berkeley: University of California Press, 1987.
Stern, Tiffany. *Making Shakespeare: The Pressures of Stage and Page*. London: Routledge, 2004.
Sternfeld, Jessica. *The Megamusical*. Bloomington: Indiana University Press, 2006.
Taylor, Millie and Symonds, Dominic. *Studying Musical Theatre*. London: Palgrave, 2014.
Van Kampen, Claire. 'Music and Aural Texture at Shakespeare's Globe' in Carston, Christie and Karim-Cooper, Farah (eds), *Shakespeare's Globe: A theatrical Experiment*. Cambridge: Cambridge University Press, 2008, 79–100.
Vermette, Margaret. *The Musical World of Boublil and Schoenberg*. London: Applause Books, 2007.
Warren, Roger, ed. *The Two Gentlemen of Verona*. The Oxford Shakespeare. Oxford: Oxford University Press, 2008.
Weiner, Albert. 'The Function of the Tragic Greek Chorus'. *Theatre Journal* 32(2), (1980), 205–212.
Wells, Stanley and Gary Taylor (eds). *William Shakespeare: A Textual Companion* (Revised ed.). Oxford: Oxford University Press, 1997 [1987].
Wells, Stanley, Taylor, Gary, Jowitt, John and Montgomery, William (eds). *The Oxford Shakespeare: The Complete Works* (2nd ed.). Oxford: Oxford University Press, 2005 [1986].
Willett, John (Ed. and Trans.). *Brecht on Theatre*. London: Eyre Methuen, 1974.
Wilson, Christopher R. 'Shakespeare and Early Modern Music' in Wray, Ramona et al. (eds), *The Edinburgh Companion to Shakespeare and the Arts*. Edinburgh: Edinburgh University Press, 2011.
Woolfenden, Guy. 'The Composer – Guy Woolfenden' in Sally Beauman (ed), *The Royal Shakespeare Company's Centenary Production of Henry V*. Pergamom Press, 1976, 46–51.
Zuccarini, Carlo. 'The (Un)Pleasure of Song: On the Enjoyment of Listening to Opera' in Dominic Symonds and Millie Taylor (eds), *Gestures of Music Theater: The Performativity of Song and Dance*. Oxford and New York: Oxford University Press, 2014, 22–36.

Audio-Visual and Sound Recordings

A Shakespeare Celebration. CD. Chandos Digital: CHAN9812, 2000.
Cymbeline: Music and Speeches. CD. RSC Enterprises: RSCE014, 2016.
Henry IV Parts I & II: Music and Speeches. CD. RSC Enterprises: RSCE 004, 2014.
Hess, Nigel. 'Interview with Nigel Hess.' *Much Ado About Nothing Or Love's Labour's Won*. DVD. Opus Arte: OA 1193 BD, 2015.
John Woolf and Friends: Music for the RSC. CD. RSC Enterprises, 2011.

Love's Labour's Lost: Music and Speeches. CD. RSC Enterprises: RSCE 007, 2014.
Love's Labour's Lost. DVD. Royal Opera House Enterprises Ltd: OA1185D, 2015.
Love's Labour's Won: Music and Speeches. CD. RSC Enterprises: RSCE 008, 2014.
Love's Labour's Won. DVD. Royal Opera House Enterprises Ltd: OA1186D, 2015.
Matilda. Original Cast Recording. CD. RSC Enterprises: RSCE 002, 2010.
Macbeth. DVD. FremantleMedia: FHED1776, n.d.
Merry Wives: The Musical. CD. RSC Enterprises, 2006.
Richard II: Music and Speeches. CD. RSC Enterprises: RSCE 003, 2013.
Sweet Swan of Avon. CD. Meridian: CDE84301, 1995.
Tagg, Philip. *Kojak: 50 Seconds of Television Music* (Towards the Analysis of Affect in Popular Music). Vol. 2. Gothenburg: Studies from the Department of Musicology, 1979.
The Merchant of Venice. DVD. Royal Opera House Enterprises Ltd: OA 1202D, 2016.
The Songs of Ariel. From the 1978 Royal Shakespeare company production of *The Tempest*. CD. Ariel Music, 1978.
The Tempest: Music and Speeches. CD. RSC Enterprises: RSC 016, 2016.
The Winter's Tale. DVD. Heritage Theatre Ltd and Royal Shakespeare Company, n.d.
Two Gentlemen of Verona. DVD. Opus Arte: OA1168D, 2015.
Two Gentlemen of Verona: Music and Speeches. CD. RSC Enterprises: RSCE 005, 2014.

Archival References and Online Reviews

ACGB. 'RST Balance Sheet' 2nd December 1972. Arts Council of Great Britain (ACGB) papers, V&A Theatre Archive.
Barnett, Laura. 'Cicely Berry, Voice coach to the stars.' *The Guardian*, 24 July 2011. https://www.theguardian.com › Arts › Stage › Royal Shakespeare Company 24 July 2011 [Accessed 23 April 2017].
Billington, Michael. 'Matilda – review'. *The Guardian*, 10 December 2010. http://www.guardian.co.uk/stage/2010/dec/10/matilda-musical-review. [Accessed 23 September 2016].
Billington, Michael. 'Merry Wives: The Musical'. *The Guardian*, 13 December 2006. https://www.theguardian.com/stage/2006/dec/13/theatre.rsc. [Accessed 21 August 2017].
Billington, Michael. '*Two Gentlemen of Verona/Julius Caesar*'. *The Guardian*, 22 October 2004.
Curtis, Nick. 'Playing it for Laughs: A Midsummer Night's Dream Barbican.' *Standard*, 27 April 1995.
Dickson, Andrew. 'Trevor Nunn: A Life in Theatre.' *The Guardian*, 18 November 2011. https://www.theguardian.com/stage/2011/nov/18/trevor-nunn-life-in-theatre. [Accessed 26 April 2017].

Duncan-Jones, Katherine 'Fit but not fitting'. *TLS*, 12 August 1994.
Eyre, Richard. 'Sir Peter Hall: Godfather of British theatre turns 80.' *The Independent*, 19 November 2010. http://www.independent.co.uk/arts-entertainment/theatre-dance/features/sir-peter-hall-godfather-of-british-theatre-turns-80-2137729.html. [Accessed 26 April 2017].
Griffith, David. *David Munrow: Pied Piper.*http://www.davidmunrow.org/biography.htm. Website updated 27 September 2014. [Accessed 12 February 2016].
Kelly, Dennis and Minchin, Tim. *Matilda the Musical.* RSC, 12 September 2011. https://www.youtube.com/watch?v=RR5bUzf1JVc. [Accessed 10 June 2017].
Koenig, Rhoda. 'Dreaming Colour' *Independent*, 5 August 1994.
Minchin, Tim. *Making Matilda, Episode 2: Composer Tim Minchin on Tapping into Everybody's Inner Child*. Broadway.Com, April 2013. https://www.youtube.com/watch?v=_thmK0qVzNY. [Accessed 10 July 2017].
Minchin, Tim. *Interview with Tim Minchin – Matilda the Musical*. RSC, 12 September 2011. https://www.youtube.com/watch?v=qaDSSszB92A. [Accessed 10 July 2017].
Munrow, David. 'Biography' http://www.davidmunrow.org/biography/. [Accessed 16 February 2016].
Musicians' Union. 'Agreement between the Royal Shakespeare Company and the Musicians' Union 2013'. http://www.musiciansunion.org.uk/getattachment/f44b4416-880d-4af7-9388-7a1df27434b3/.aspx. [Accessed 25 January 2016].
Musicians' Union. 'Minutes of the Midland District Council.' 4 October 1970.
Musicians' Union. 'Minutes of NEC November 1962.' Musicians' Union Archive, Stirling University.
Orme, Steve. 'Merry Wives the Musical' *British Theatre Guide*, 2006.http://www.britishtheatreguide.info/reviews/RSCmerrywives-rev. [Accessed 21 August 2017].
RSC. 'Bringing a Production to Life' *RSC Information Sheet*, January 2009.
RSC. *RSC Members' News.* September 2010.
Spencer, Charles 'Trying too hard to be merry' *The Telegraph*, 13 December 2006. http://www.telegraph.co.uk/culture/theatre/drama/3657104/Trying-too-hard-to-be-merry.html. [Accessed 21 August 2017].
Tims, Anna. 'How We Made *Les Misérables*' *The Guardian*. Tuesday 19 February 2013. https://www.theguardian.com/stage/2013/feb/18/how-we-made-les-miserables. [Accessed 03 July 2017].

Interviews and Emails

Brown, Richard. Interview, National Theatre Foyer, London, 12 September 2014.
Brown, Stephen. Telephone interview, 14 December 2015.
Butler, David G. Email exchange, January 2016.

Collison, David. Email exchange, March 2016.
Dunn, Jeremy. Interview, Sound office at RSC, 3 August 2016.
Hess, Nigel. 'Interview with Nigel Hess.' *Much Ado About Nothing Or Love's Labour's Won.* DVD. Opus Arts: OA 1193 BD, 2015.
Howells, Roger. Numerous interviews at the Birthplace Trust Archive between August 2013 and August 2017.
Jones, James. Telephone interview, 22 January 2016a.
Jones, James. Email follow-up, 23 January 2016b.
Klein, Beverley. Interview at Chichester Festival Theatre. 7 September 2017.
Lee, Adrian. Email exchange. 29 September 2017.
Leibovici, Leo. Telephone interview, 17 March 2016.
Leonard, John. Interview, Jerwood Space, London. 7 February 2016.
O'Neil, Bruce. Interview, Rehearsal room at The Courtyard Theatre, 12 September 2016.
Peaslee, Richard. *A Midsummer Night's Dream.* Score, 1970.
Reynolds, Ian. Email exchange, December 2015 and January 2016a.
Reynolds, Ian. Telephone interview, 14 March 2016b.
Sandland, Richard. Email exchange, February/March 2015.
Savran, David, Email exchange. 11/12 October 2017.
Sekacz, Ilona. Interview, At her home near Stratford, 25 April 2016.
Stone-Fewings, Andy. Telephone interview, 19 December 2015.
Woolfenden, Guy, Tubbs, Michael, & Woolfenden, Jane. Group Interview at Woolfenden's home, 21 November 2013.
Yershon, Gary. Backstage at Old Vic Theatre, London, 3 October 2016.

Index[1]

A

Actor musician, 155, 159, 165, 166, 171, 173, 191
Adaptation, 25, 55, 59, 65, 81, 103, 140, 181n3, 185–187, 198–203, 206–208
Added value, 67, 93
Addenbrooke, David, 40
Aesthetics, 6, 9, 10, 12, 52, 97, 139, 176, 180–189, 197, 221, 224
Alarum, 72, 73, 77, 78
Aldwych Theatre, 15, 16, 23, 33, 38, 100, 103, 109, 111
Alford, Geraldine, 176, 183
Alice in Wonderland, 44, 196
Alienation, 149, 170, 188, 194
Allam, Roger, 203, 204
All's Well That Ends Well, 19
Antony and Cleopatra, 18
Armstrong, Alun, 203, 204
Armstrong, Craig, 21, 85, 87, 87n20
Arts Council, 15, 15n5, 33, 34, 35, 35n23, 104, 112, 207
Atmosphere, 5, 6, 9, 49, 54, 58, 59, 68, 80, 83, 93, 109, 118, 119, 126, 134, 136–145, 148, 154, 164, 190, 192, 194, 212, 224
Attenborough, Michael, 18, 20, 123
Auden, W.H., 158, 189, 190
Audio visual continuum, 225
Audio visual illusion, 67
Audio visual imagery, 59
Aural dramaturgy, 96
Authentic instruments, *see* Period instruments
Authenticity, 8, 63, 65, 116, 149, 150, 154, 156, 157
Authentic production, 63
Avatar, 10, 128, 217, 218, 218n3, 219, 220

---

[1] Note: Page numbers followed by 'n' refer to notes.

B

Band box, 38, 40–44, 48, 137, 188, 219
Barbican theatre, 16, 17, 26, 35, 44, 45, 58, 101, 103, 104, 113n8, 115, 125, 202, 203, 206, 217
Barton, John, 19, 43, 120, 176
BBC Radiophonic Workshop, 70, 71
Beauty and the Beast, 44, 196
Beech, Julian, 40, 111
The Beggar's Opera, 14, 196, 197
Bell Helicoptor, 150, 171
Bellowhead, 21
Berry, Cicely, 176, 176n1, 177–179
Birmingham Conservatoire, 30
Blackfriars' playhouse, 396
Blezard, William, 118, 119
Boden, John, 21
Bogdanov, Michael, 162, 163
Bolt, Ranjit, 198
Boublil, Alain, 202
Boyd, Michael, 16, 20, 21, 54, 85, 87, 90, 177, 178
The Boys from Syracuse, 149, 185
Brecht, Bertolt, 112, 164, 172, 201
Bridgewater, Leslie, 13, 17
Bristol Old Vic, 102, 103, 123
Brook, Peter, 54, 61, 69, 76, 90, 102, 109, 110, 116, 118, 119, 125, 126, 165, 166, 168, 170, 177–179, 195, 216
Brown, Richard, 16–18, 20, 26, 44, 44n34, 45, 46n35, 57–60, 68, 125, 183, 184, 186, 187, 197
Bruce, Andrew, 202
Bruce, Michael, 21, 57, 65, 67, 96, 102, 123, 187, 188
Buffini, Fiona, 67
Burgon, Geoffrey, 80

C

Cage, John, 2, 44, 56, 70, 119, 131
Caird, John, 119, 121, 125, 195, 197, 202–204, 207
Cameron, John, 202
Catch (round), 63, 66, 66n6, 221
The Caucasian Chalk Circle, 19
Chion, Michel, 67, 93, 94, 133, 138, 146, 148
Christian tradition, 84
Christmas shows, 6, 44, 196, 198, 201, 208
City of Birmingham Symphony Orchestra (CBSO), 30
Click tracks, 129, 130, 222
A Clockwork Orange, 142
Cole King, Helen, 110, 166, 171, 179
Collaboration, 3–5, 8, 9, 11–49, 52, 54, 57, 58, 60, 65, 71, 72, 82, 91, 94, 97, 102, 110, 112, 115, 120, 122, 128, 130, 132, 136, 140, 154, 165, 173, 202, 207, 215, 216, 222–224
Collaborative practice, 8
Collison, David, 72, 97–100, 102, 104, 105, 109–111, 116, 120, 122, 124, 142
The Comedy of Errors, 21, 43, 103, 110, 114, 145, 147, 148, 153, 154, 171, 172, 185–187, 195–197
Comic stings, 150, 151
Commercial sponsorship, 34
Commercial transfers, 35, 210
Company ethos, 8, 178
Conductor, 11, 13, 18, 30, 32, 45, 47, 130
Contemporary pop, 181, 186, 212
Cooke, Dominic, 20
Coriolanus, 70, 71, 95, 111, 119
Cork, Adam, 21, 123, 129
Coveney, Michael, 206
Covent Garden, 34, 110
Creativity theory, 12, 48
Cross, Ian, 47, 140
Curtin, Adrian, 3n1, 6, 95, 114, 115, 141, 172, 181, 182
Cymbeline, 13, 26, 33, 33n20, 117, 159n5, 196

D

Dance (dancing), 1–3, 9, 12, 22, 55, 57, 58, 60, 61, 66–68, 69n10, 75, 78, 81, 88, 95, 127, 131, 137, 150, 155, 157–159, 168, 171, 185–187, 200, 201, 218
Darnley, Lyn, 176–178, 176n1, 183
Davey, Shaun, 21, 22, 152, 186, 198
Davies, Howard, 20, 44, 58n2, 123, 153
Davis, Carl, 19
Delia Derbyshire, 70, 70n12, 71, 96
Dench, Judi, 44, 79n15, 185
Deputies (deps), 30
Devine, George, 69, 117–119, 143
Digital echo effects, 218
Digital instruments, 9, 105
Digital keyboards, 105
Doran, Gregory, 10, 16, 18, 19, 21, 131, 132, 155, 198, 199, 217
Doubling, 23, 36, 75, 76, 161, 205
  See also Musicians' Union; Trebling
Dramaturgy, 4, 9, 12, 38, 60, 96, 117, 135, 154, 155, 158, 190, 191, 210, 213–215
  See also Music, dramaturgical
Dress rehearsal, 25, 53, 58, 102
Dunn, Jeremy, 41, 101, 106, 108, 113, 115, 124, 128–132, 217, 220–222
Dynamic shape of performance, 222

E

Eacott, John, 152
Early modern period, 7, 8, 22, 39, 52, 63, 64, 66, 81, 149, 175, 181–184
Early modern theatre, 7, 38, 68, 79, 95, 95n1
Economics of music, 12, 28–38
Edward II, 145
Edward IV, 14

Electro-acoustic, 7, 70, 95
Electronic generation, 18, 124
Electronic instruments, 105
Elgar's Rondo, 163
Elizabethan madrigals, 201
Employment practices, 12
Employment rights, 33
Englishby, Paul, 19, 128, 198, 199, 217
English National Opera, 34
Ensemble practice, 201, 203, 215
Experimental music theatre, 2
Eyre, Richard, 19, 178

F

Fanfare, 31, 40, 73, 75–78, 80, 81, 100, 119, 122, 127, 137, 153
Farah, Abd'Elkader, 42, 42n32, 43, 58
Farce, 150, 199, 200
Feedback loop, 141
Fenton, George, 20, 25, 44, 199, 200, 211
Fenton, James, 203
Filter Theatre, 5, 6n3, 155, 165, 172, 181, 182
Flourish, 68, 72, 73, 76–78, 80, 120, 209
Franks, Andrew, 128, 217, 220
Functions of song, *see* Song

G

Garham, Bill, 103
Gerhard, Roberto, 69–71, 81, 82, 116, 117, 117n11, 118, 119, 119n12, 128, 143, 214
Gershwin, George, 65, 68
Gielgud, John, 195
Gilkes, Denne, 176, 183
Gill, Peter, 20, 20n9
The Globe, 6, 7, 19n8, 26, 39, 63, 64, 95, 117, 158, 181, 206

Godwin, Simon, 67, 187
Goodbody, Buzz, 177, 178
Gorbman, Claudia, 4n2, 137, 146, 151
Graphic score, 55
Group flow, 12
Groupmind, 46, 48

H
Hack, Keith, 19
Hall, Charlie, 108
Hall, Peter, 13–16, 19, 24, 39, 60, 69, 71, 80, 90, 99, 100, 109, 109n6, 118, 119, 178
Hamlet, 57, 71, 145, 182
Hammerton, Richard, 123
Hands, Terry, 16, 19, 42, 58, 60, 90, 111, 122
Henry IV Pt 1, 198
Henry IV Pt 2, 192
Henry V, 31, 58, 71, 72, 120, 121, 130, 142, 144, 198, 199
Henry VI, 14
Henry VIII, 153
Hess, Nigel, 16–18, 53, 54, 57, 184
Hierarchical relationship, 56, 91
Higgins, Sonia, 100, 111, 190n7
Hip Hop Shakespeare Company, 178
The Histories, 54
HMS Pinafore, 221
Hodgson, Brian, 71, 72
Home-Cook, George, 5, 139, 223
House of Desires, 188
Howells, Roger, 38n26, 40, 41, 43, 99, 109–111
Hugo, Victor, 201, 202, 204

I
Indoor theatres, 23, 39, 45, 75
Inpoints and outpoints, 58
Instrumental colour, 57, 58, 127

Instrumentation, 14, 18, 25, 27, 28, 30, 54, 57, 59, 67, 79, 82, 146, 187
Interdisciplinarity, 9
Intertextual, 66, 68, 77, 134, 146, 168, 181, 200, 221, 224
Irony, 66, 190
The Island Princess, 21

J
Jackson, Barry, 97
Jerry Springer the Opera, 216
The Jew of Malta, 40
Johnson, Bruce, 182
Jones, James, 21, 22, 25, 37n25, 38, 47, 54, 55
Judge, Ian, 184, 197
Julius Caesar, 15, 19, 20

K
Kelly, Dennis, 209, 211, 212
King John, 19, 33, 33n20
King Lear, 21, 55, 56, 81, 91, 109–111, 117–119, 132, 153, 184
The King's Men, 8, 39
Kiss Me Kate, 44, 196
Klein, Beverley, 204, 205, 207
Kneehigh Theatre Company, 155, 165
Koch, Martin, 202
Kretzmer, Herbert, 203, 205

L
Lee, Adrian, 21, 24, 54, 82, 83, 145, 149
Leibovici, Leo, 102, 111, 112, 115, 123
Leigh, Mike, 20
Leitmotif, 151

Leonard, John A., 100–104, 108, 111–114, 123, 123n15, 125
Leppard, Raymond, 13, 14, 19, 71
Les Misérables, 27, 90, 103, 104, 114, 195, 196, 196n10, 201–207, 208n17, 209, 210, 213–216
Levitin, Daniel, 140, 141
Lighting design, 109, 161, 202, 209
Lindley, David, 7, 22, 23, 38, 39, 61, 66, 69, 72, 73, 75, 170, 181–184, 190–192, 196
Linehan, Conor, 67
The Lion, The Witch and The Wardrobe, 30, 44, 106, 107, 196–198
A Little Night Music, 185
Liveness, 2, 134, 136, 156, 173, 222, 223
    dynamics of, 136
Lloyd, Phyllida, 20, 195, 201
Lloyd Webber, Andrew, 195, 201
London Road, 216
The Lorenzaccio Story, 19
Love's Labour's Lost, 13, 19, 40, 154
Love's Labour's Won, 19
Lyrical, 88, 119. 152, 178, 180, 185, 187, 195, 200, 212, 213
Lyricism, 215
Lyric quality, 180
Lyric time, 180

M
Macbeth, 1–10, 34, 40n29, 52, 68–90, 94, 96, 119, 124, 134, 137, 142, 148, 153, 167, 175–216, 224
Mackintosh, Cameron, 202, 203, 207, 209, 214
Magical, 51, 93, 114, 126, 150, 154, 166, 184, 217–220
Manchester Royal Exchange, 20
Marling, Laura, 21, 61, 130, 181, 188

Matilda: The Musical, 18, 196, 207, 210
McMillin, Scott, 180
McWhinnie, Donald, 69
Measure for Measure, 15, 19
Meckler, Nancy, 188
Melodrama, 95, 134, 168
Mendelssohn, Felix, 66, 119, 126, 143, 168, 170, 170n9
The Merchant of Venice, 19, 20, 39, 40, 140, 147, 153, 159, 177, 225
Merry Wives of Windsor, 195, 198
Merry Wives: The Musical, 18, 44, 195, 196, 198–200, 208, 211
Metadiegetic, 151
Metaphorical, 142, 180, 195
Metaphysical, 78, 79, 85, 126, 133, 154
A Midsummer Night's Dream, 19, 54, 66, 73, 125, 133, 143, 145, 146, 165–167, 169, 177, 200, 216
Military signalling, 22, 33, 69, 77, 80, 89
Mimetic acting, 193
Minchin, Tim, 208, 209, 211–213
Mode (States, Bert)
    collaborative, 160, 162
    representative, 110
    self-expressive, 160, 161, 163
Montage, 148
Mother Courage, 44, 196
Much Ado About Nothing, 18, 19, 43, 187
'Sigh no more,' 187
Muldowney, Dominic, 163
Munrow, David, 7n4, 24, 30, 64
Music
    acoustic, 7, 70, 108
    advisor, 13, 17
    anempathetic, 138, 142, 143
    atmospheric, 45, 137, 141–146, 149, 164

Music (*cont.*)
  atonal, 171, 220
  authentic, 7, 64, 77
  bluegrass, 156, 158
  chase, 150
  conceptual, 138, 151, 155–158
  contextual, 2, 138, 146–151, 155, 181
  diegetic, 136, 138, 156, 158, 159, 161–164
  dramaturgical, 135, 136, 151, 157, 158, 189, 195, 211, 215, 224, 225
  Elizabethan, 7, 63, 64, 178, 199–201, 219, 221
  empathetic, 138, 142, 143
  film, 58, 67, 135–138, 140, 145, 147, 152, 154
  folk, 116, 147, 156, 218
  incidental, 2, 3, 15, 24, 25, 61–63, 66, 69, 70, 72, 80, 116, 117, 161, 170n9, 196
  Jacobean, 7, 63
  library, 5
  management, 12–18
  Manager, 17
  non-diegetic, 136
  Officer, 17
  operatic, 19
  polyphonic, 105, 119, 126, 144, 219, 221
  recorded, 29, 63, 72, 97, 110, 111, 115, 129
  religious, 79, 84
  spotting, 58, 59, 71
  theatrical, 138, 164, 165
  tonal, 3
  world, 18, 81, 82, 90
Musicality, 4, 10, 165, 175–180, 195, 215, 225
Musical motifs, 82, 151
Musical theatre (musicals), 2, 6, 9, 40n30, 51, 53, 130, 176, 180, 182, 184–186, 189, 190, 192, 193, 195, 196, 198–201, 203, 206, 207, 208n16, 212, 214–216, 224, 225
Musicians' Union (MU)
  agreement, 26, 27n12, 36
  contract, 17, 26, 30, 32, 35
  Midland District Council, 29
  National Executive Committee (NEC), 28, 29
  policy, 26
  subsistence, 30, 35
Music theatricality, 164–172
Mutual implication, 137

N
Narrative context, 5
National Theatre (NT), 2, 5, 6, 15n5, 20, 26, 34, 81, 110, 158, 216
Naturalistic theatre, 4
Newcastle-upon-tyne, 45
Nicholas Nickelby, 202, 204, 206, 216
Nicholls, Peter, 198
Niebur, Louis, 72, 78, 117
Nightingale, Benedict, 202, 204, 206
Nightingale, Christopher, 213
Noble, Adrian, 16, 19–21, 27, 38n27, 64n3, 80, 90, 125, 144, 153, 154, 161, 164, 177, 182–184, 186, 190, 198
Nunn, Trevor, 16, 19, 33, 34, 40, 43, 73, 85, 90, 100, 149, 163, 177–180, 184–187, 195, 201–204, 207, 209

O
Oliver, Stephen, 19, 25, 43, 55, 125
O'Neil, Bruce, 17, 18, 21, 28, 45, 60, 61, 130, 152, 154, 188, 196, 208, 209, 211, 213, 214
Onstage appearance, 29, 36

Orpheus, 51
Othello, 19, 113, 191
  'Willow Song,' 184, 190
The Other Place, (TOP), 16, 19, 25, 27, 32, 38, 79, 102, 111, 112, 125, 149, 178, 195, 205
Outdoor theatres (Amphitheatres), 22, 39, 69, 94

P

Panatrope, 62, 97, 98, 98n3, 99, 119, 143
Panning, 137, 161
Pantomime, 2, 129, 130, 172, 199–201, 208
Pastiche, 147, 164, 168, 182, 197
Peaslee, Richard, 54, 166, 166n7, 166n8, 167, 169–171
Peer Gynt, 19
Performativity, 135, 136
Perfume Genius, 21
Pericles, 19, 20, 118
Period instruments, 7, 63, 64
Perkins, Laurie, 213
Peter Pan, 19, 195, 196
Physical, 71, 84, 85, 89, 112, 141, 150, 151, 154, 160–163, 166, 172, 179, 186, 205, 217, 218, 218n3, 222
Piaf, 112, 115, 196, 198
Piccadilly Theatre, 16
The Pit, 1, 15, 16, 39, 44, 44n34, 97, 139
Poetic, 142, 165, 178, 180, 193–195, 203, 213, 224
Poeticisation of language, 195
Poeticisation of space, 194, 215, 225
Poizat, Michel, 194
Poppy, 196, 198
Porter, Cole, 65, 68, 181n3
Posner, Lindsay, 20

Post-dramatic theatre, 193
Pre-production, 57, 158
Preview, 25, 53, 58, 102, 158, 202, 206
Priestman, Brian, 13, 14
Privates on Parade, 196, 198
Production timeline, 52–53, 62
Psychology (of drama), 47, 48, 85, 90

R

Rehearsal period, 14, 53, 54, 58, 59, 158, 171, 203, 210
Reynolds, Ian, 21, 24–26, 30, 32, 33, 35, 37n25, 42, 45, 46n35, 47, 48, 112, 129, 161–164
Richard II, 19, 33n20
Richard III, 14, 22, 54n1, 61
Ringham, Ben, 123, 129
Ringham, Max, 123, 129
Rodenburg, Patsy, 176n1, 179
Roesner, David, 2–4, 6
Romeo and Juliet, 19, 43, 71, 87, 116, 147, 153, 200
Rough aesthetic, 180
Royal Charter, 15, 16
Royal Shakespeare Company (RSC), 1–174, 217–232, 1475–216
Royal Shakespeare Theatre (RST), 15–17, 19, 27, 33n19, 44, 67, 69, 99, 110
Russolo, Luigi, 2

S

Saint-Denis, Michel, 176
Salome, 21
Samplers, 14, 21, 96, 98, 105, 106, 123–125, 127, 129, 131, 144
Sandland, Richard, 17, 87
Savran, David, 166, 170, 171
Sawyer, R. Keith, 12, 46

242   INDEX

Schonberg, Claude-Michel, 195, 202, 206
The Secret Garden, 44
Sekacz, Ilona, 21, 53–56, 58, 81, 82, 91, 107, 124–126, 132, 142, 144, 145, 153, 155–158, 184, 188, 192, 197
The Shakespeare Birthplace Trust, 6, 42, 70n12, 103, 114, 165n6, 191, 207n15
Shakespeare Festival, 13
Shakespeare Memorial Theatre, 13, 15, 24
Shakespeare Memorial Theatre Orchestra, 24
Shakespeare Memorial Theatre Wind Band, 24
Shakespeare's Globe Theatre, 6, 63, 64
Shakespeare, William, 3, 6, 7, 9, 11–13, 15, 17, 19n8, 20, 23, 24, 26, 28, 37, 38, 42, 63, 64, 64n3, 65, 66, 66n5, 67–69, 70n12, 79, 94, 103, 114, 116, 134–136, 141, 147–149, 154, 158, 165, 165n6, 171, 175, 176n1, 177–183, 186–189, 191, 192, 195, 196, 198, 199, 201, 207n15, 212, 214, 224
Sher, Antony, 21
Sibelius software, 55
Singing
  aesthetics, 9, 10, 12, 52, 97, 176, 180–189, 197, 221, 224
  operatic, 19, 147, 168, 171, 198, 221
  training, 123, 176–180, 183, 185, 196, 215, 224
Slocombe, Paul, 108
Smith, Bruce R., 7, 95, 182
Song
  called-for, 158, 189, 190

extant, 66
functions of, 189–193
impromptu, 189, 190
mad, 182
operatic, 171
performing, 40, 135, 191
spotting, 57
work, 182, 206
See also Singing; Voice
Sound
  acoustic, 40, 97, 108
  cues, 3, 73, 78, 79, 89
  design, 2, 3, 3n1, 4–9, 48, 57, 60, 72, 81, 82, 90, 91, 94, 96, 102, 105, 106, 108–110, 112, 114, 116, 118, 119, 122, 123, 128, 129, 131, 132, 134, 137, 141, 151, 155, 173, 194, 202, 207, 214, 218, 220–224
  designers, 5, 6, 9, 57, 60, 72, 81, 82, 91, 94, 96, 105, 106, 109, 112, 114, 116, 118, 122, 123, 128, 129, 131, 132, 137, 141, 155, 173, 194, 202, 207, 214, 221, 223, 224
  digital, 218, 220
  electronic, 9, 21, 40n29, 72, 90, 93–132, 134, 197, 214
  world, 3, 4, 9, 10, 18, 21, 56, 57, 59, 64, 65, 70, 79, 81, 82, 87, 89, 95, 96, 115–117, 123, 125, 126, 131, 132, 140, 148–150, 154, 156, 158, 166, 171, 178, 214
Soundscape, 5, 7, 96–98, 105, 108n5, 115, 125, 127, 128, 131, 177, 194
Stage management, 12, 49, 59, 95, 98, 101, 106, 110, 111
States, Bert O., 160
Stone-Fewings, Andy, 27, 27n11, 36
Subsidised theatre, 216

INDEX 243

The Swan Theatre, 16, 27, 44, 163
Synthesisers, 14, 21, 57, 60, 96, 105, 106, 120n14, 123–127, 123n15, 127n18, 129, 131, 144, 202

T
Tagg, Philip, 146
The Taming of the Shrew, 19, 30, 71, 73, 117, 152, 159, 160, 162
Technical rehearsal, 25, 45, 53, 54, 58, 60, 115, 158
Television rights, 34
The Tempest
  'Come unto these yellow sands,' 218
  'Flout 'em and scout 'em,' 221
  'Full Fathom Five,' 218, 219
  'No more dams,' 220
  'Where the Bee Sucks,' 218, 220
Thacker, David, 20, 57, 65, 181, 184
Theatre and Aural Attention, 5
TheatreGoRound (TGR), 16
Theatre production, 2, 8, 9, 59, 70
Theatre Projects, 72, 110
Theatricality, 4, 5, 9, 87–90, 135, 137, 138, 159, 164–173, 212, 222, 224
  See also Music theatricality
Tis Pity She's A Whore, 19
Titus Andronicus, 61, 118
Touring, 16, 23, 27, 29, 30, 34, 35, 39, 67, 108, 113, 158, 166, 167
Tragedy (tragedies), 3, 63, 64n3, 127, 134
Trebling, 36
  See also Doubling; Musicians' Union
Trevis, Di, 20, 163
Troilus and Cressida, 43, 53, 142
Tubbs, Michael, 15, 15n4, 16–18, 25, 26, 30, 36, 53, 112, 126

Twelfth Night
  'Come Away Death,' 159, 184, 191
  'O Mistress Mine,' 191
Two Gentlemen of Verona, 59, 65–68, 146, 147, 181n3, 187

U
Underscore, 54, 84, 87, 126, 130, 136, 140, 144, 145, 149, 157, 181, 193, 197, 198, 208, 213, 216, 220
Undertow, 88, 122, 142, 144, 145, 220
Unheard music, 62
Unit Delta Plus, 72, 119

V
Van Kampen, Claire, 6, 7n4, 63
Venetian Twins, 163
Vernacular, 150
Verse speaking, 176, 178, 180, 215
Vibrans, Mark, 20
Vocal practices, 3, 176, 179, 179n2, 190, 215
Vocal qualities, 180, 188, 218
Voice
  aesthetic, 176, 180–189
  department, 2, 3, 12, 14, 40, 49, 53, 91, 95, 96, 103, 104, 111–113, 115, 120, 123, 128, 220
  training, 176–180, 197

W
Waits
  London, 23
  Town, 23
Warbeck, Stephen, 17, 21, 162
Warchus, Matthew, 20, 57, 155, 156, 209

The Warehouse Theatre, 16
Warren, Iris, 65n4, 176
The Wars of the Roses, 14, 71, 120
Wedding masque, 218, 221
Weill, Kurt, 201
West End rates, 26
  See also Musicians' Union
West Side Story, 185, 200
White Devil, 21
Williams, Clifford, 195
Wind band, *see* Royal Shakespeare Company
The Winter's Tale, 19–21, 40, 43, 106, 107, 147, 152, 153, 155, 156, 159n5, 186, 187, 190, 196
Wishart, Peter, 110, 195
The Wizard of Oz, 44, 196, 197
Woolf, John, 17, 18, 21, 125
Woolfenden, Guy, 14–19, 14n2, 21, 22, 24–26, 30, 31, 40, 43, 54, 58, 60, 61, 64, 65, 66n5, 71, 72, 74, 78, 79, 85n18, 90, 103, 110, 114, 119–122, 125, 136, 142, 144, 158, 181n3, 185, 187, 197, 203, 220, 222
Working agreement, *see* Musicians' Union
Working practices, *see* Musicians' Union
Workshops, 70, 71, 117, 118, 120n14, 123, 208–212, 215, 216
Writing process, 54–59
Wyndham's Theatre, 16

Y

Yershon, Gary, 20, 21, 56, 57, 129, 131, 153–157, 180, 184, 194
Young Vic, 81

Z

Zinovieff, Peter, 71, 72